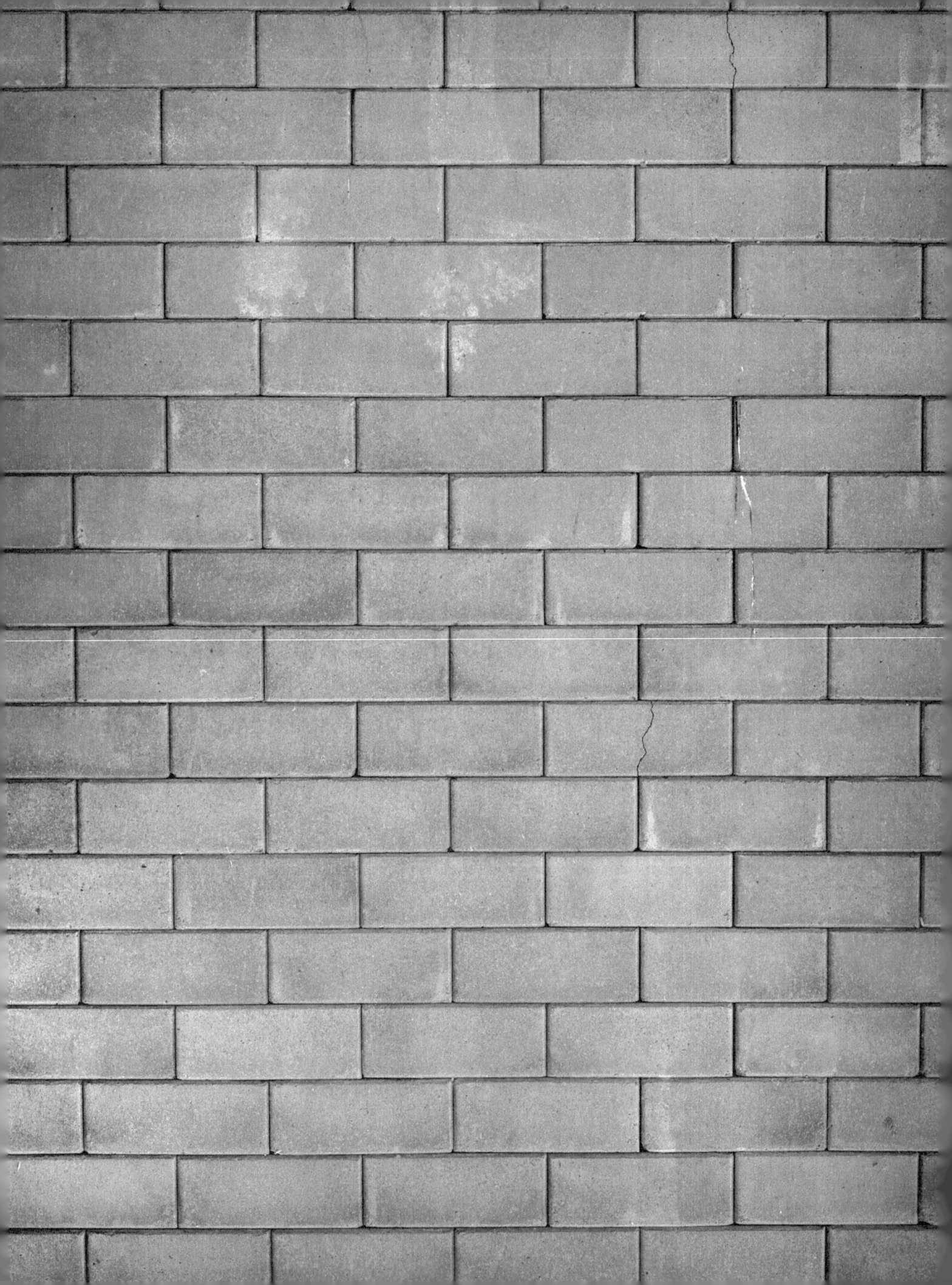

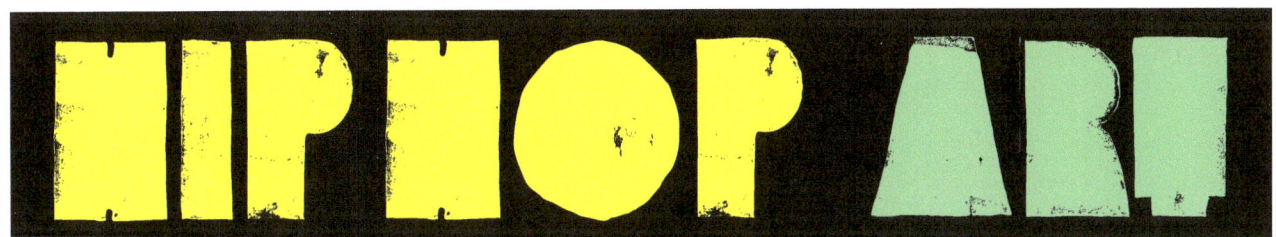

VOLUME 1

edited by PAUL STEWART
and BLACKPANTHER

HIP HOP ART VOLUME 1
2016 © Copyright by Over The Edge
Over The Edge Publishing

ISBN - 978-1-944082-28-4
Cover, Design & Layout by Michael Ziobrowski / @XIsTheWeapon

All rights reserved. No part of this book may be reproduced or transmitted in any form or by any means, electronic or mechanical, including photocopying, recording, or by information storage and retrieval systems, without the written permission of the publisher, except by a reviewer who may quote brief passages in a review. Printed in the United States of America.

overtheedgebooks.com

SECTIONS

0 - F	G-M	N-Y
50 CENT	GHOSTFACE	NAS
AALIYAH	GORILLAZ	OL DIRTY BASTARD
ASAP FERG	ICE CUBE	PETE ROCK
ASAP ROCKY	ISAIAH RASHAD	PHIFE DAWG
ASAP YAMS	J COLE	PUBLIC ENEMY
ASEOP ROCK	JAY ROCK	PUSHA T
ATMOSPHERE	JAY Z	Q TIP
BADU	JOEY FATTS ASTON MATTHEWS	QUASI DOOM
BEASTIE BOYS	KANYE WEST	RAKIM
BIG KRIT	KENDRICK LAMAR	REDMAN
BIG PUN	KID N PLAY	REVERAND RUN
BIGGIE	KRS1	RICK ROSS
BIZ MARKIE	LARGE PROFESSOR	RUSSELL SIMMONS
BLACK THOUGHT	LE$	RZA
BUSTA RHYMES	LIL JON	SADE
CHANCE THE RAPPER	LIL UZI VERT	SCHOOL BOY Q
COMMON	LIL YACHTY	SEAN PRICE
DANNY BROWN	LITTLE HALF DEAD	SIR MICHAEL ROCKS
DEATHROW	LITTLE SIMZ	SLICK RICK
DE LA SOUL	LL COOL J	SLUG
DESIIGNER	LORD FINESSE	SMOKE DZA
DONAL GLOVER	MASTA ACE	SNOOP DOGG
DILLA	MAXO CREAM	SZA
DJ PREMIERE	METHOD MAN	TALIB KWELI
DMC	MF DOOM	THE GAME
DRAKE	MISSY ELLIOT	THE WKND
DRAKE & LIL WAYNE	M.O.P.	TI
EBRO	MOS DEF	TRAVIS SCOTT
EMINEM		TUPAC
EYEDEA		TYGA
EAZY E		TYLER THE CREATOR
FLATBUSH ZOMBIES		WIZ KHALIFA
FLAVOR FLAV		WU TANG CLAN
FRANK OCEAN		YOUNG THUG
FREDDIE GIBBS		

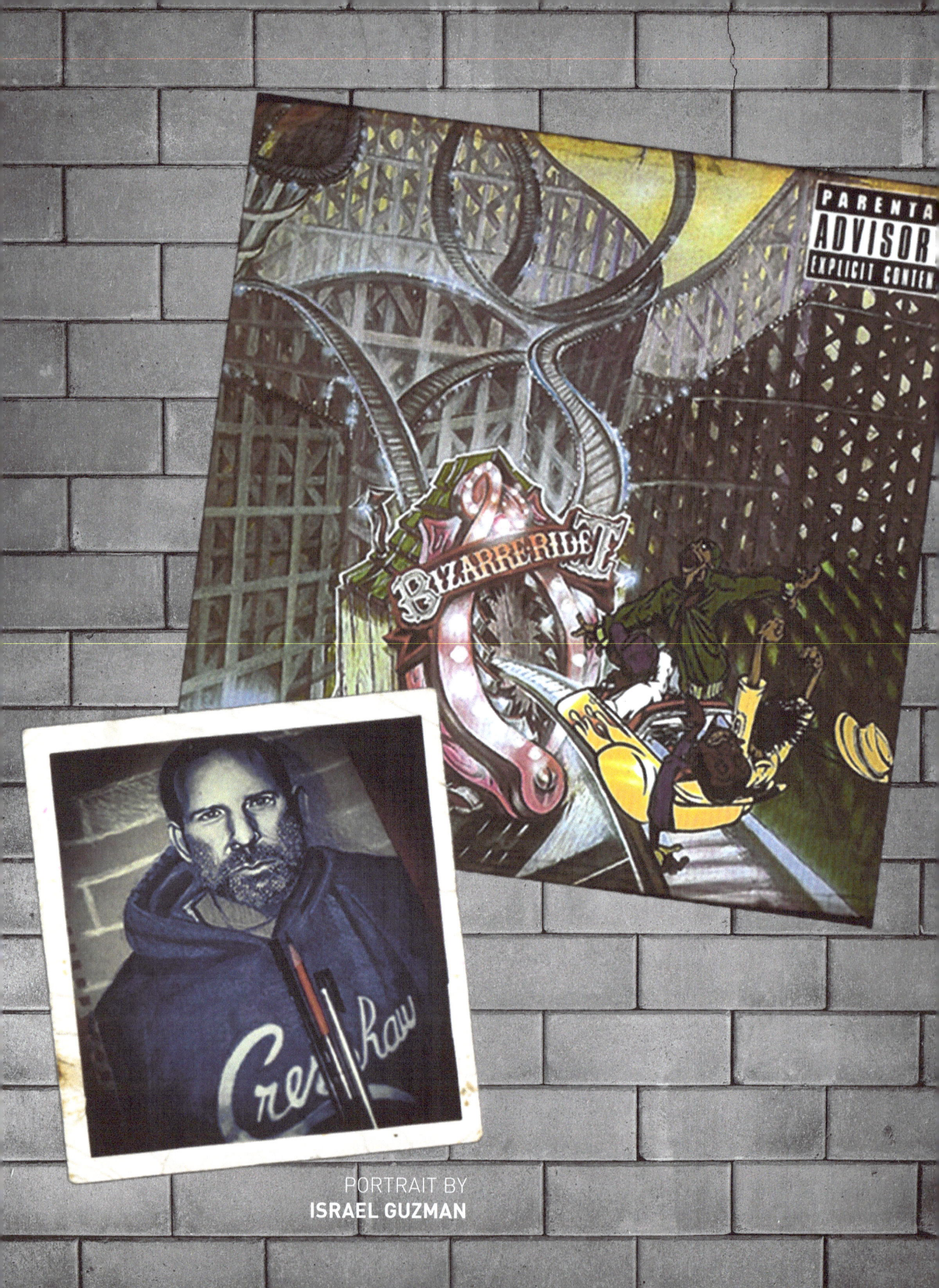

PORTRAIT BY
ISRAEL GUZMAN

As a veteran of the Hip Hop music business, I have had many accomplishments I am very proud of managing an artist who won a Grammy, music supervising a film that won an Oscar for best song but the thing I'm most proud of is as a young mgr – I connected my friend the incredibly talented Slick with my new group the Pharcyde and an amazing piece of Hip hop art was created the cover to the Pharcydes debut LP. So, a Hip Hop art book was literally like a dream come true project for me.

We at Over The Edge books are so excited to release this collection; first off I would like to thank all the artists who contributed their work to be apart of this project. This was such an amazing project for me to put together combining my love of Art and Hip Hop. We definitely made an effort to make sure we represented a wide array of artists from Rap Pioneers to the newest artists on the scene. The book has some of the most Underground artists as well as some of the most successful commercial ones. As well the artists who created the work in this book range from very established to newbies and everywhere in between but one thing that binds them is their genuine love for Hip Hop culture.

When I came up with the idea for this book I met so many talented artists on Instagram who were already doing Hip Hop art and the book kept growing, we unfortunately just had to stop at some point and save the rest we have for Vol. 2!

We hope you will check out the artists in the book all their Instagram pages are listed in the back.

Peace Out

Paul Stewart

Special shouts to BLACKPANTHER and MICHAEL ZIOBROWSKI
For helping get this book put together.

0-F

50 CENT	DEATHROW
AALIYAH	DE LA SOUL
ASAP FERG	DESIIGNER
ASAP ROCKY	DONAL GLOVER
ASAP YAMS	DILLA
ASEOP ROCK	DJ PREMIERE
ATMOSPHERE	DMC
BADU	DRAKE
BEASTIE BOYS	DRAKE & LIL WAYNE
BIG KRIT	EBRO
BIG PUN	EMINEM
BIGGIE	EYEDEA
BIZ MARKIE	EAZY E
BLACK THOUGHT	FLATBUSH ZOMBIES
BUSTA RHYMES	FLAVOR FLAV
CHANCE THE RAPPER	FRANK OCEAN
COMMON	FREDDIE GIBBS
DANNY BROWN	

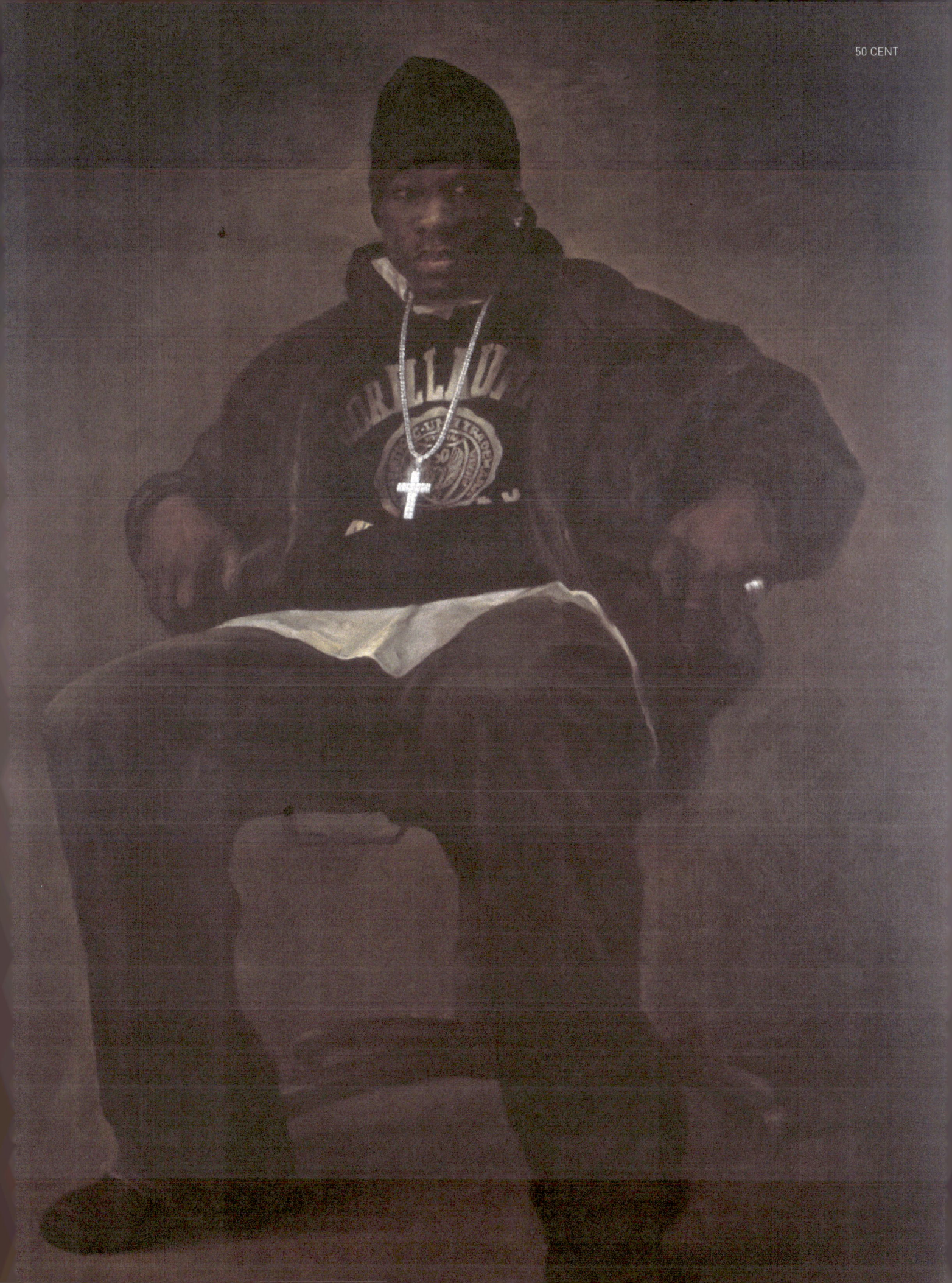
50 CENT

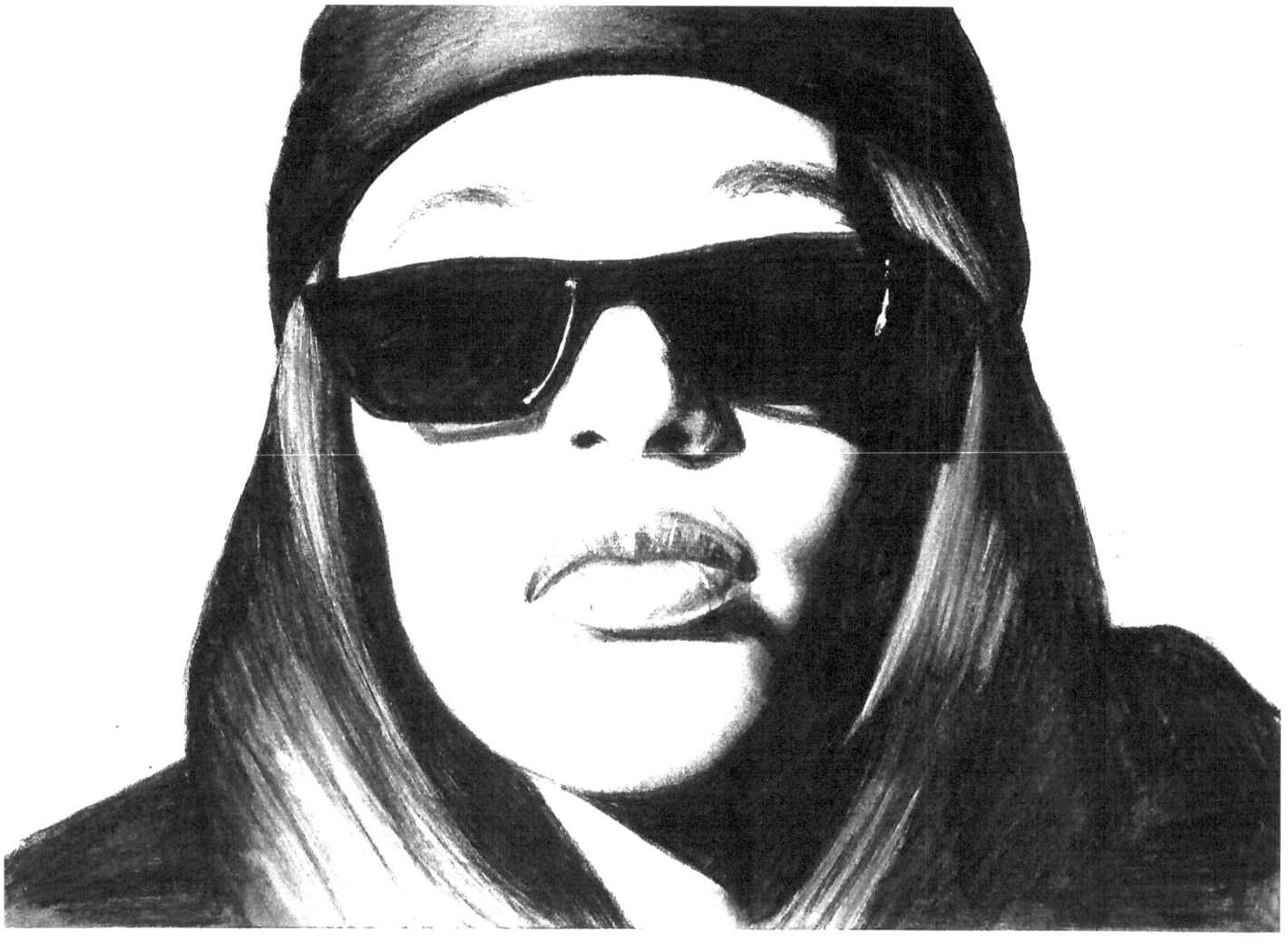

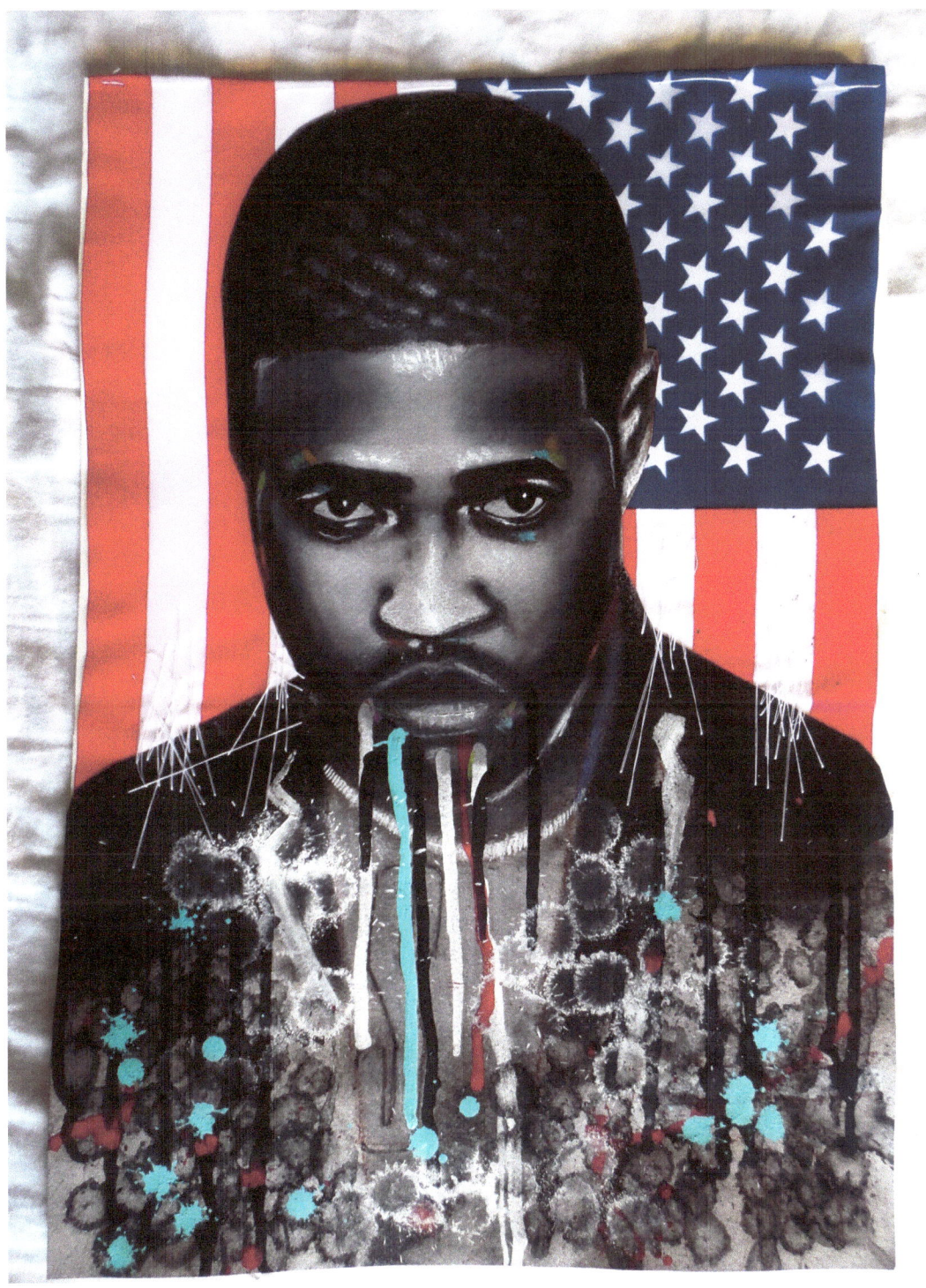

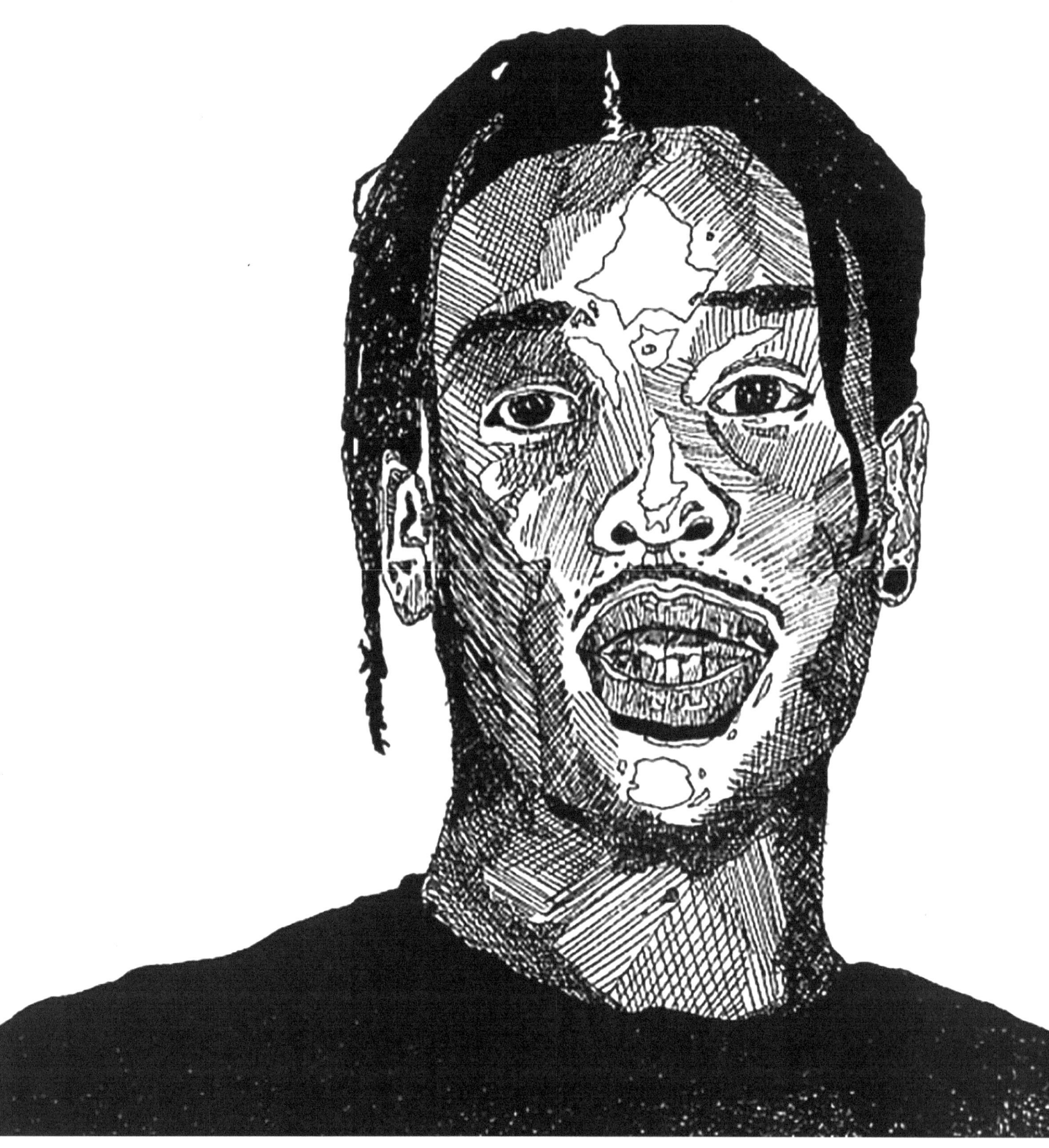

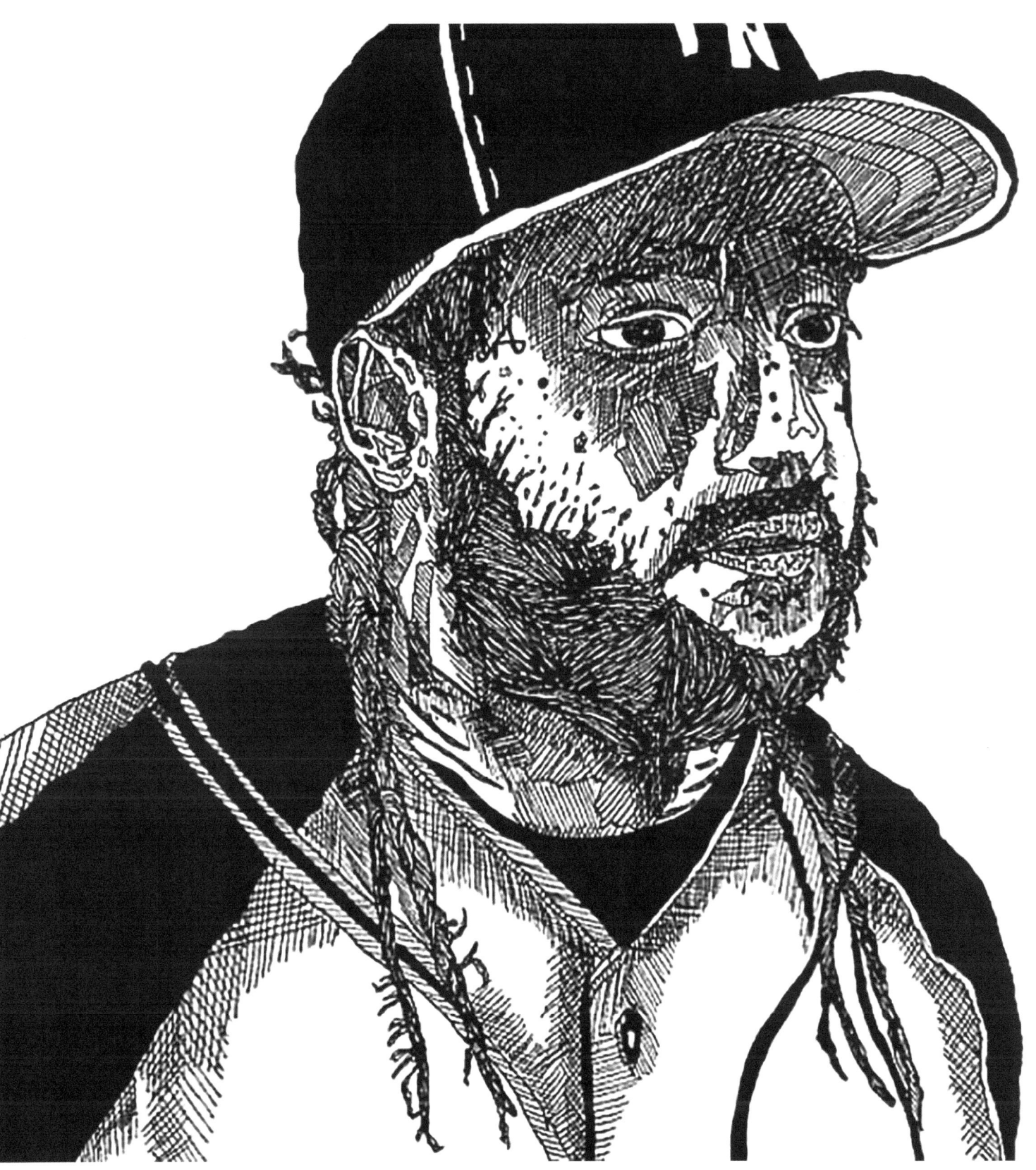
ASAP YAMS

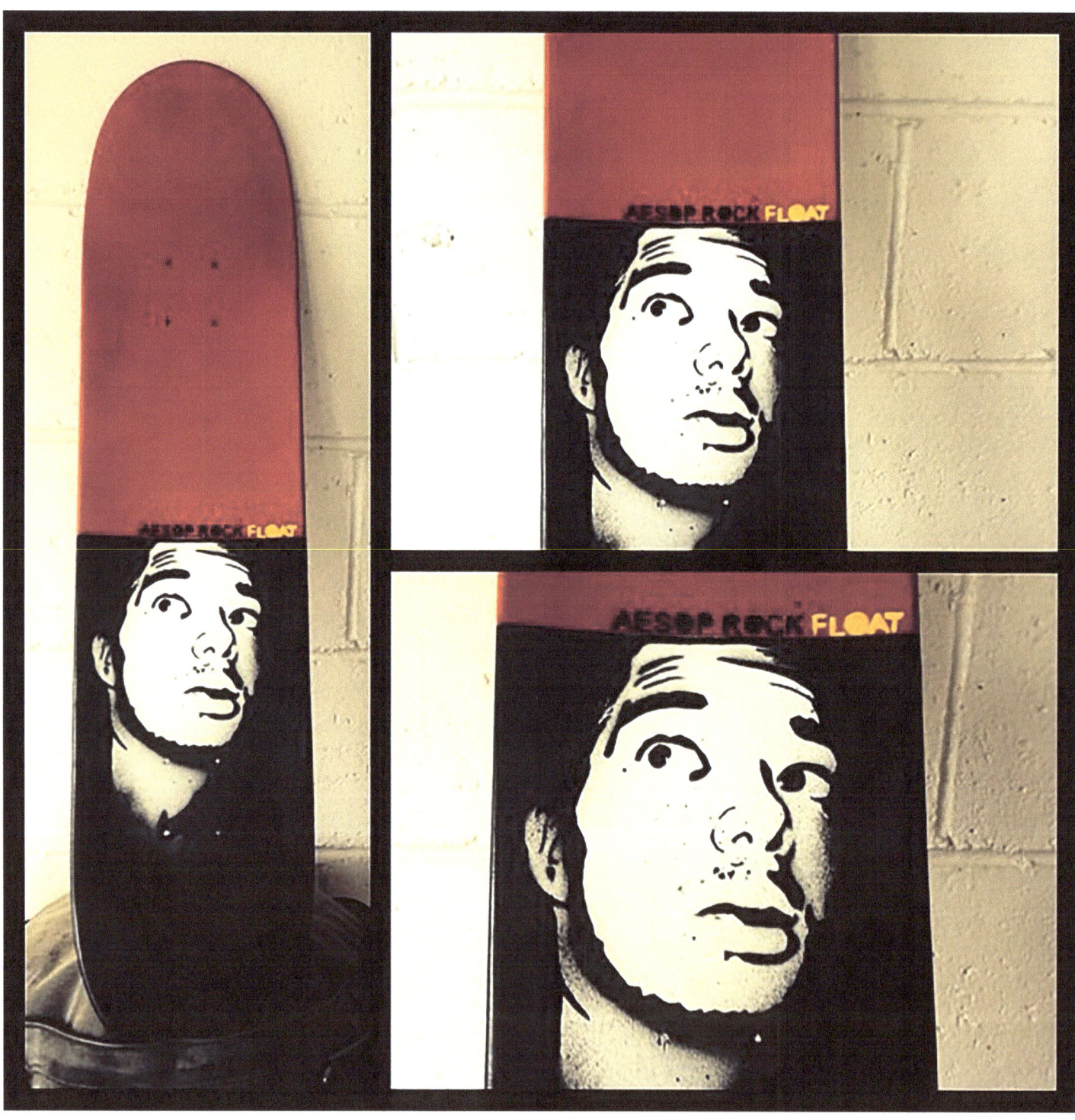

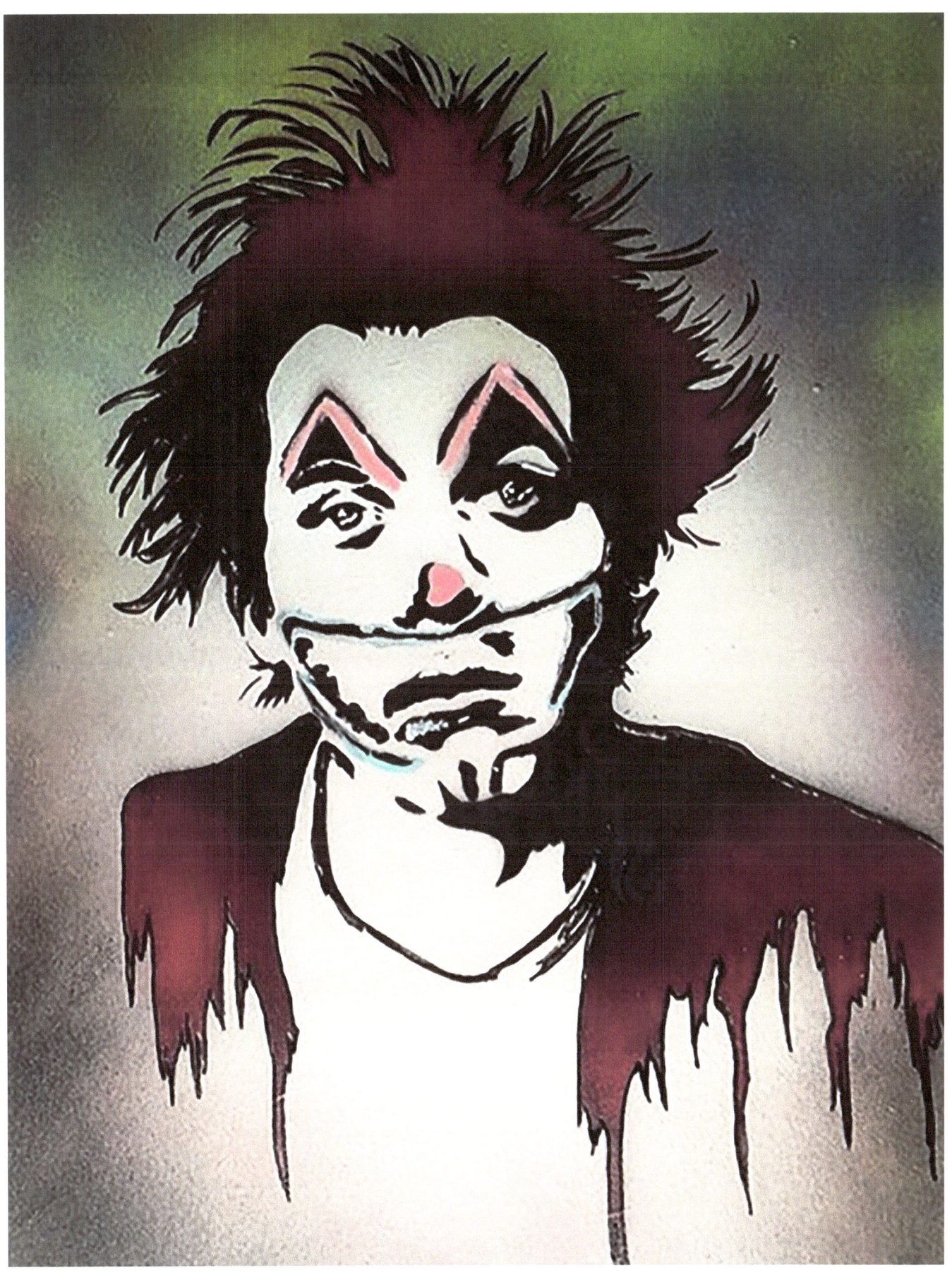

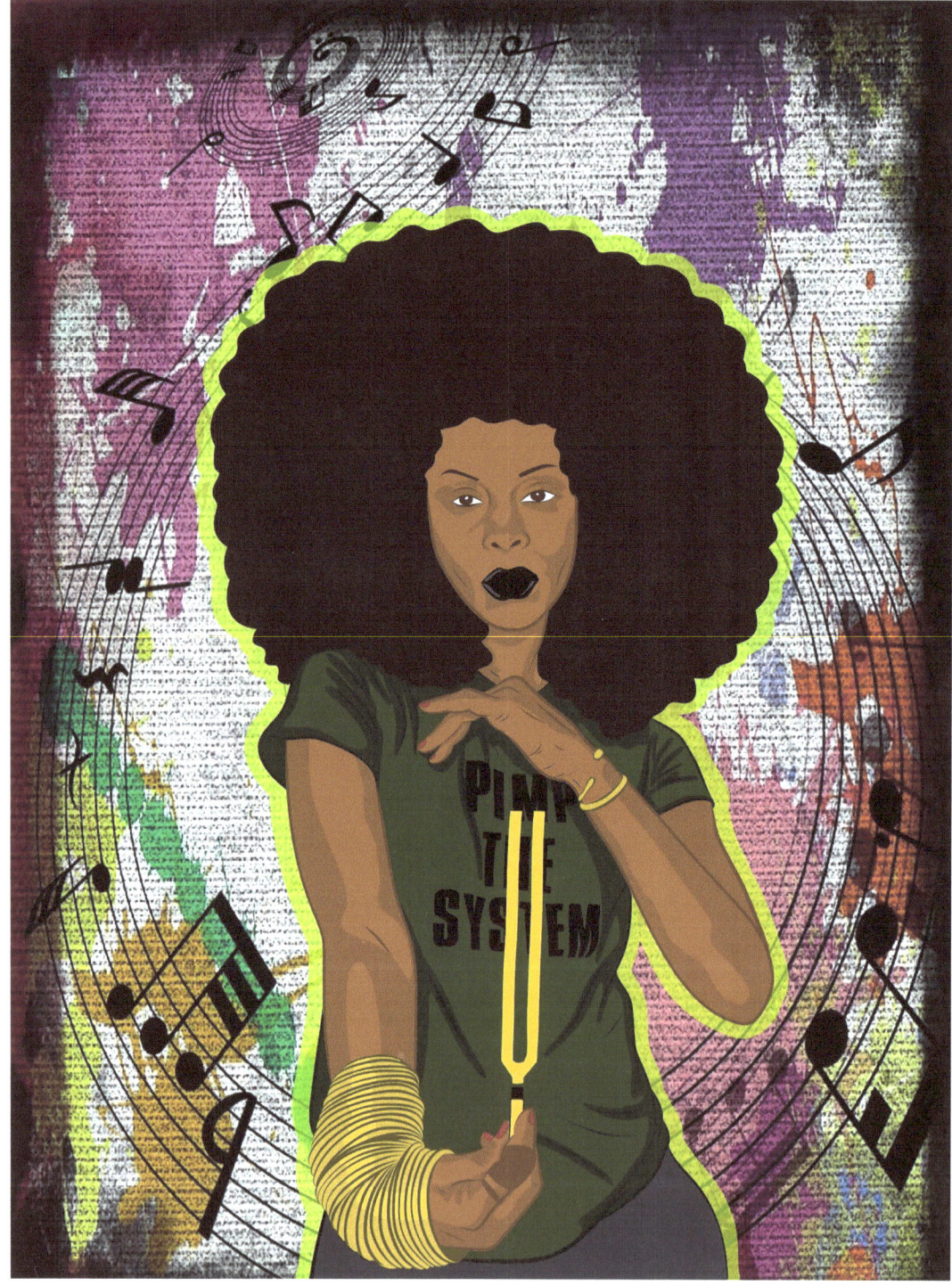

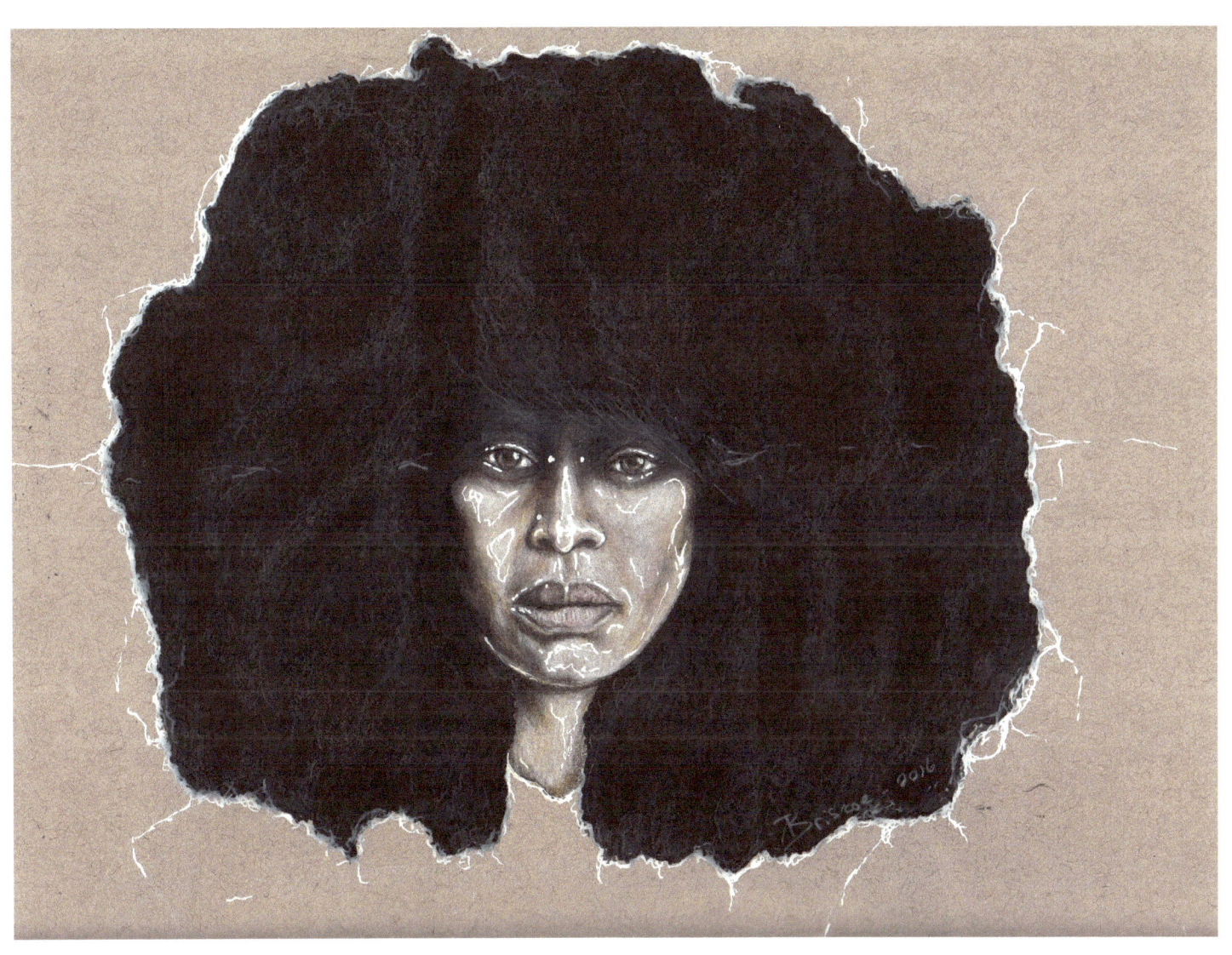

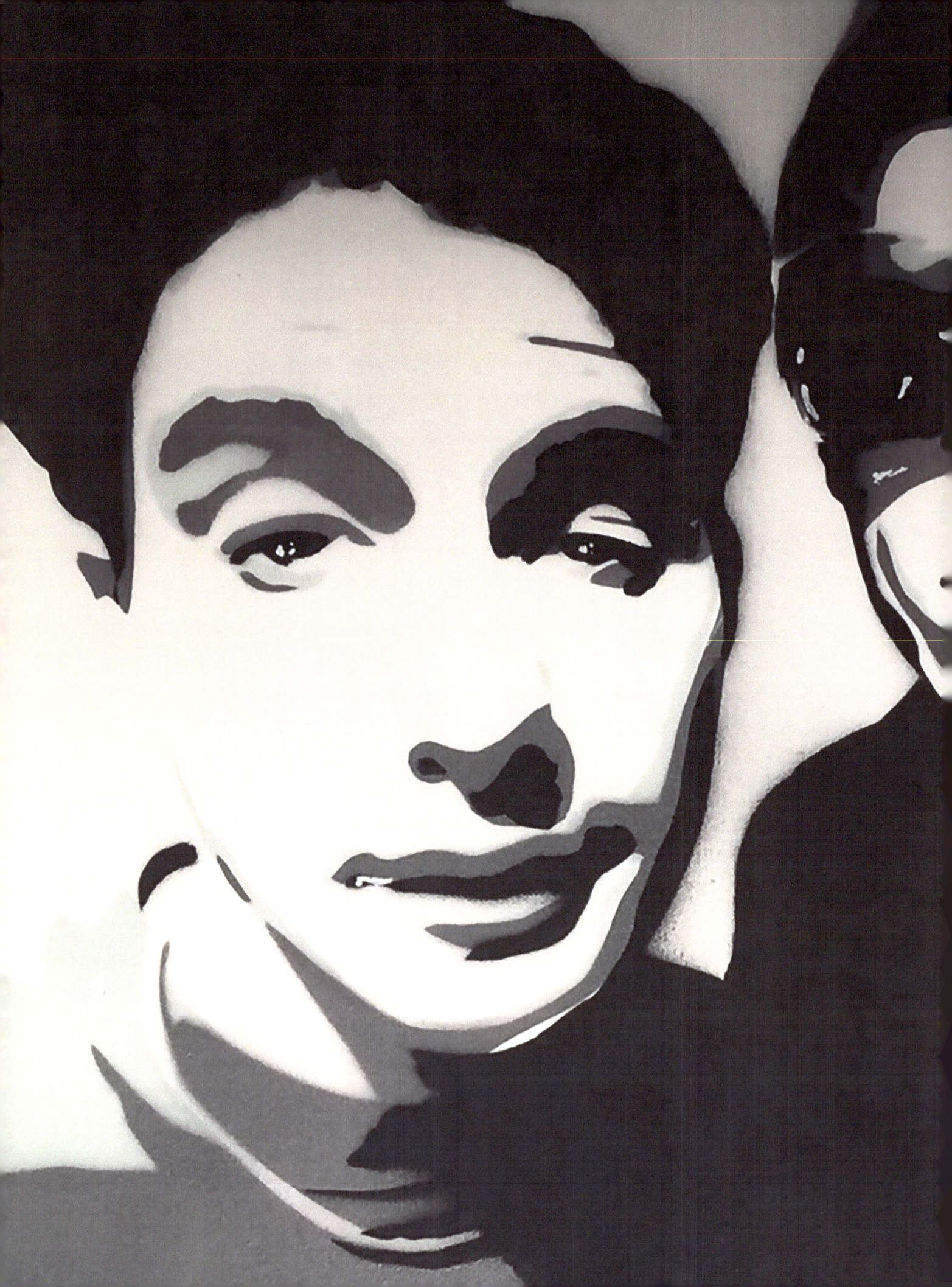

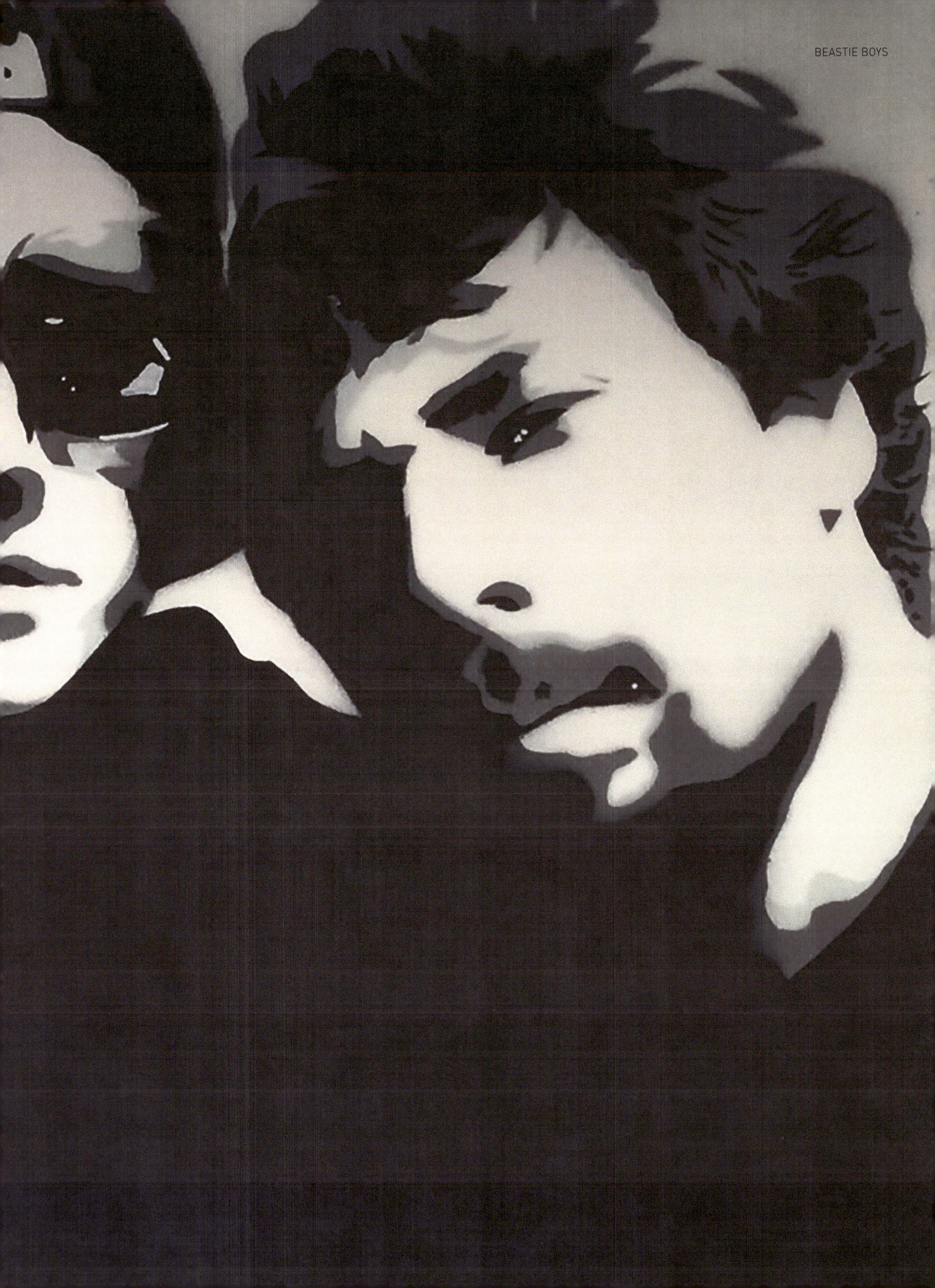

BEASTIE BOYS

BIG KRIT

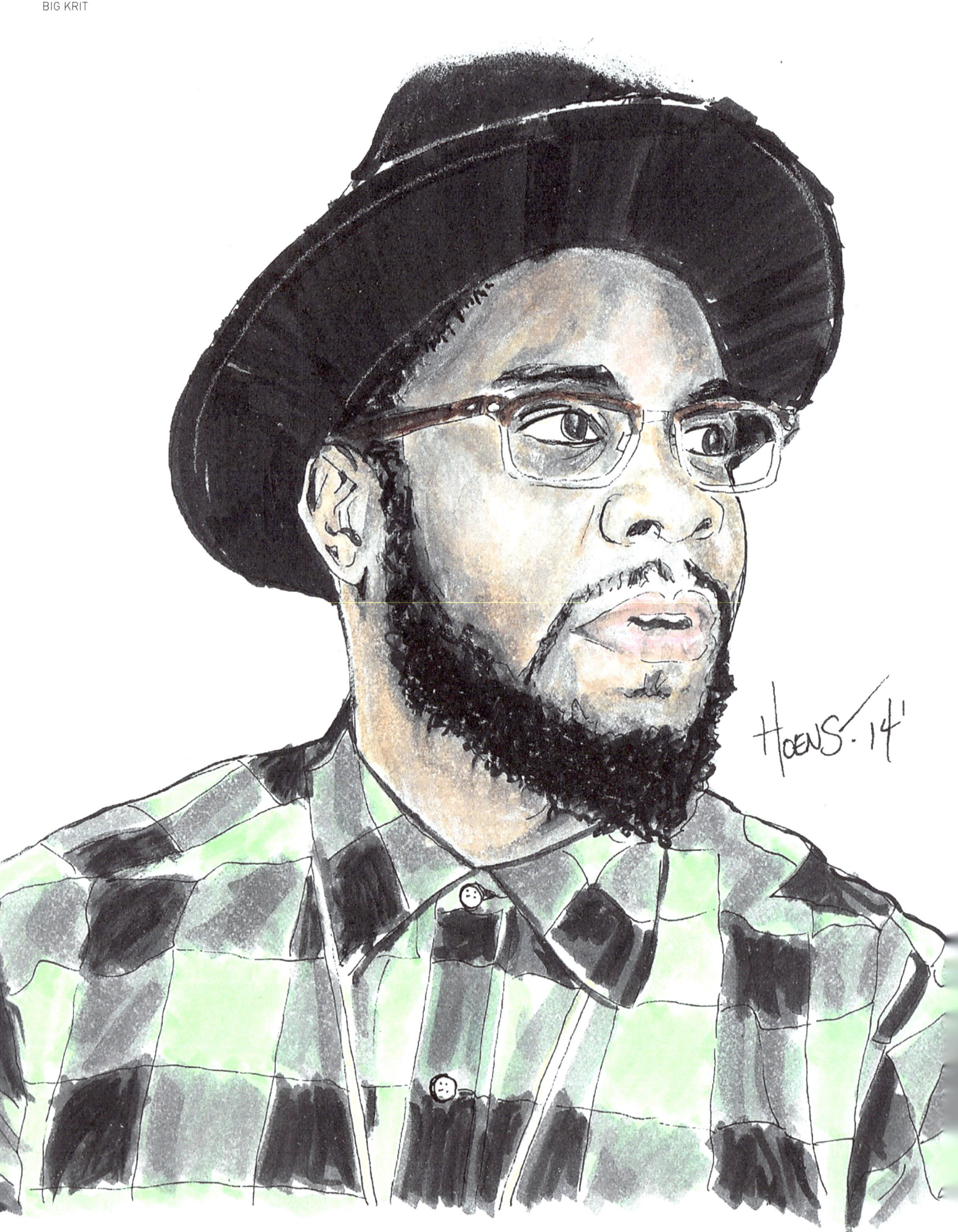

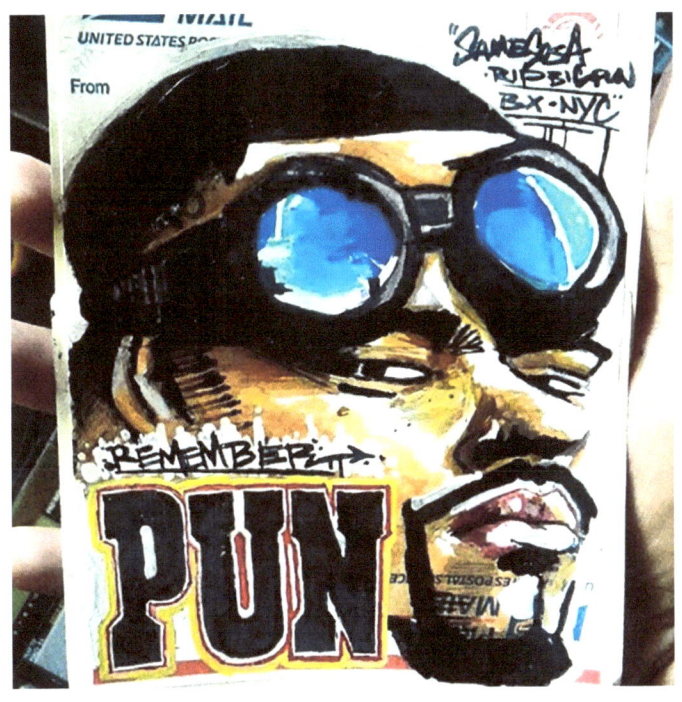
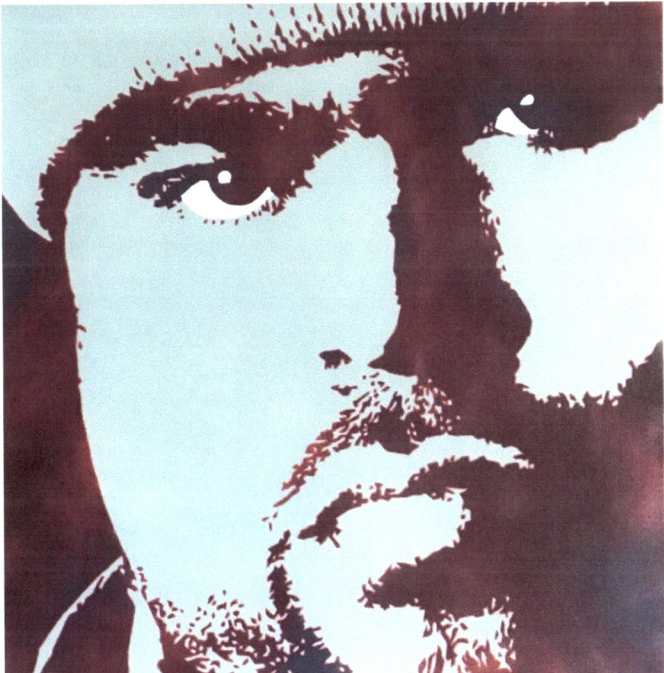
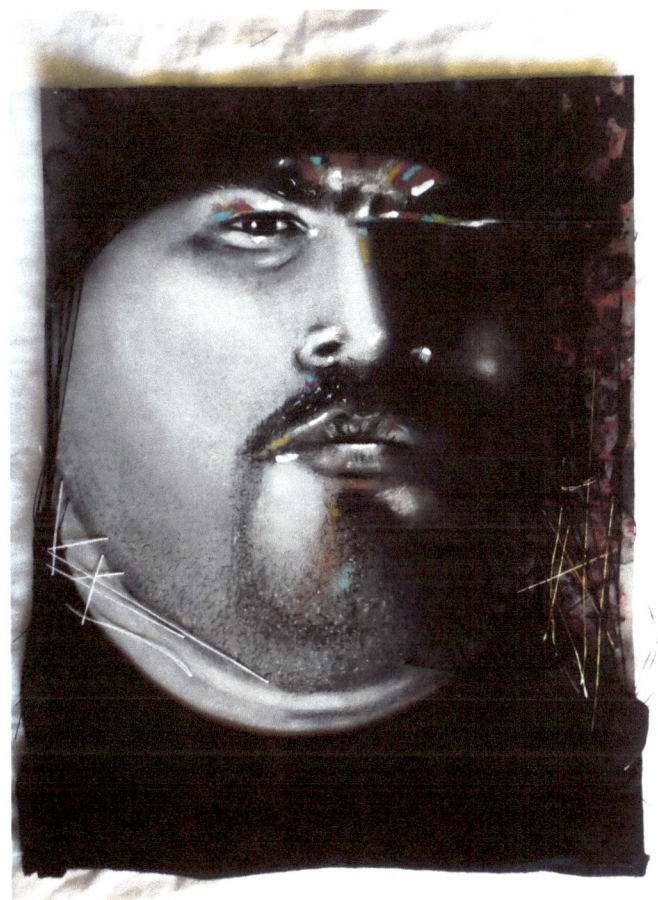

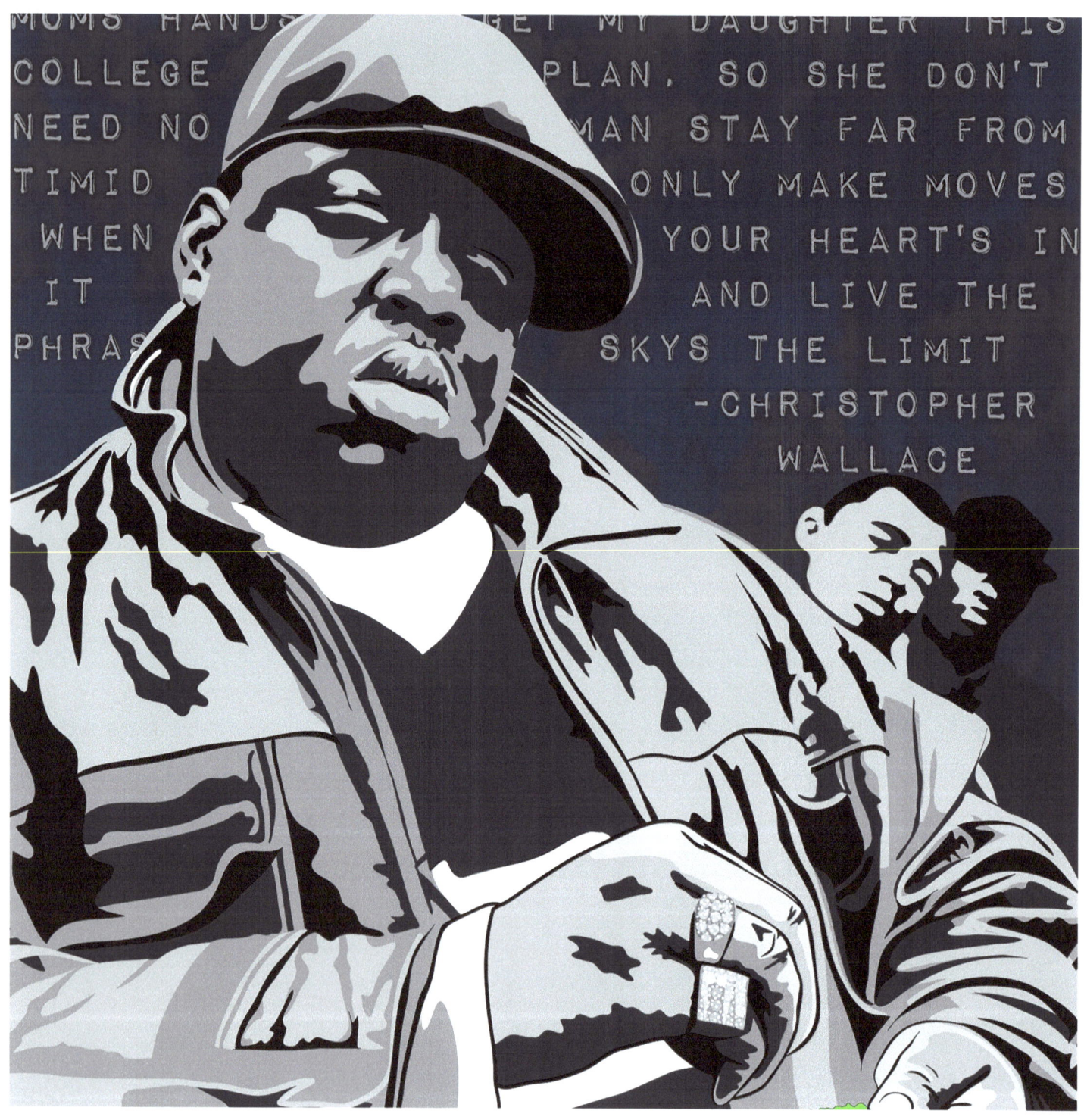

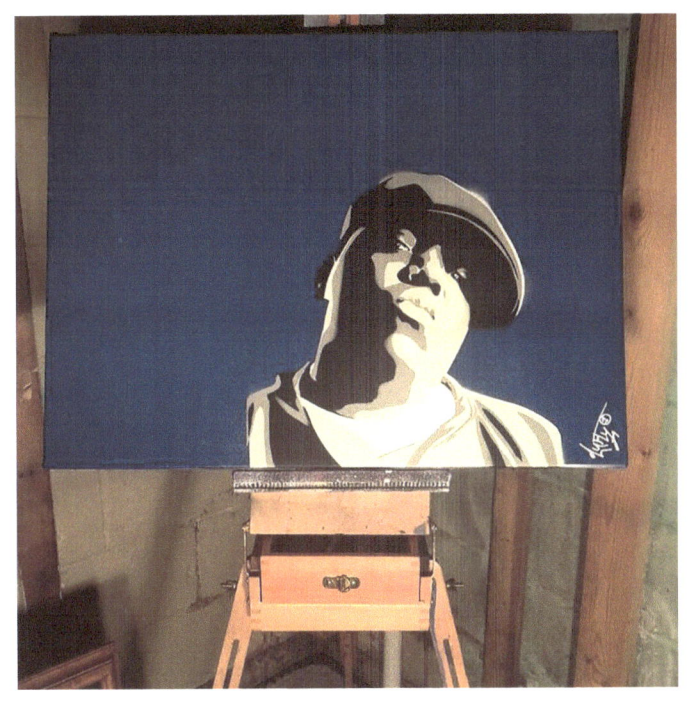
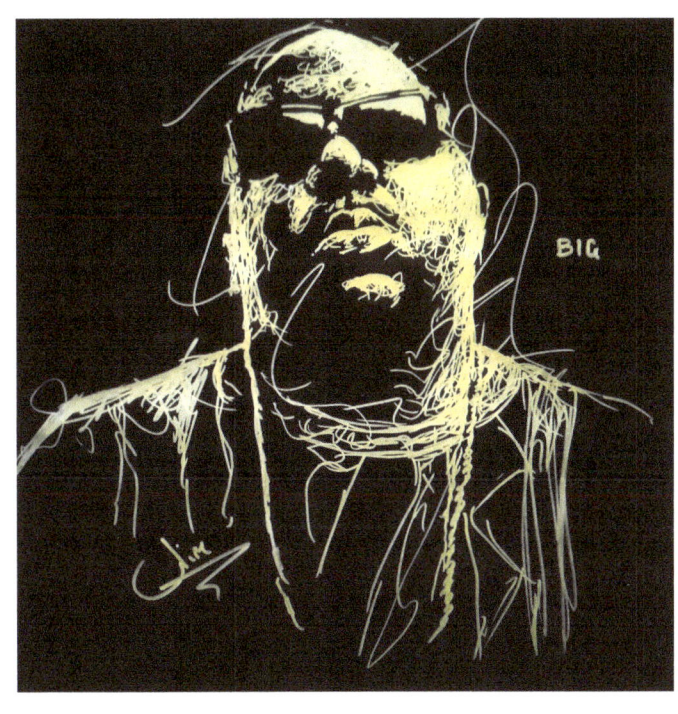
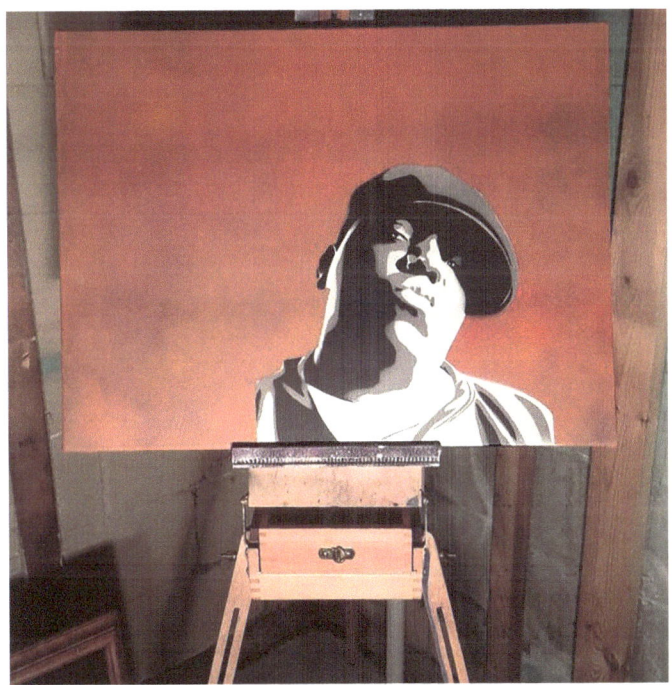
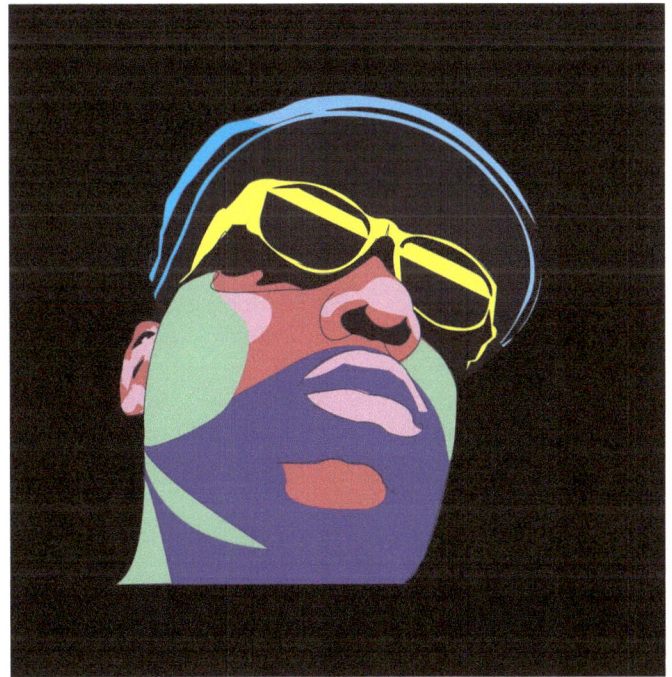

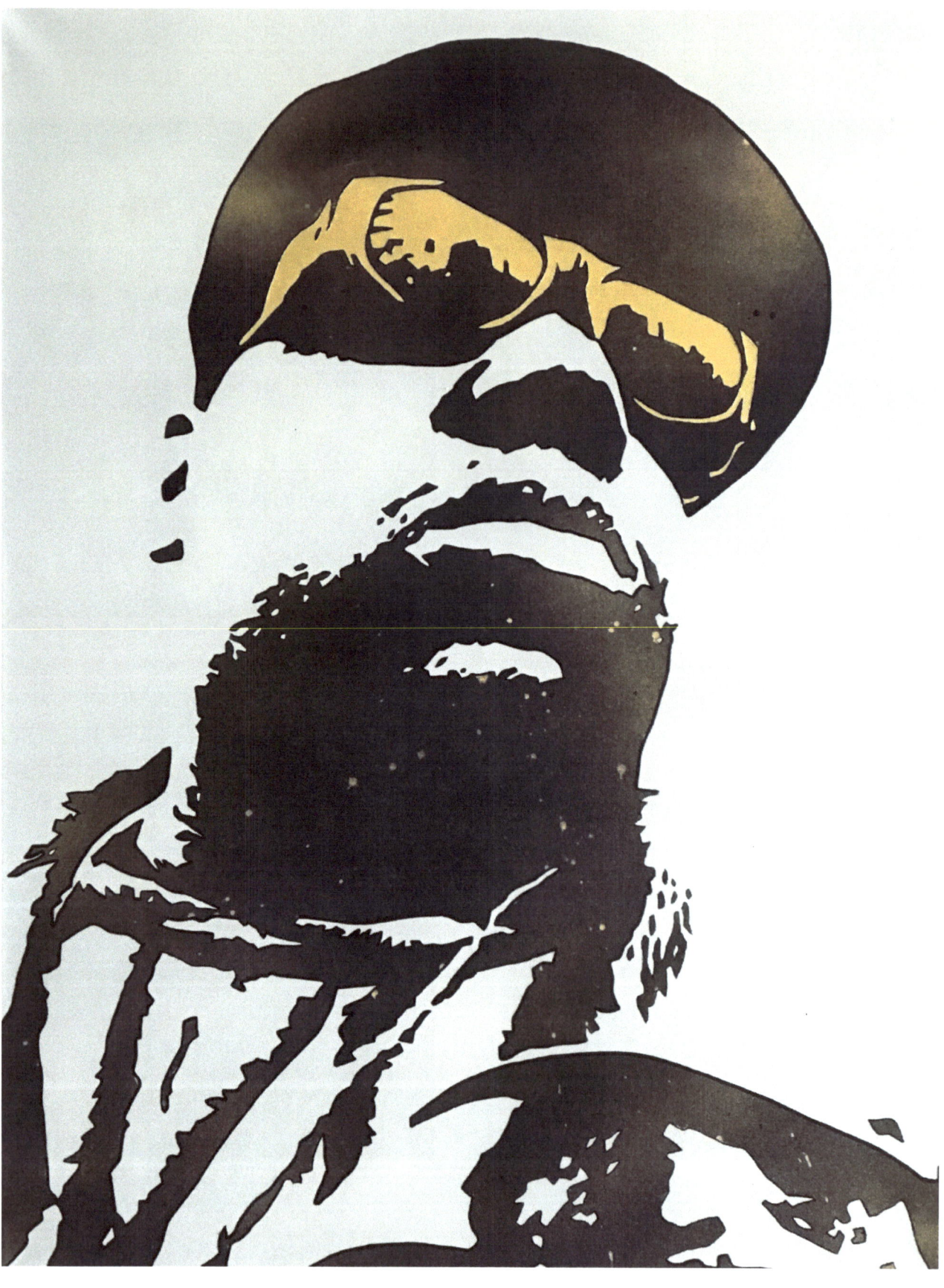

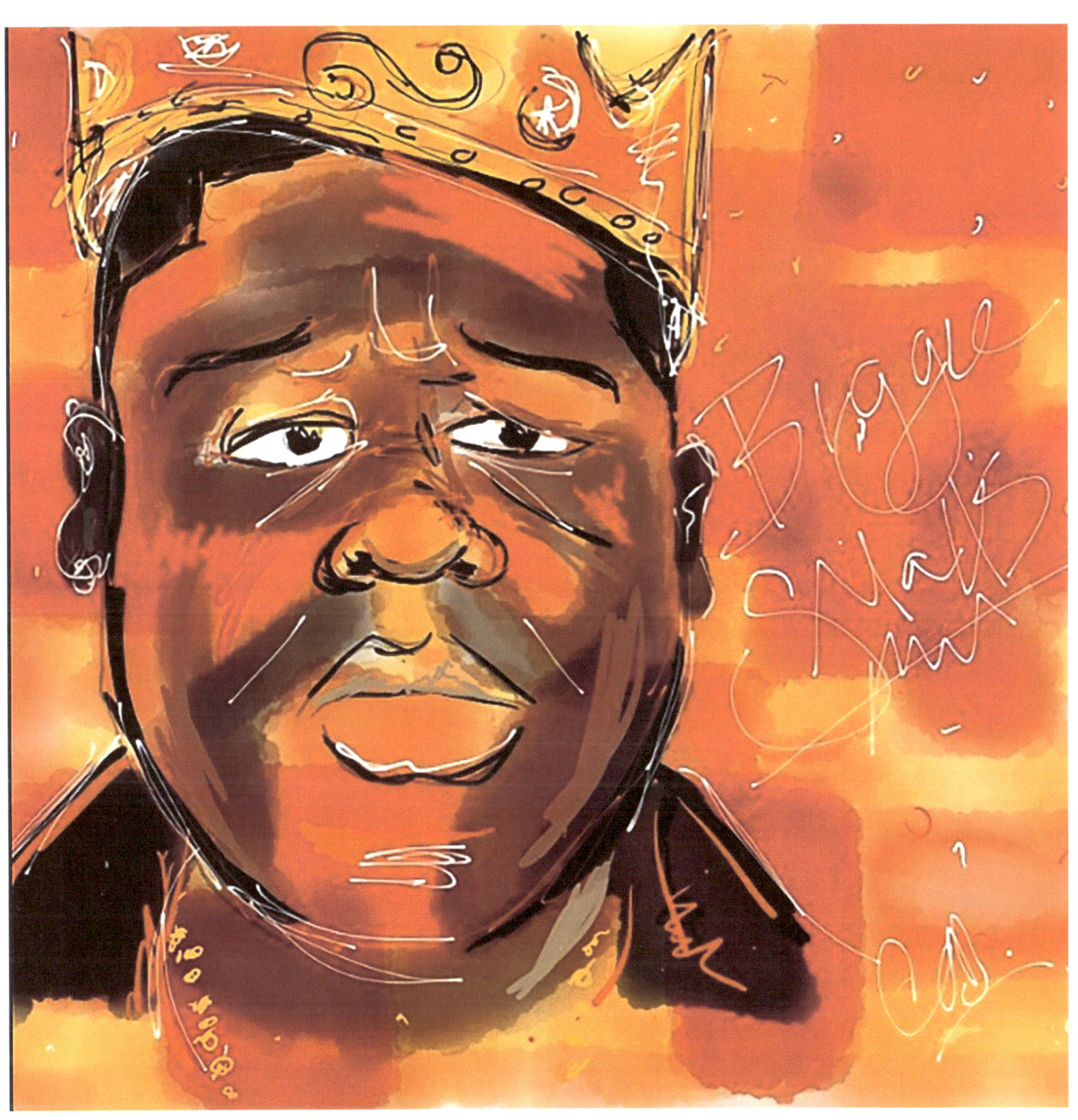

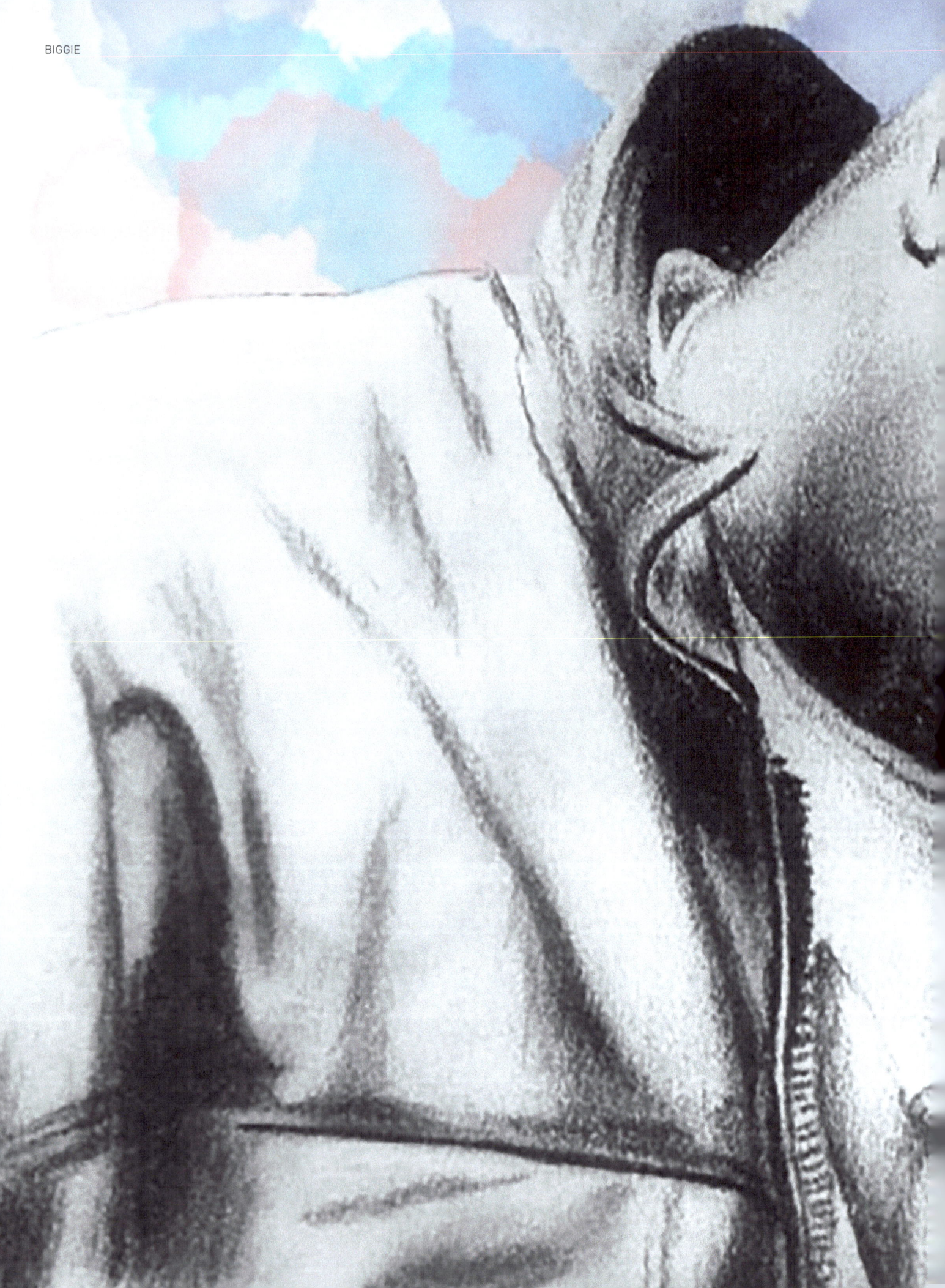

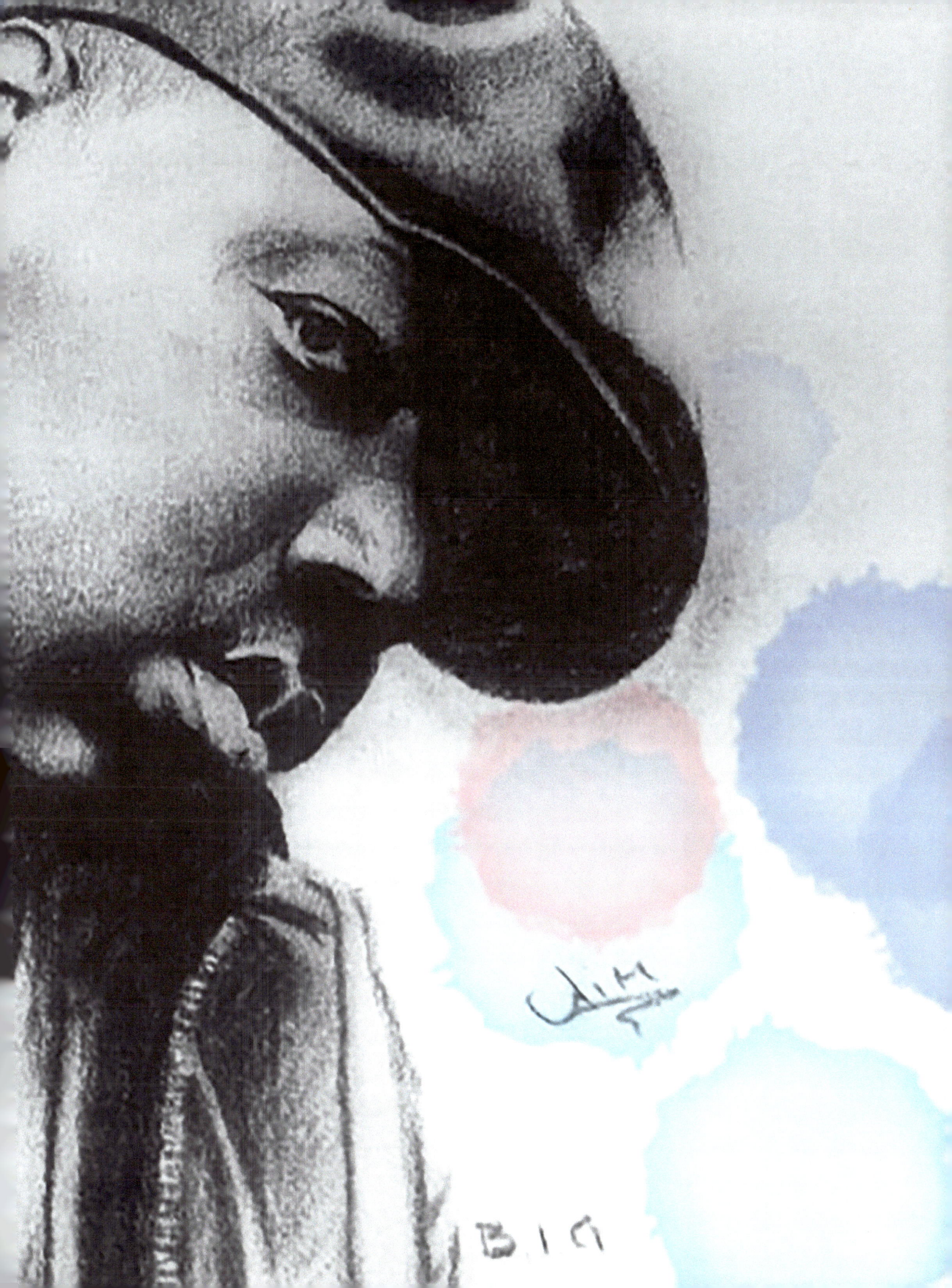

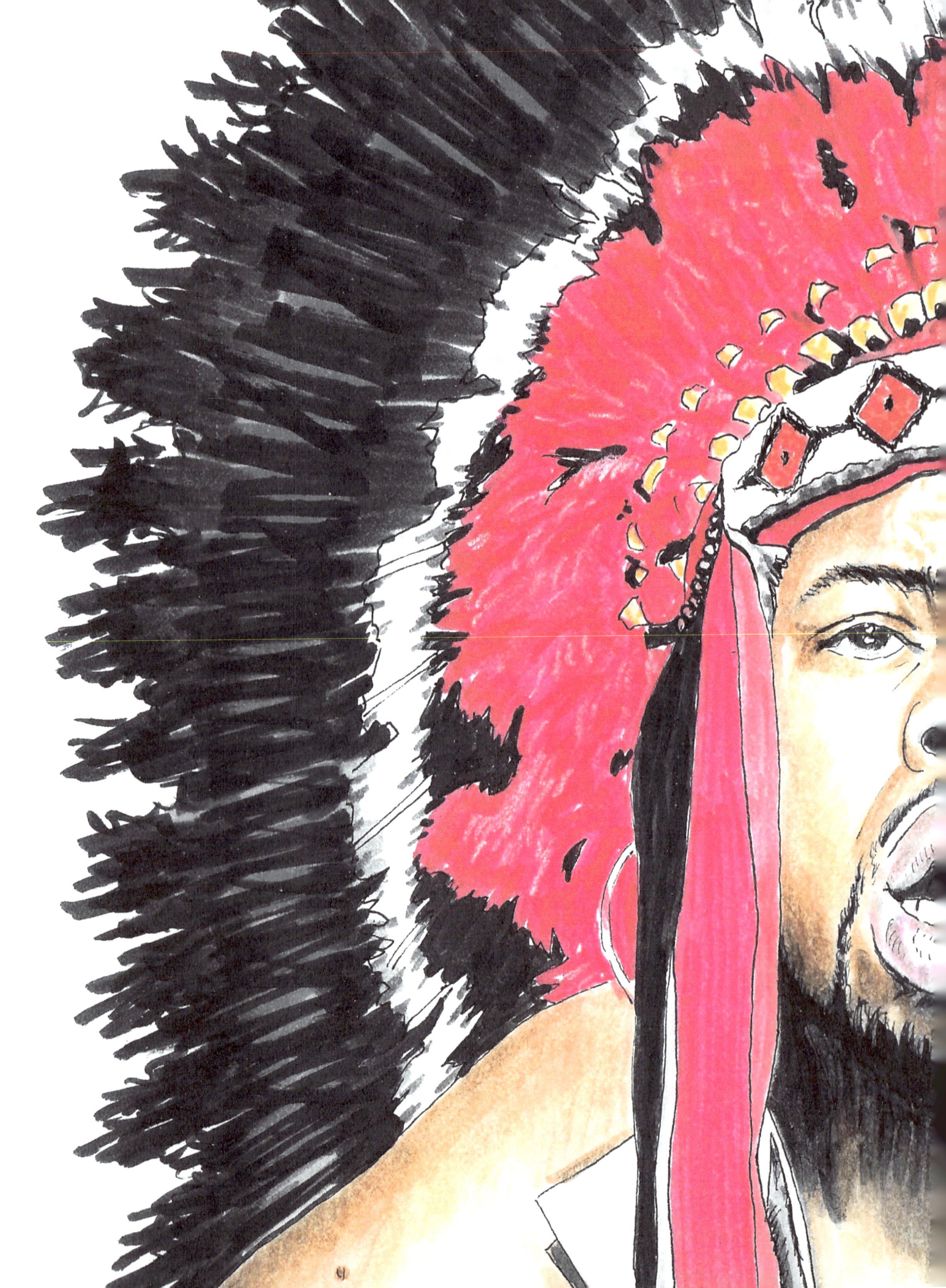

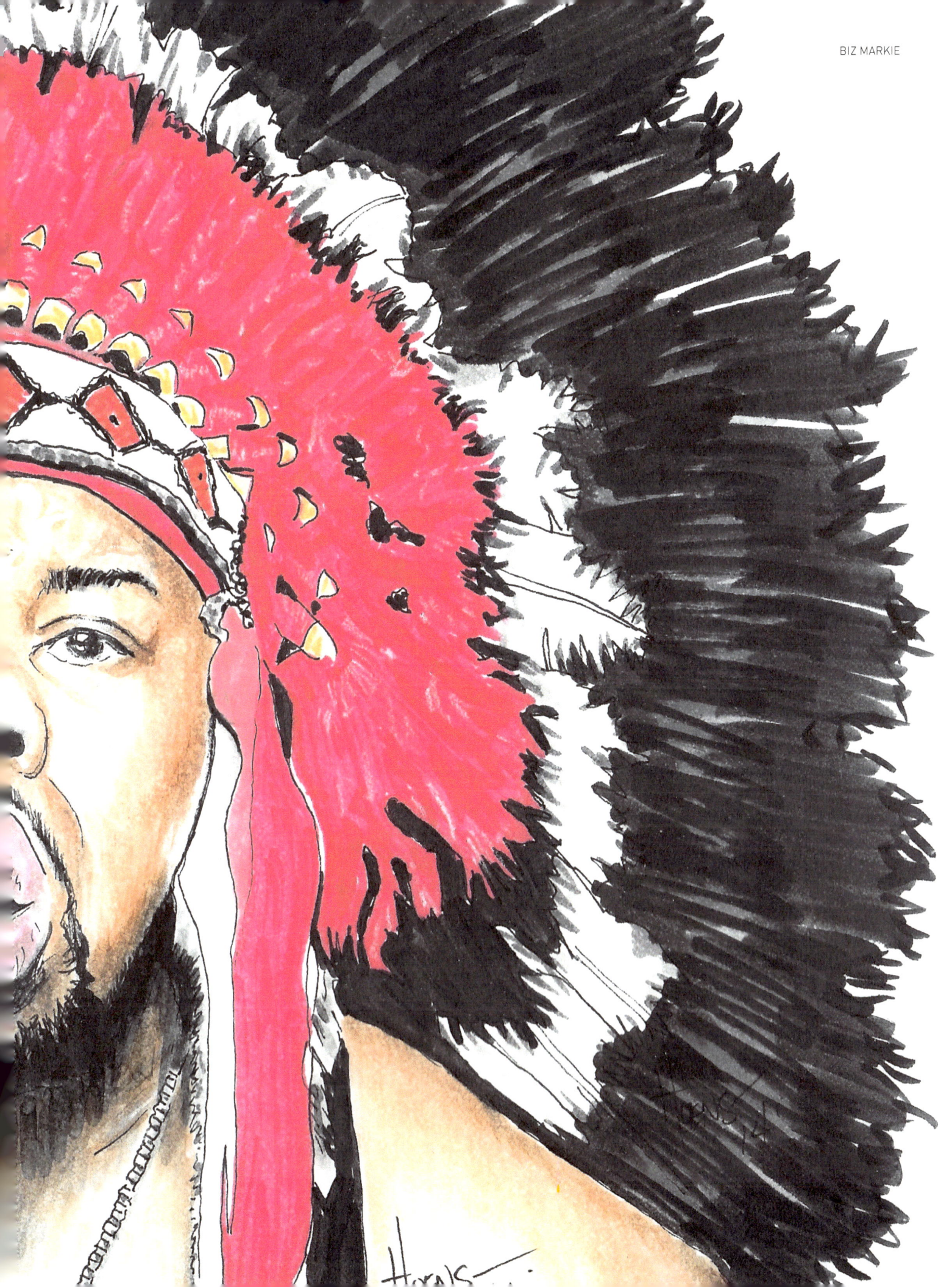
BIZ MARKIE

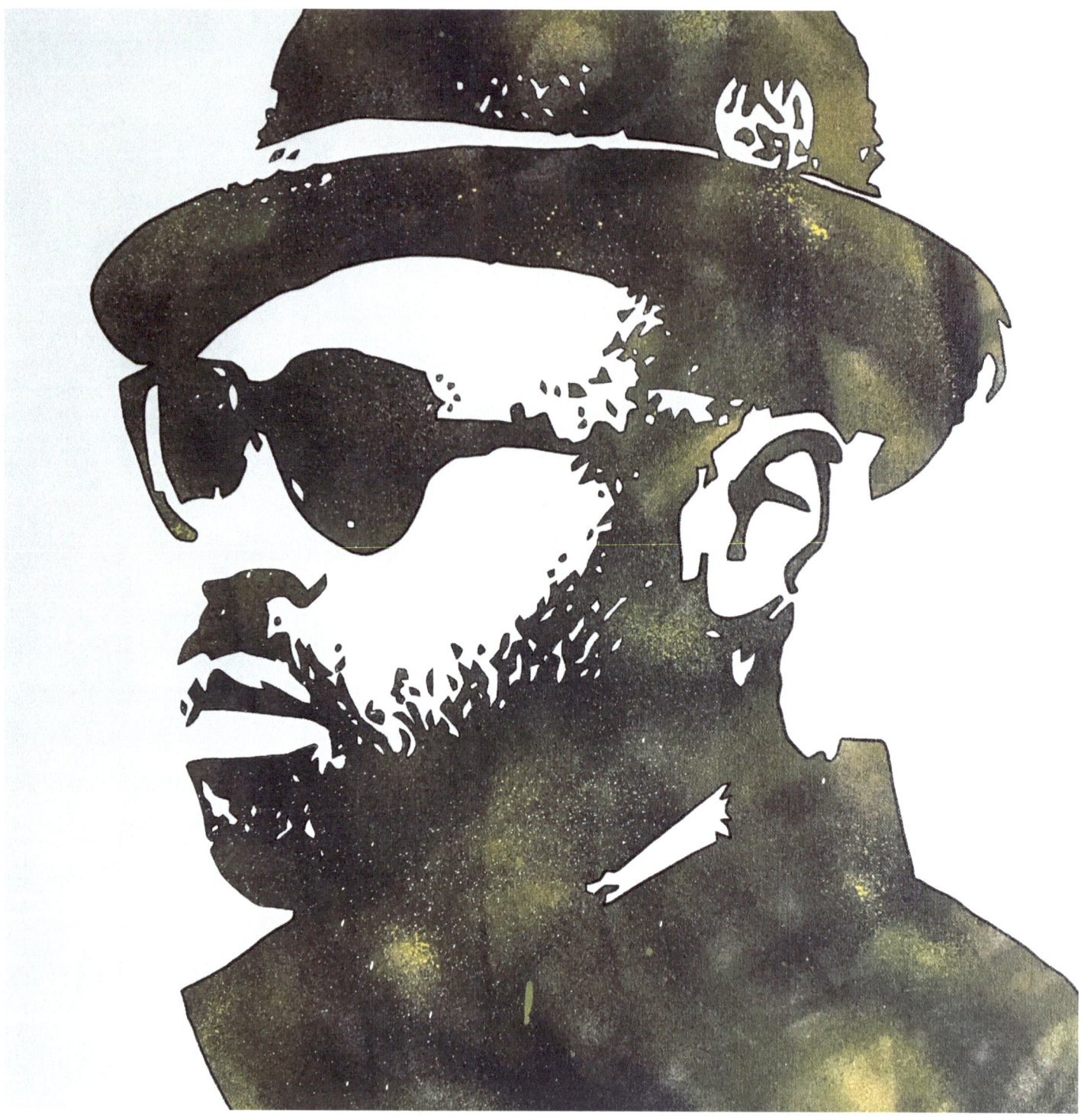

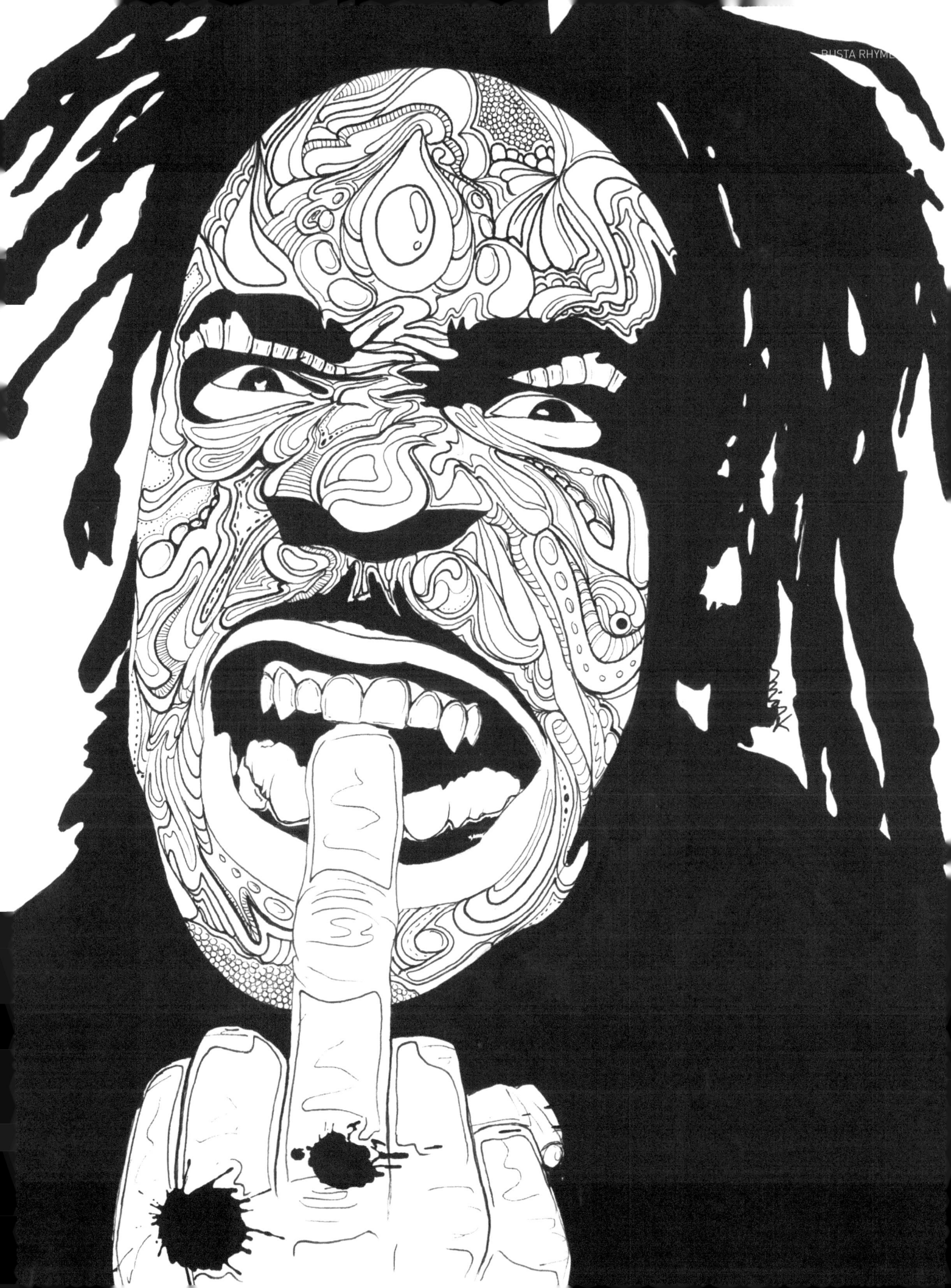

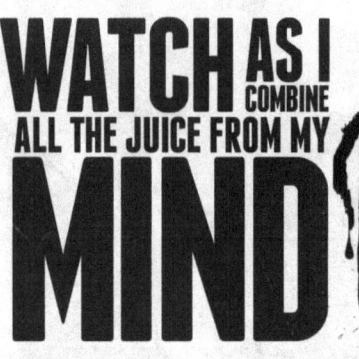

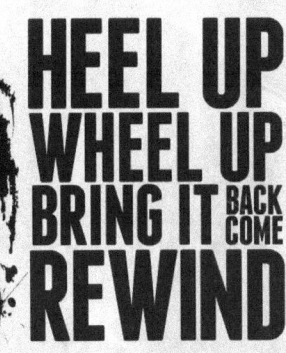
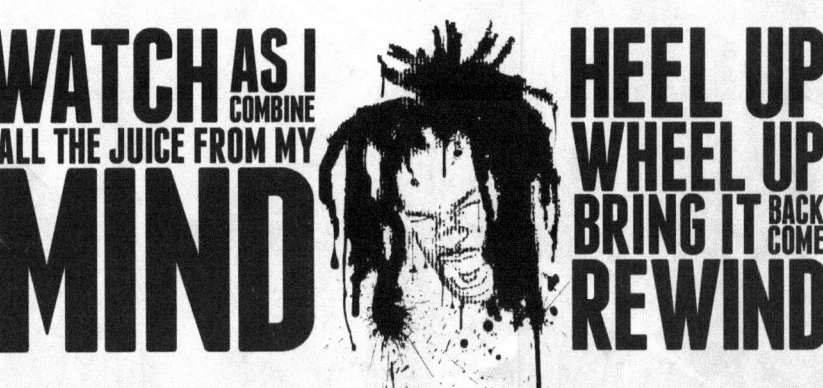
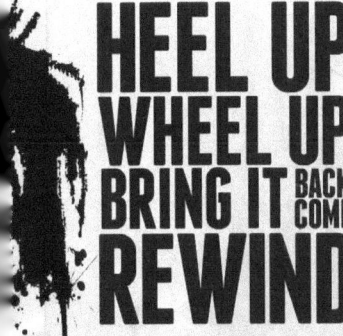
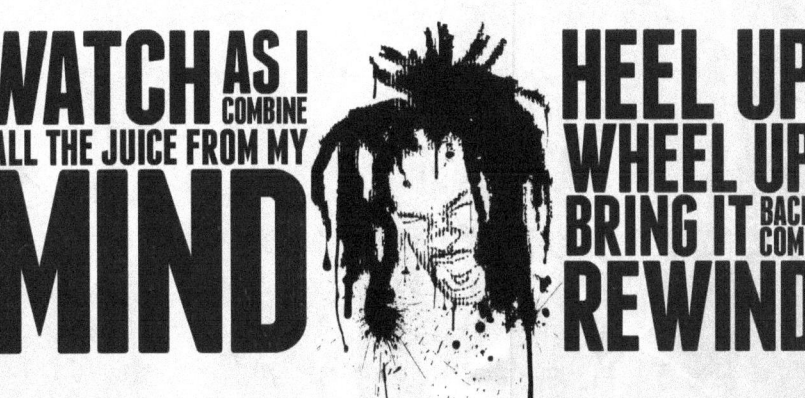
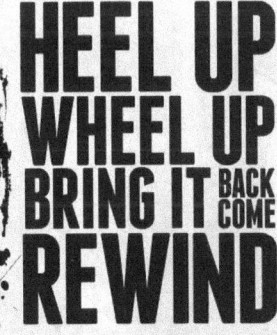
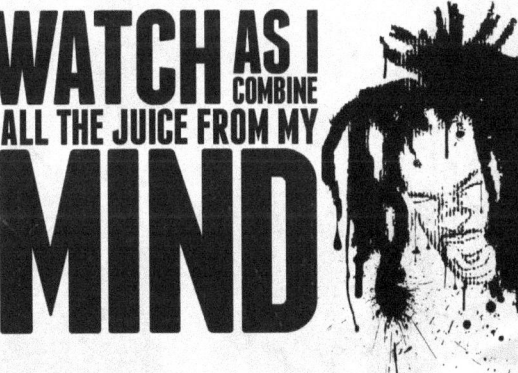
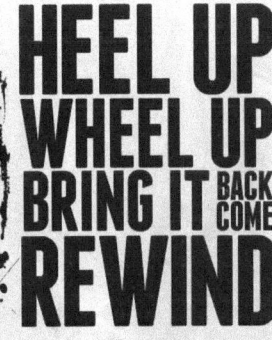
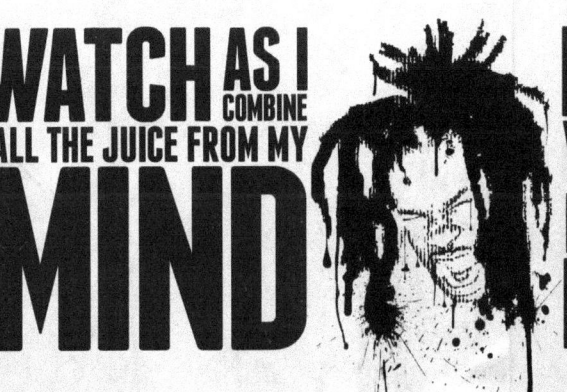

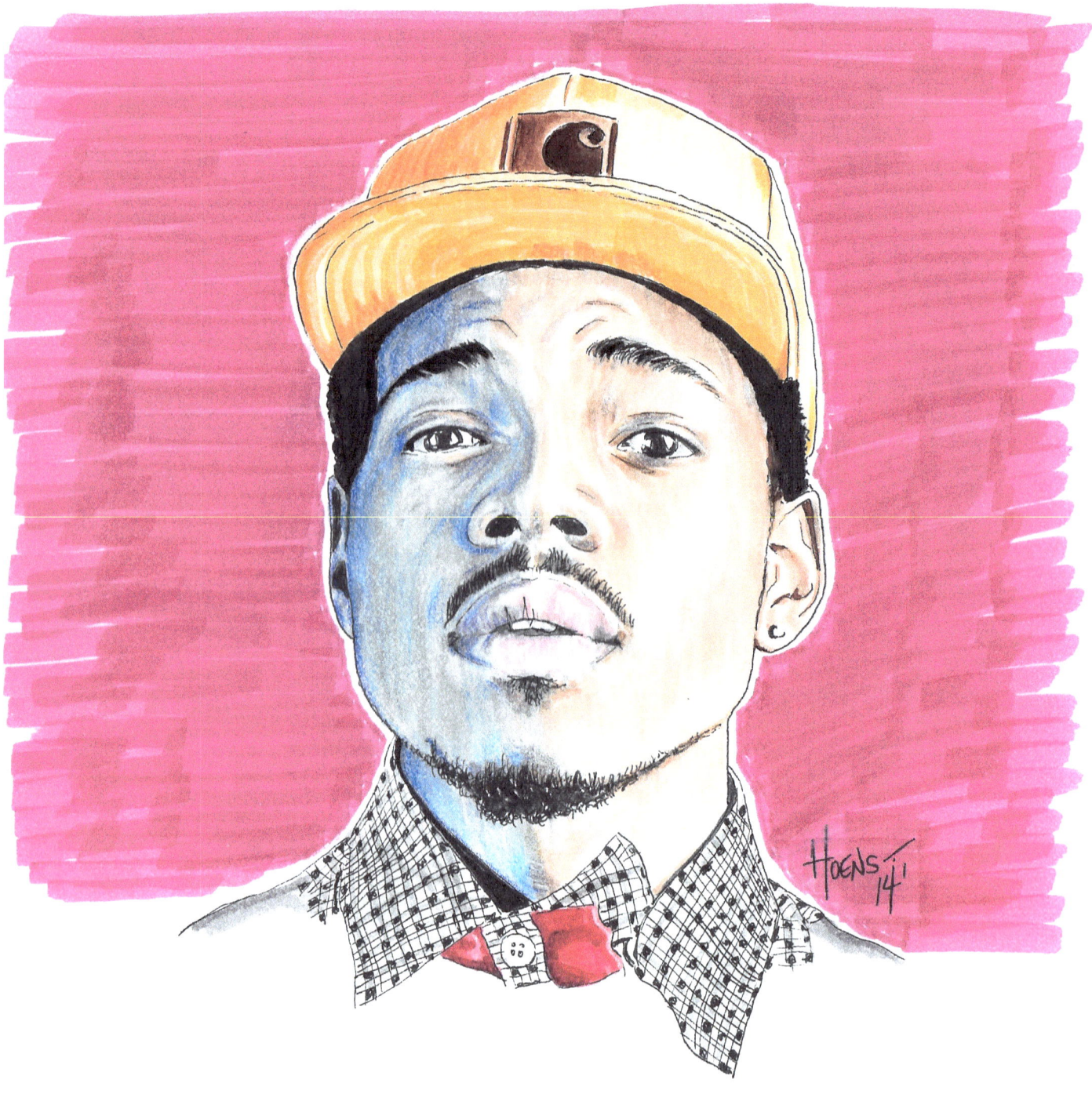

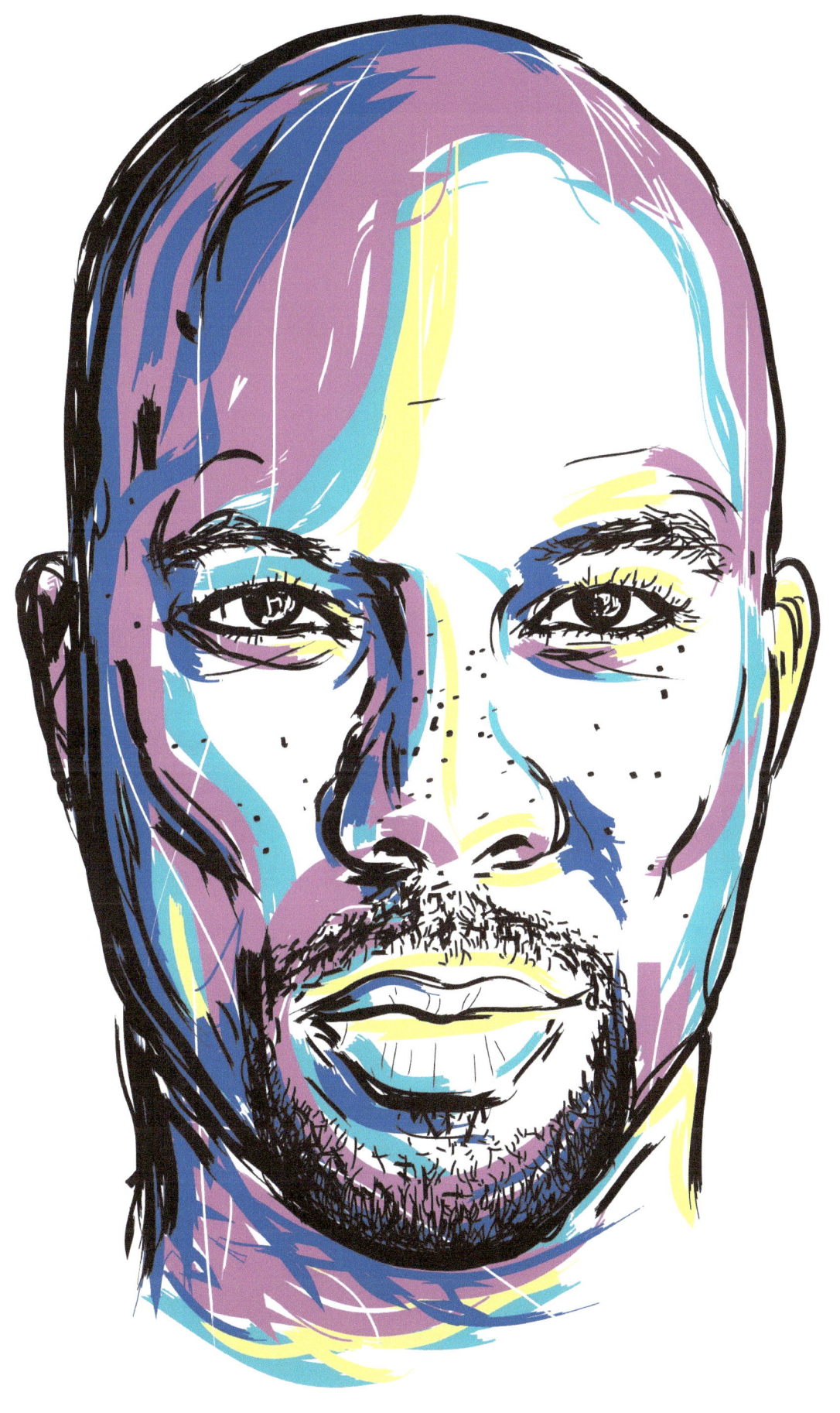
COMMON

DANNY BROWN

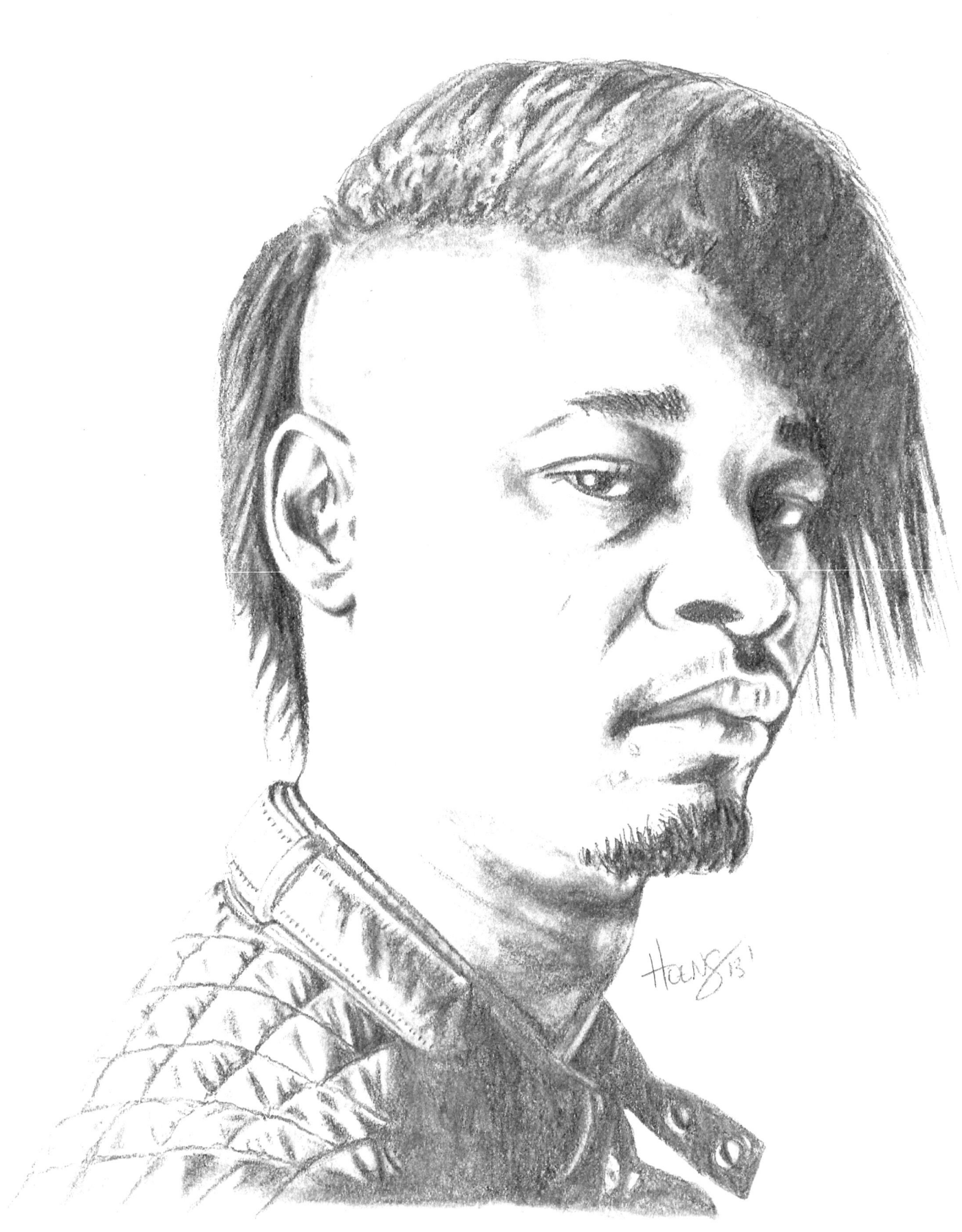

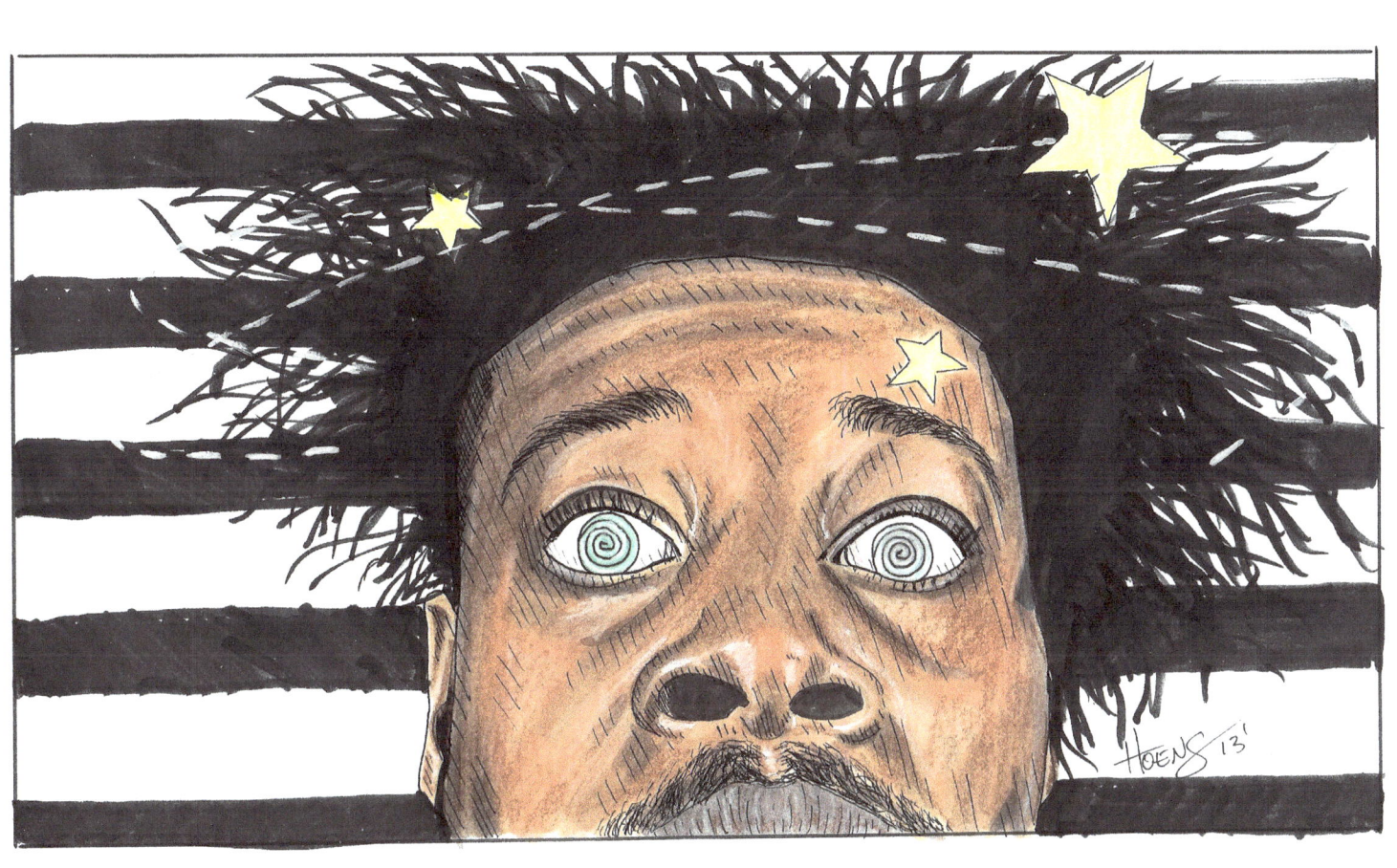

DEATH ROW

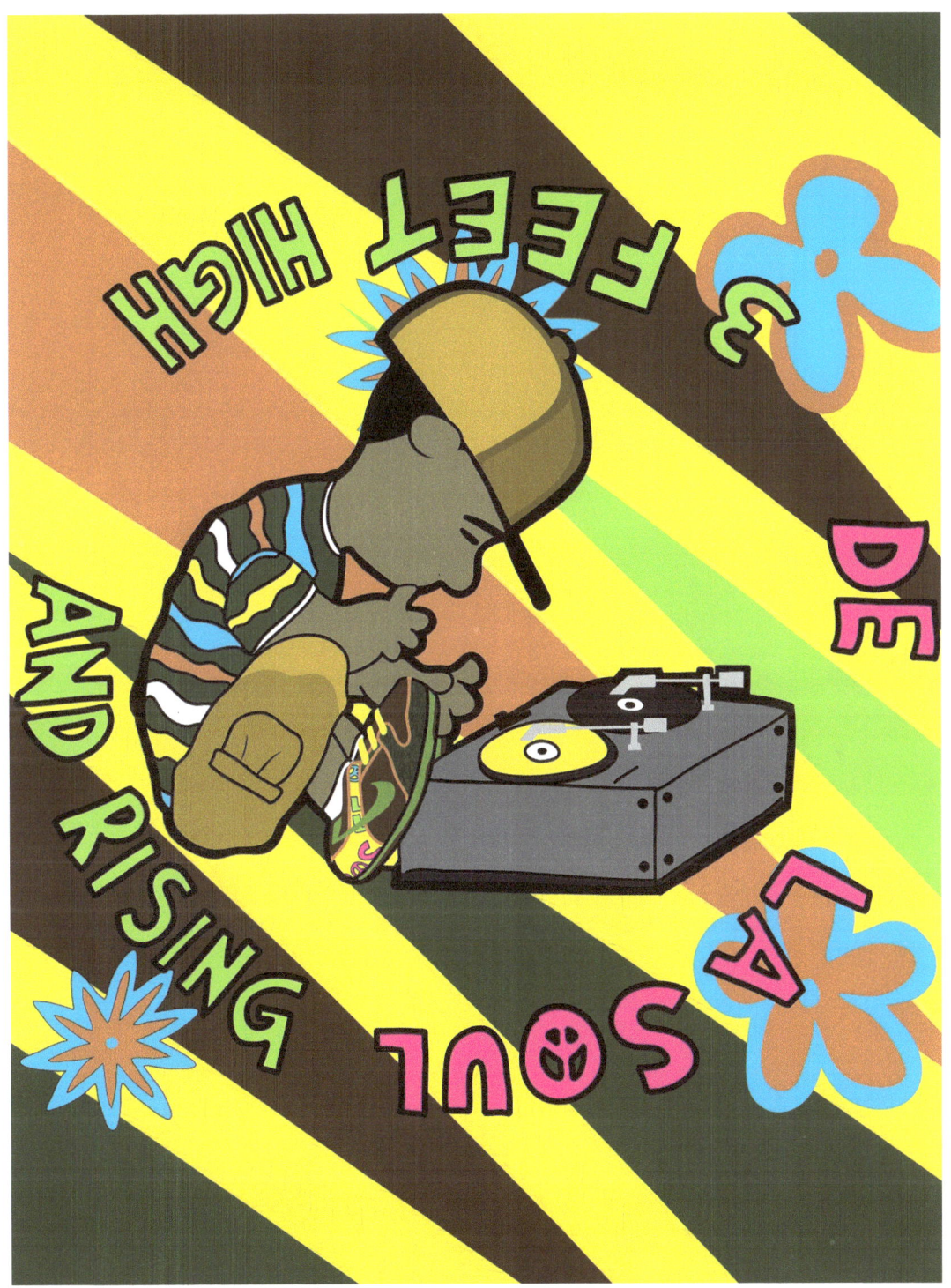

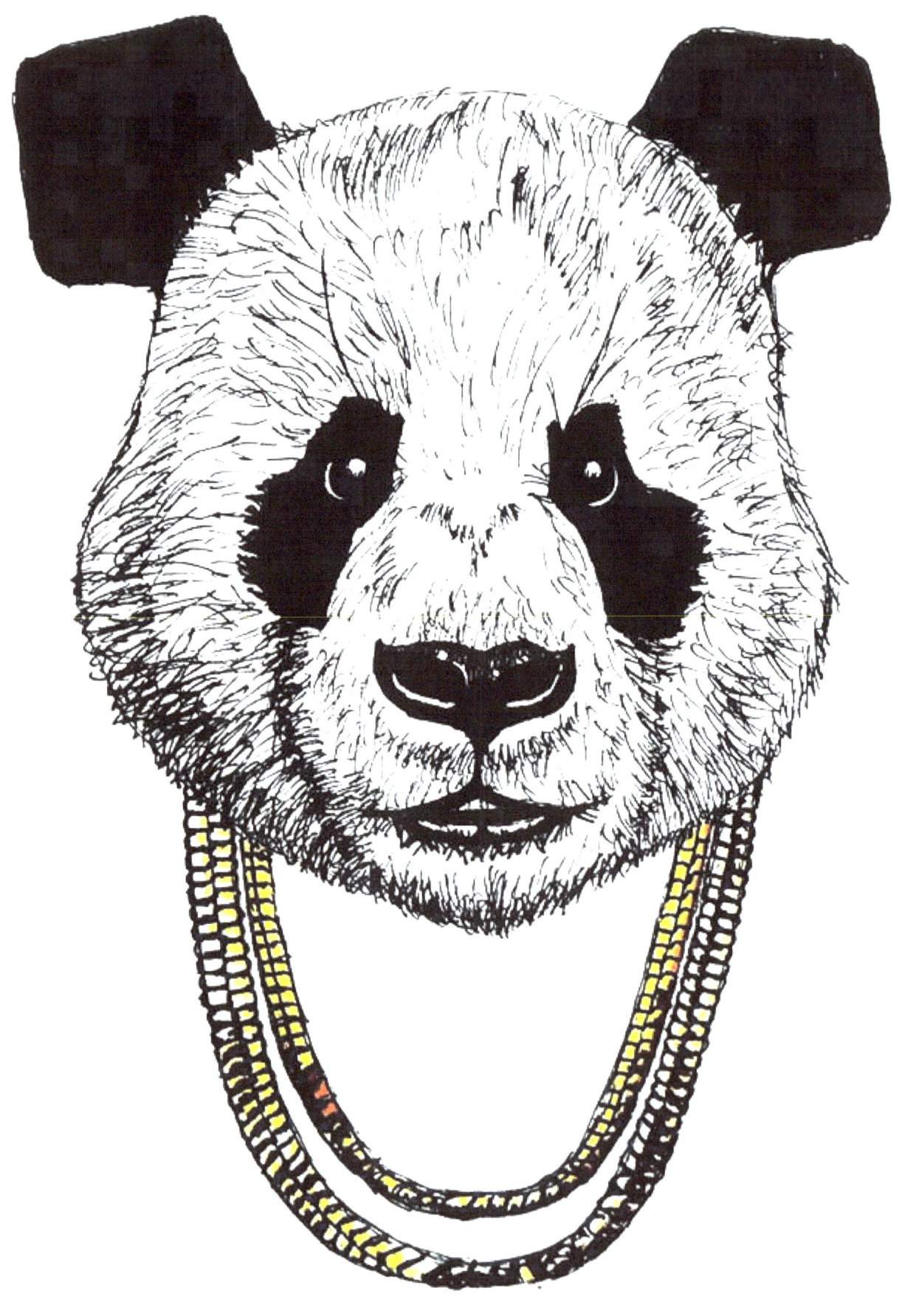

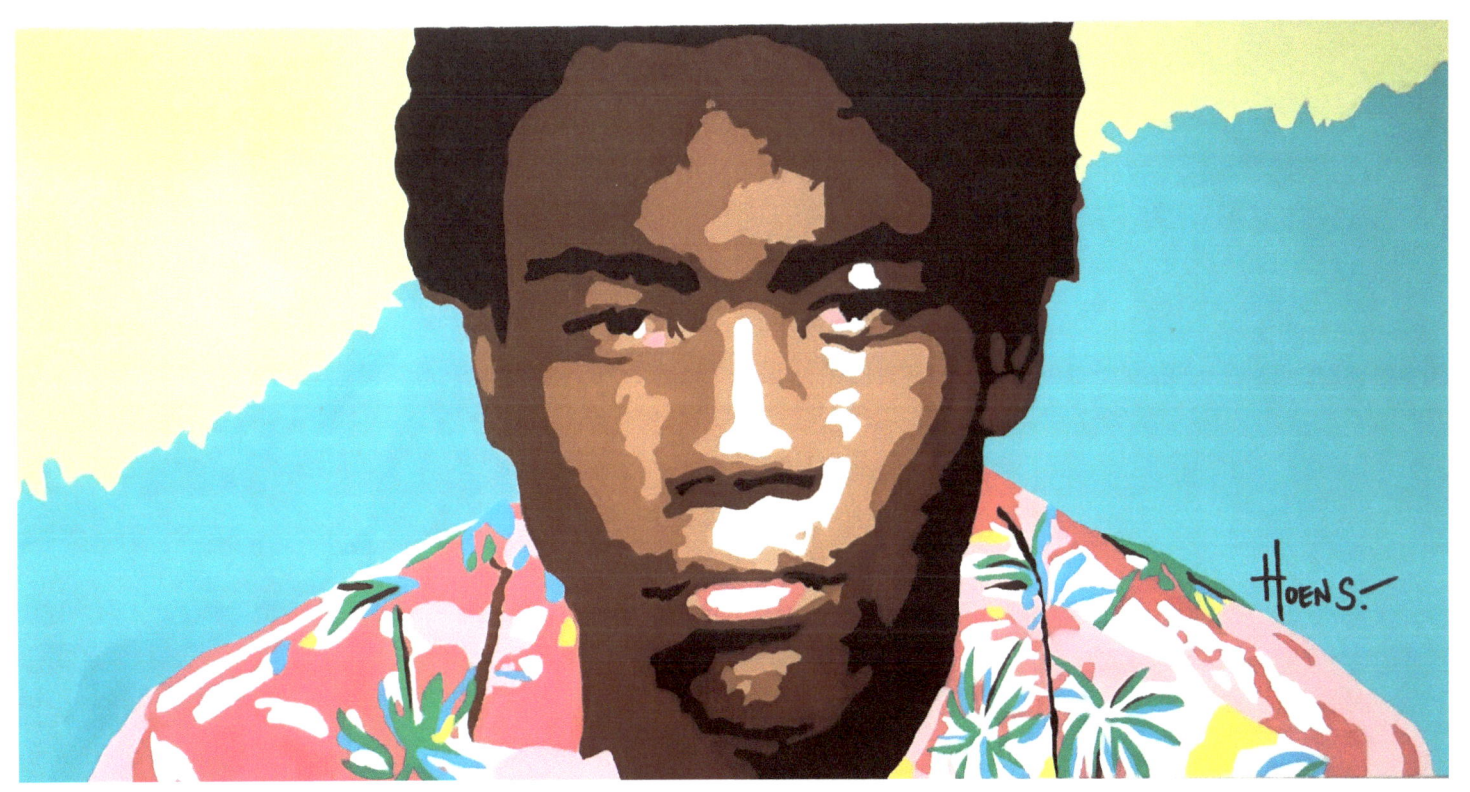

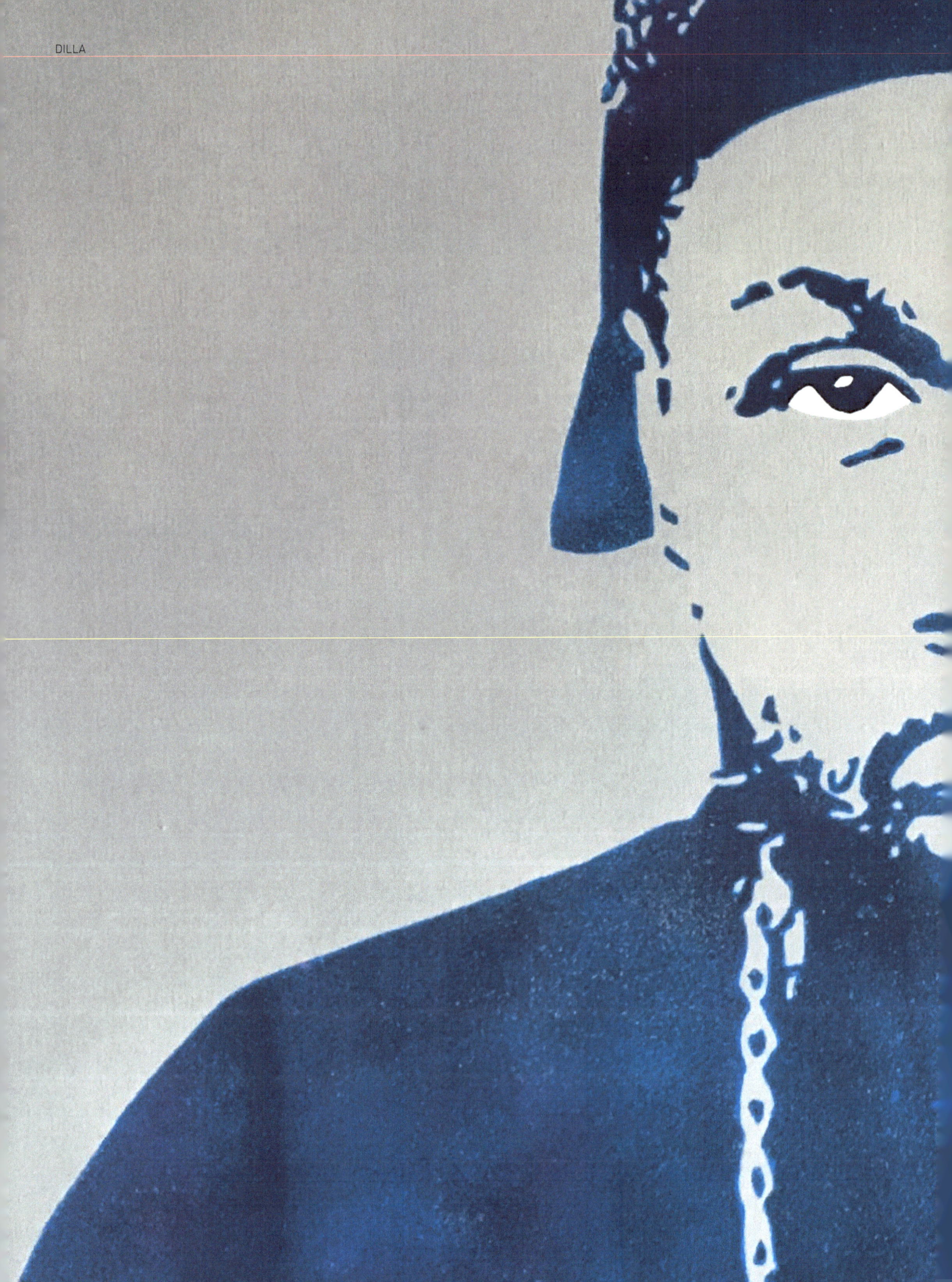

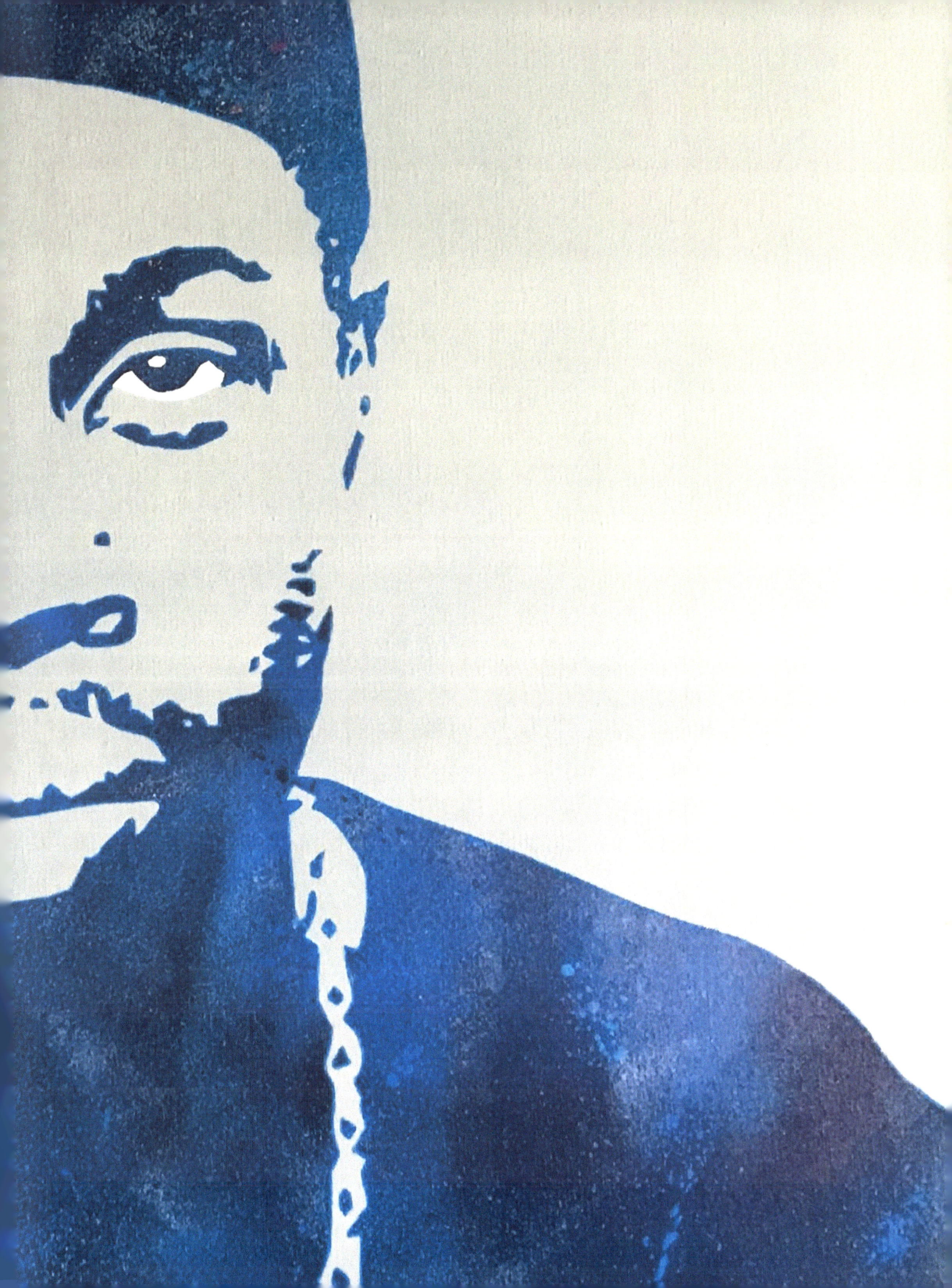

DJ PREMIERE

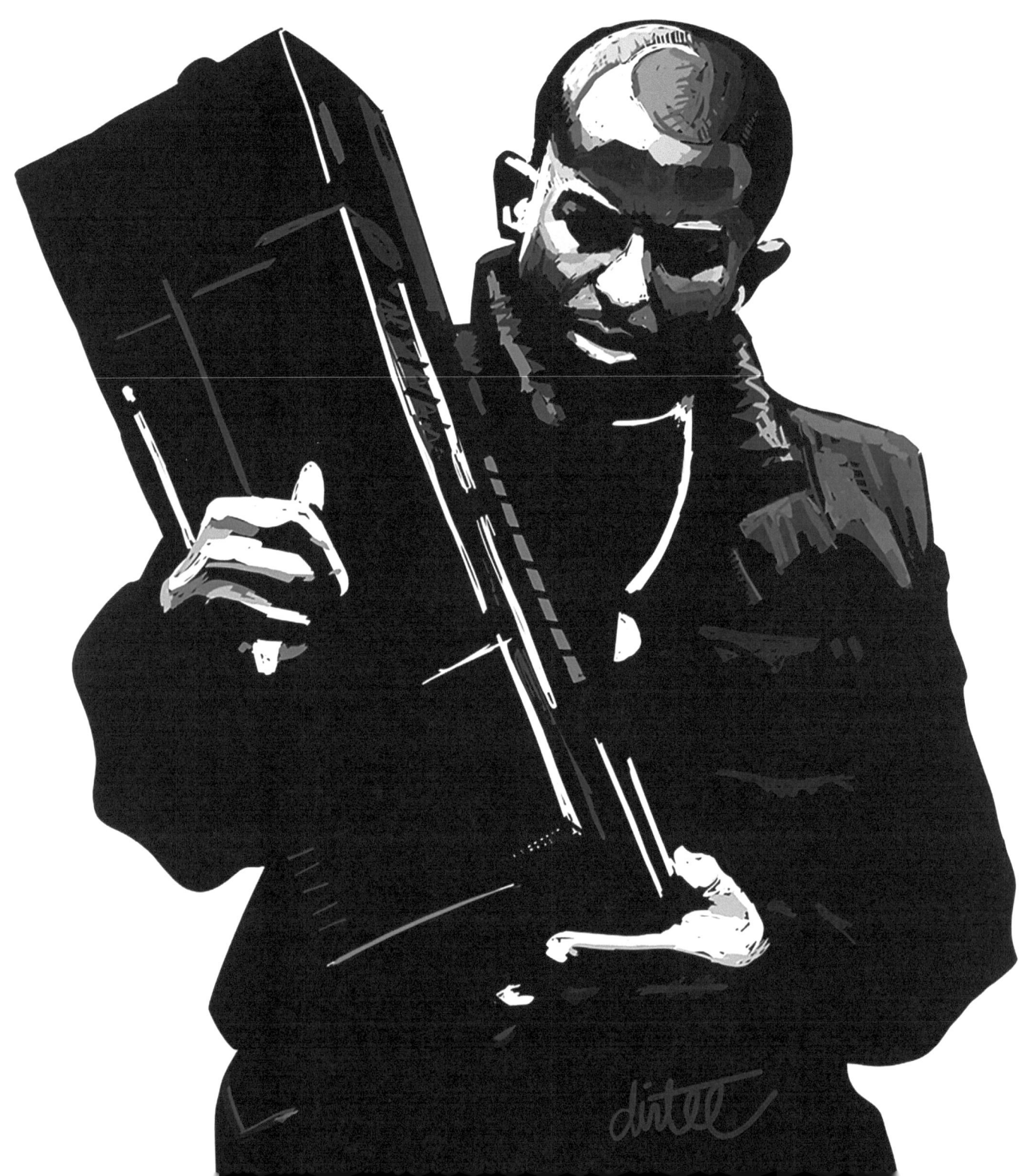

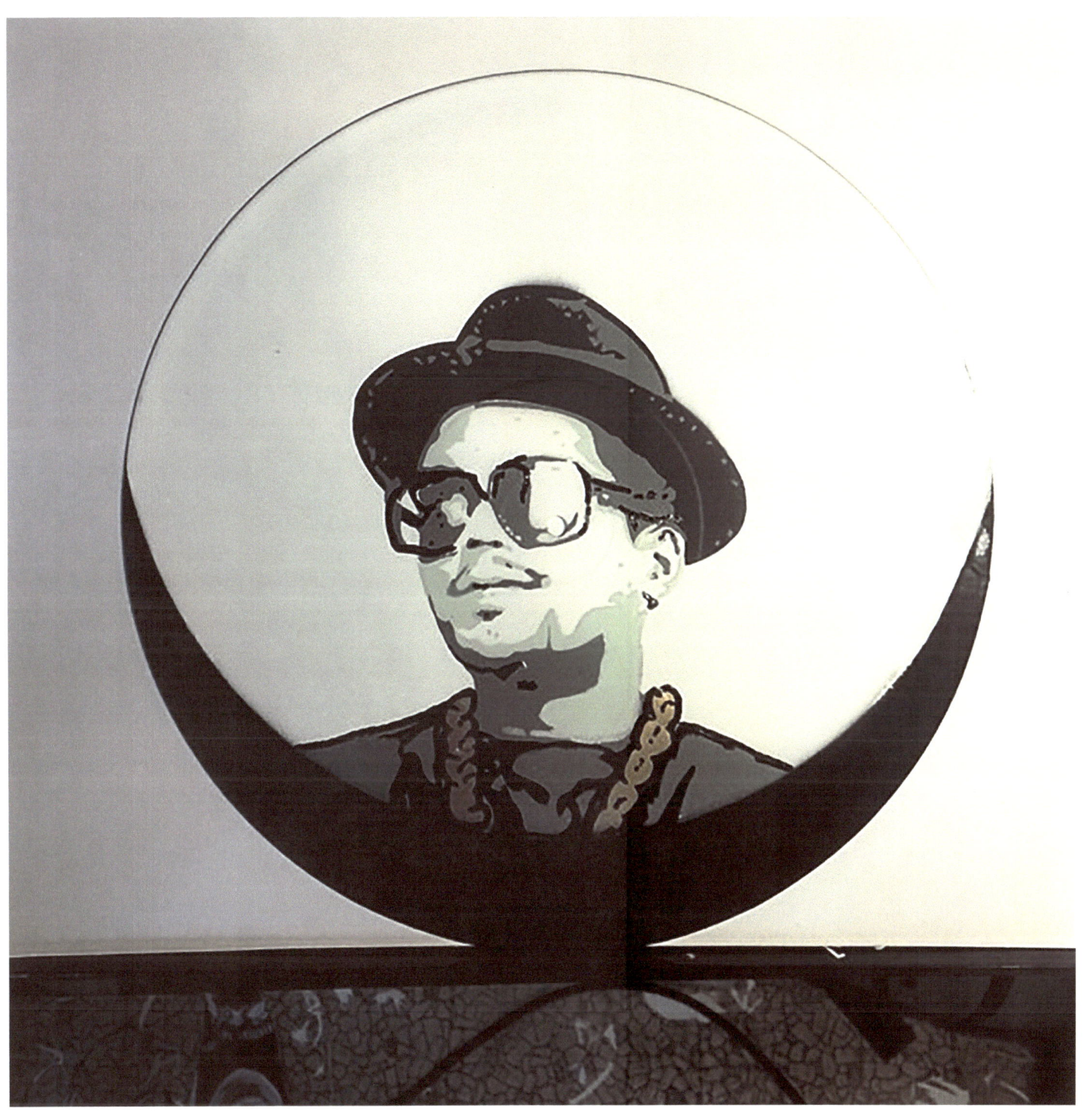

DMC

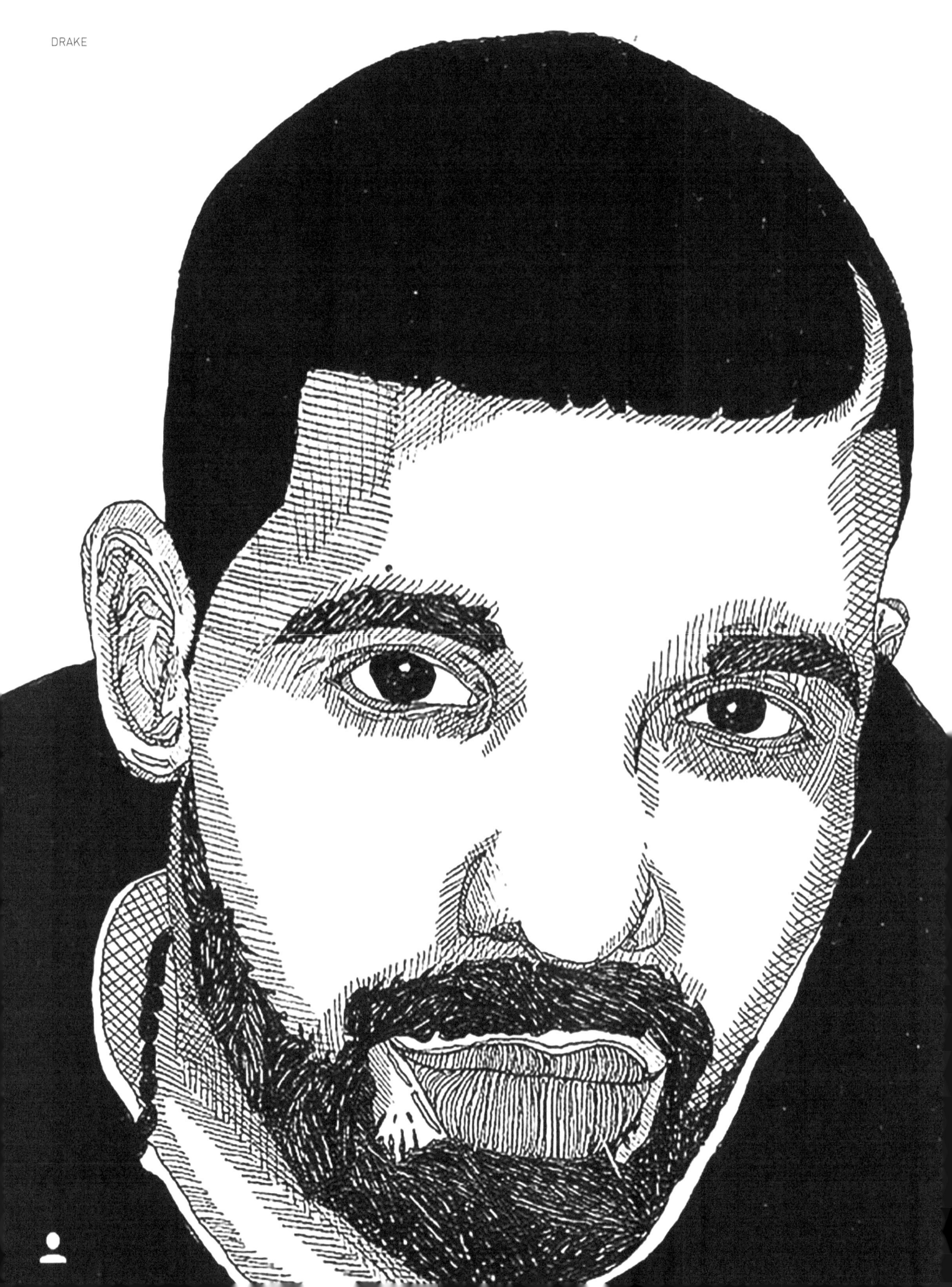

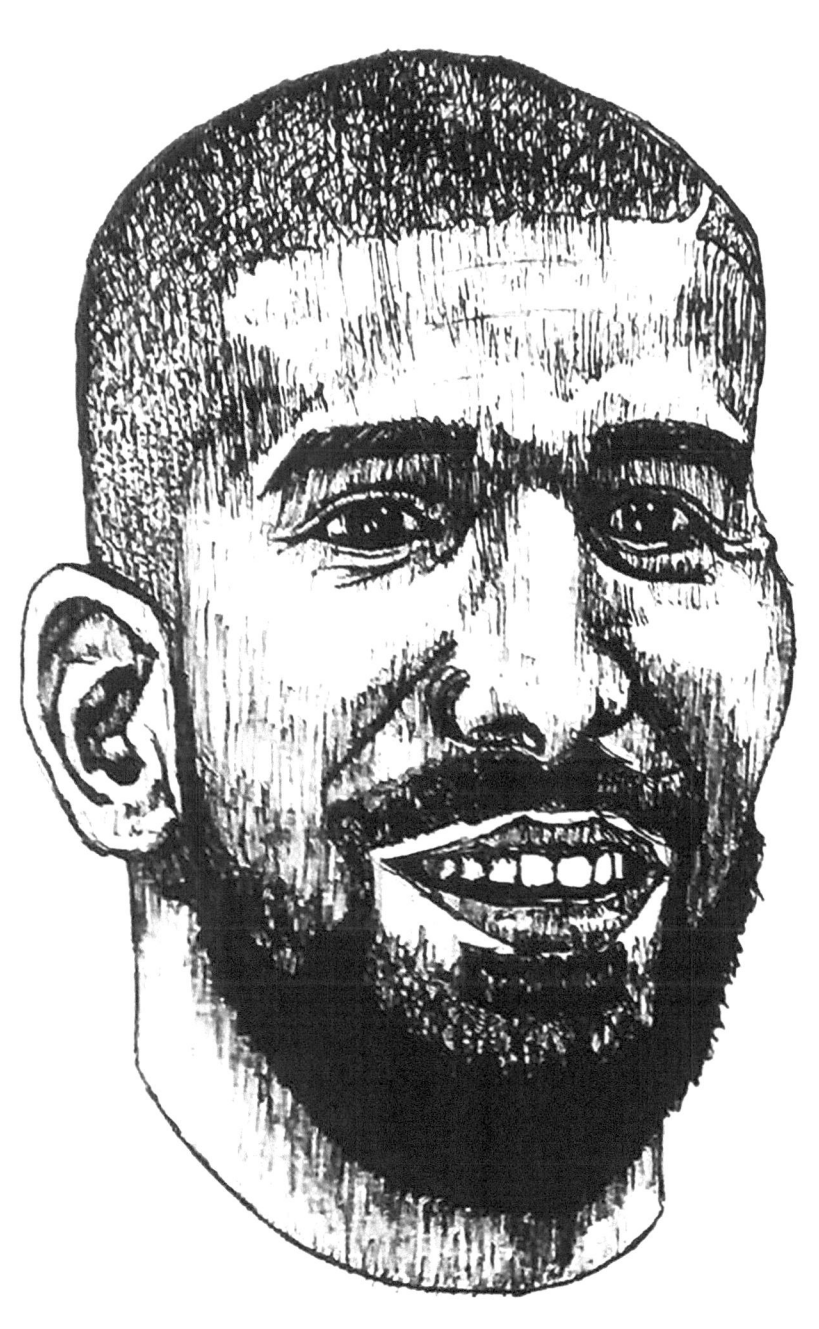

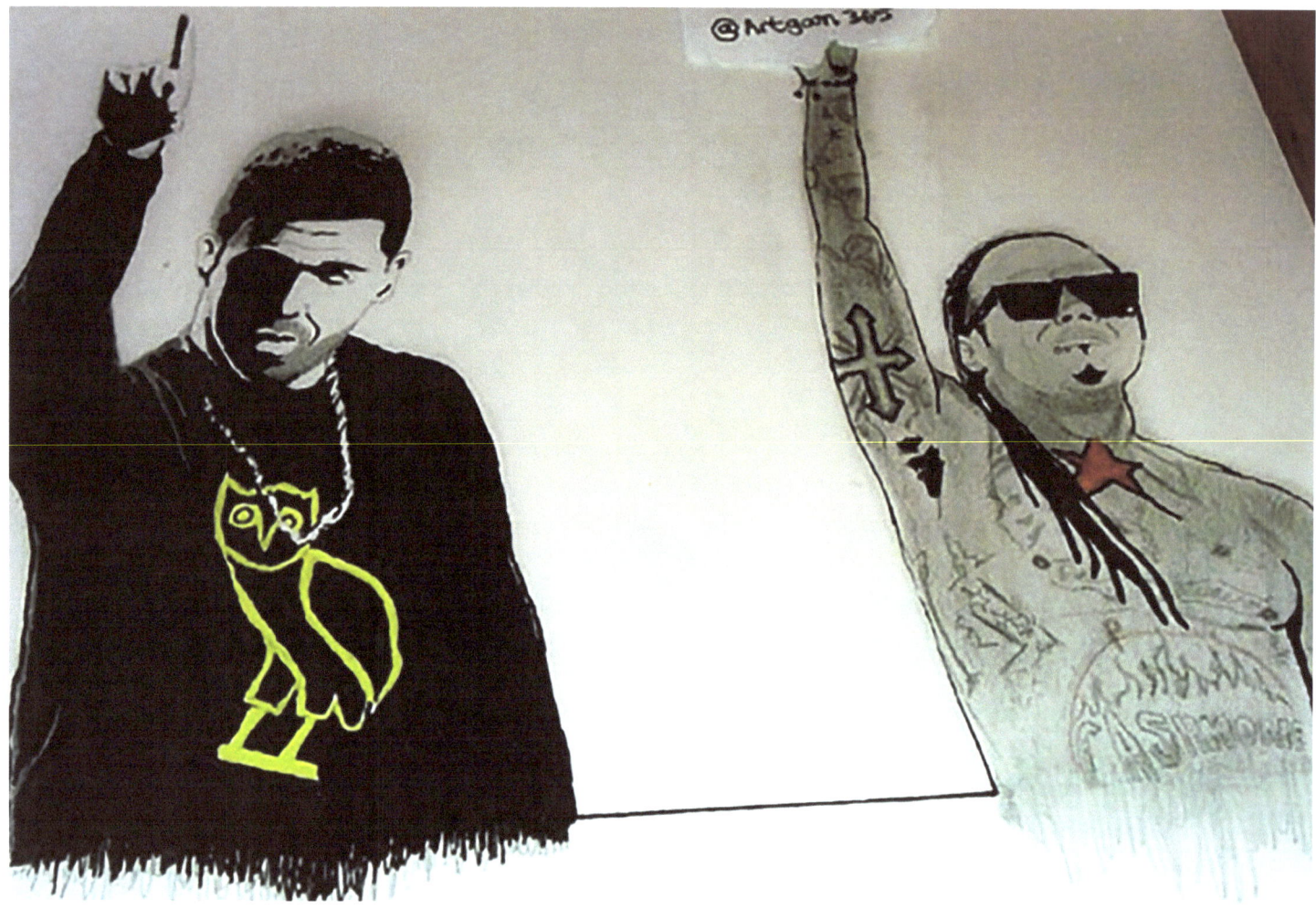

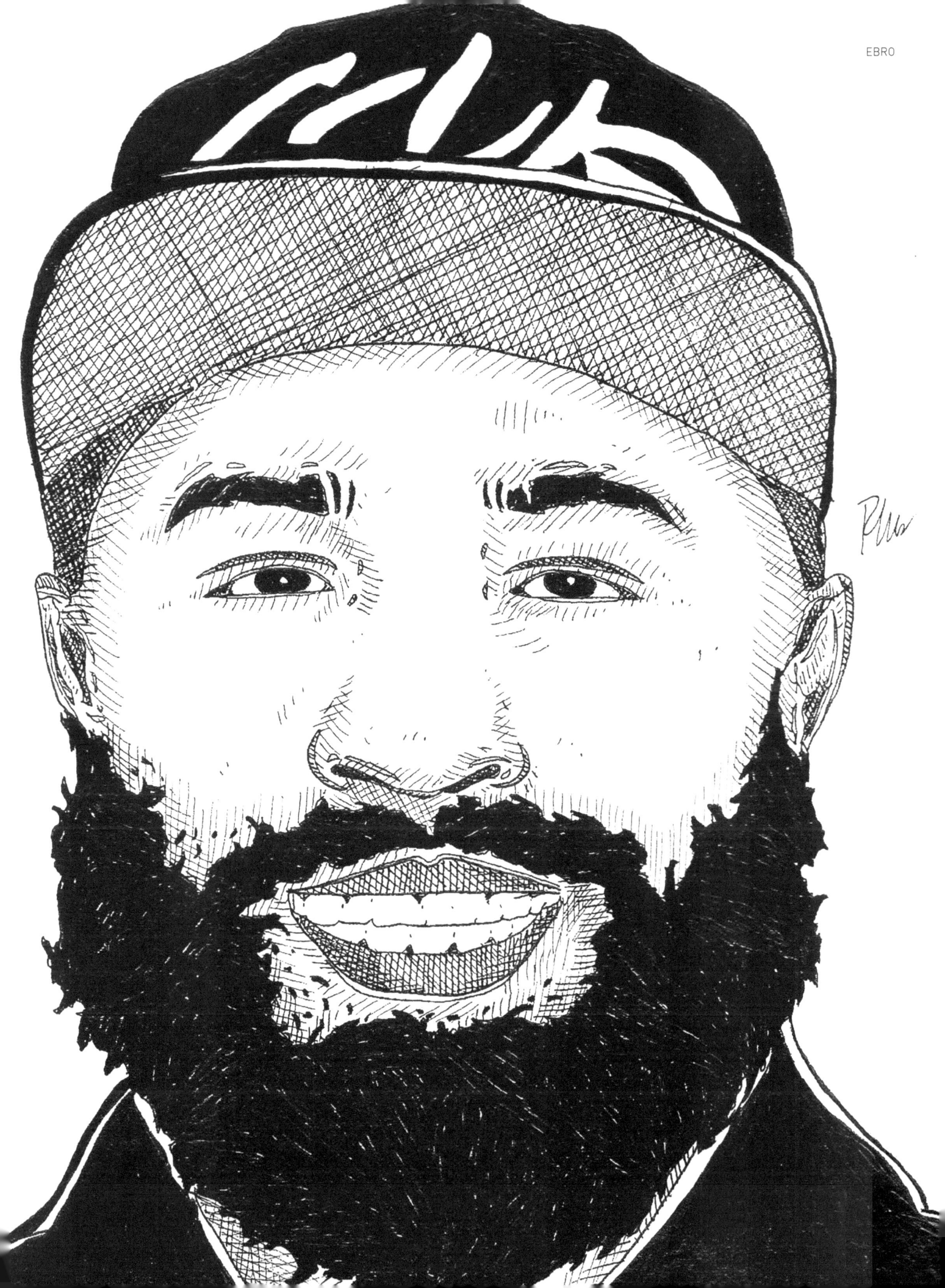

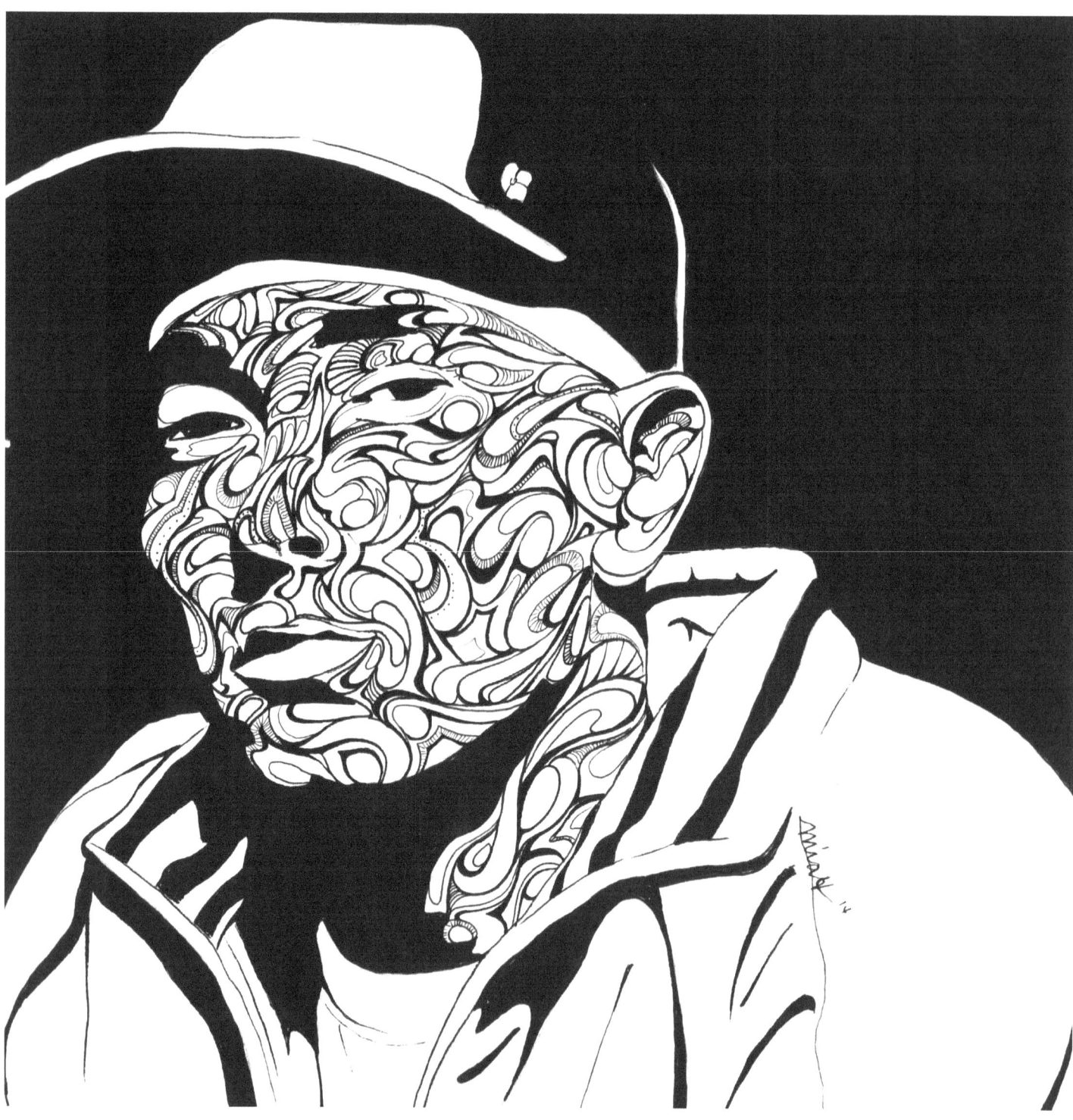

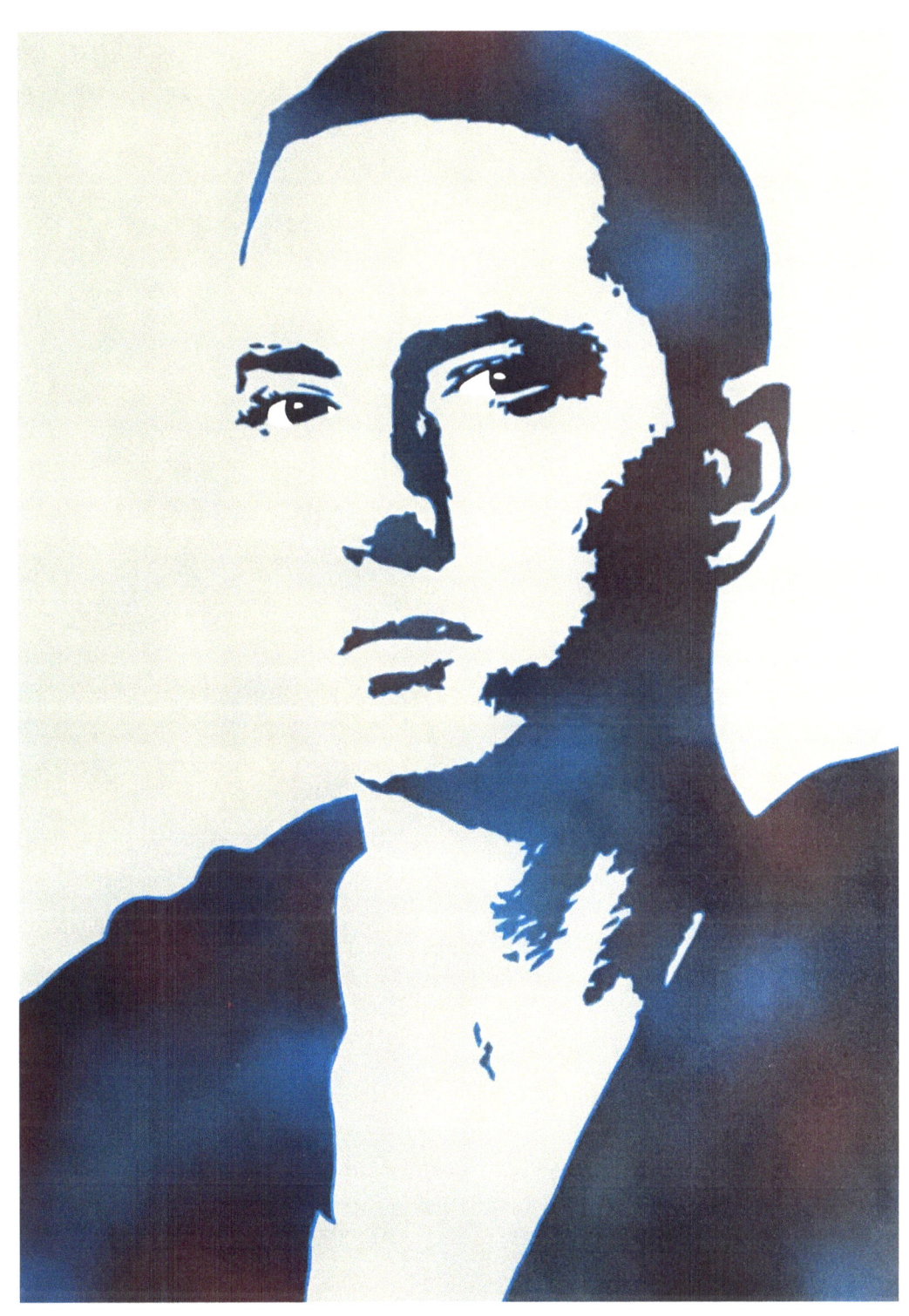

EYEDEA

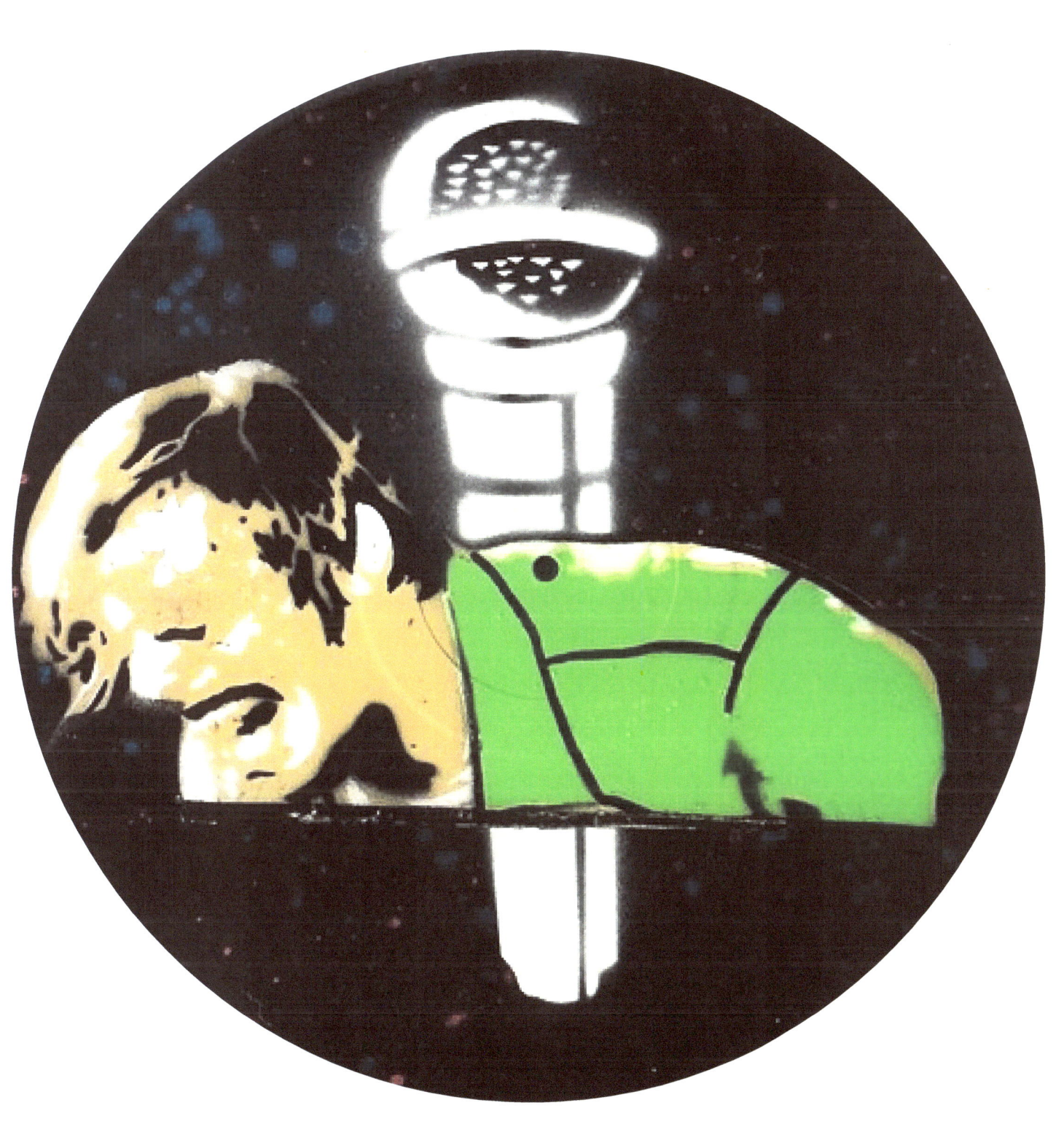

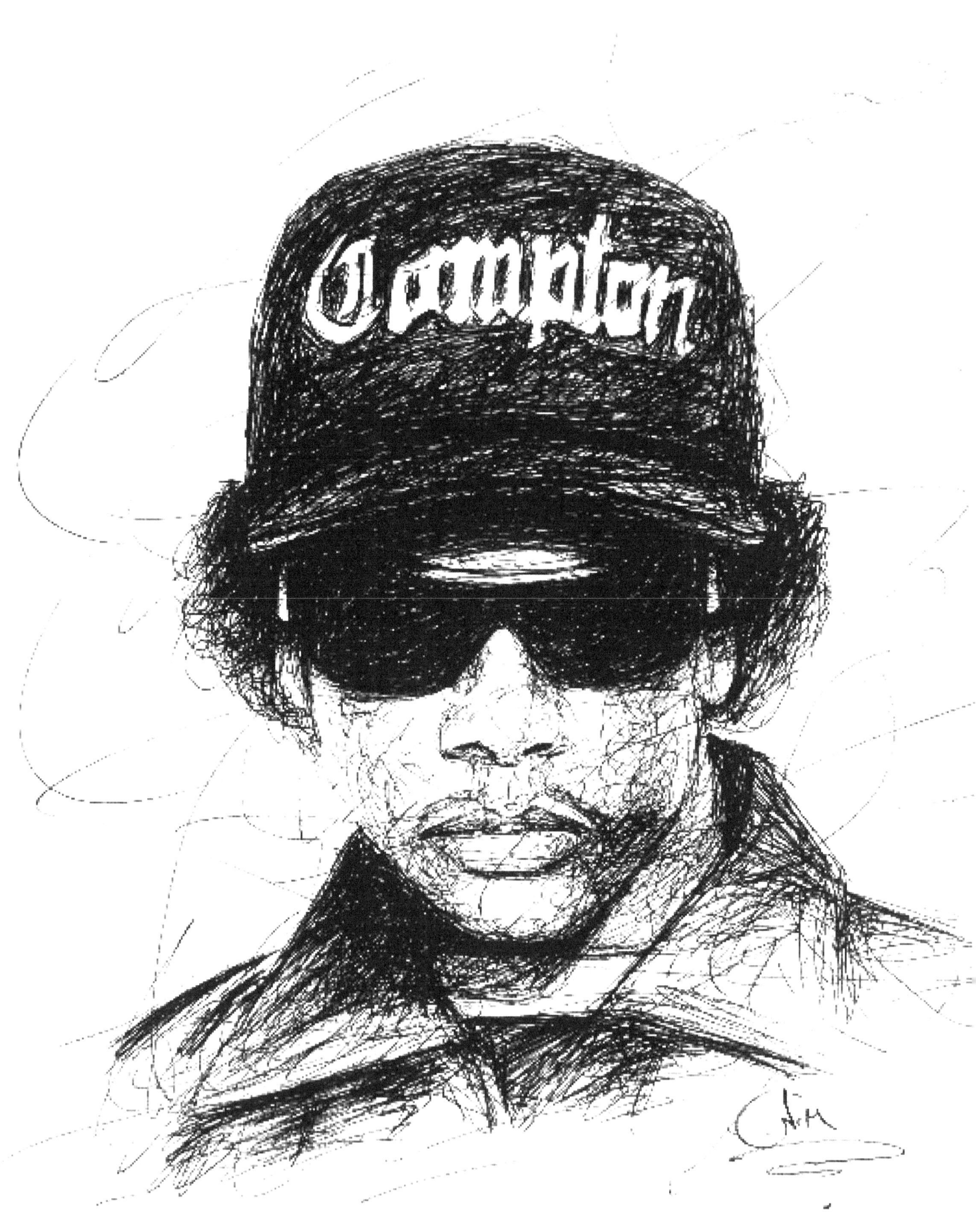

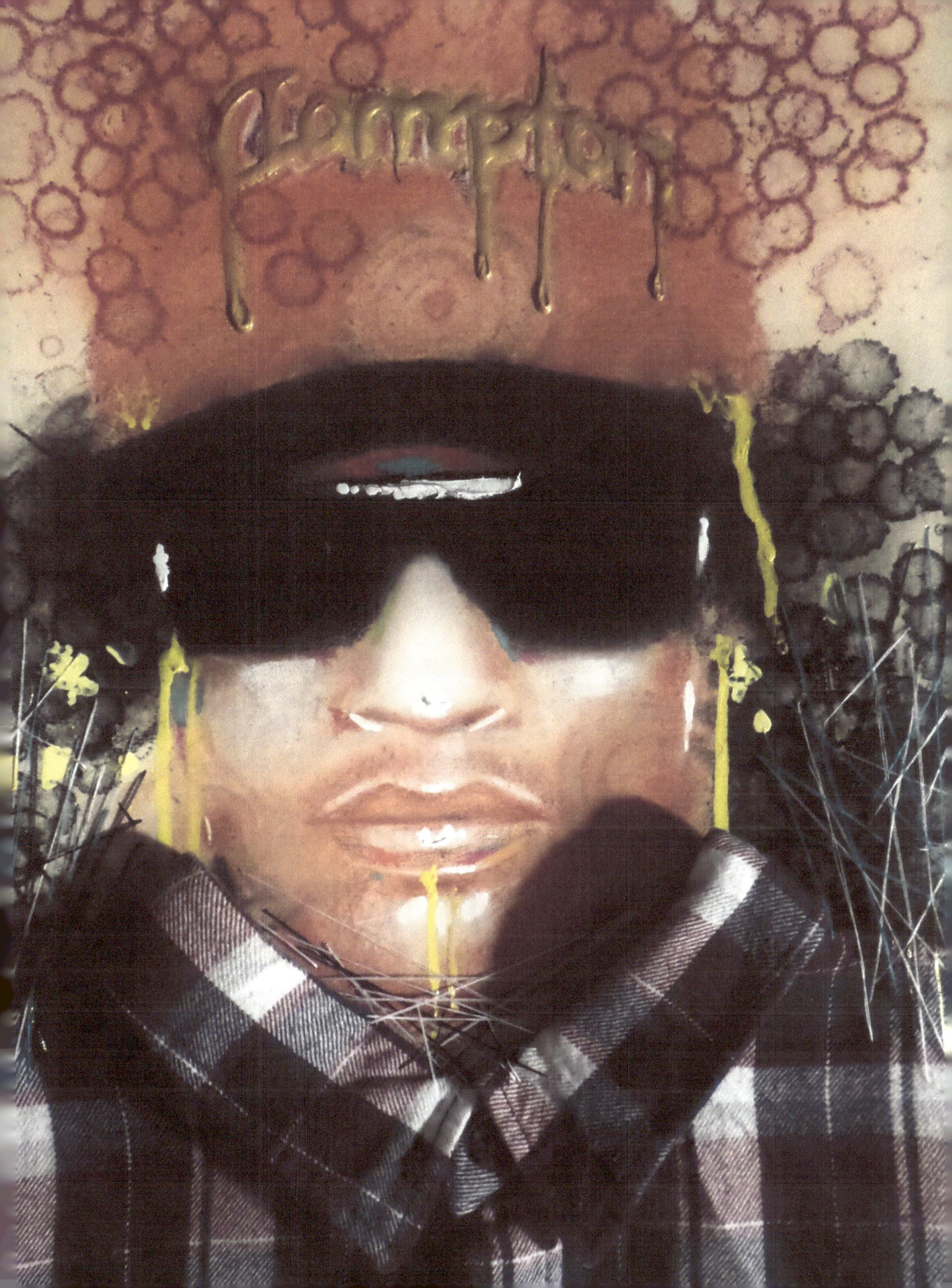

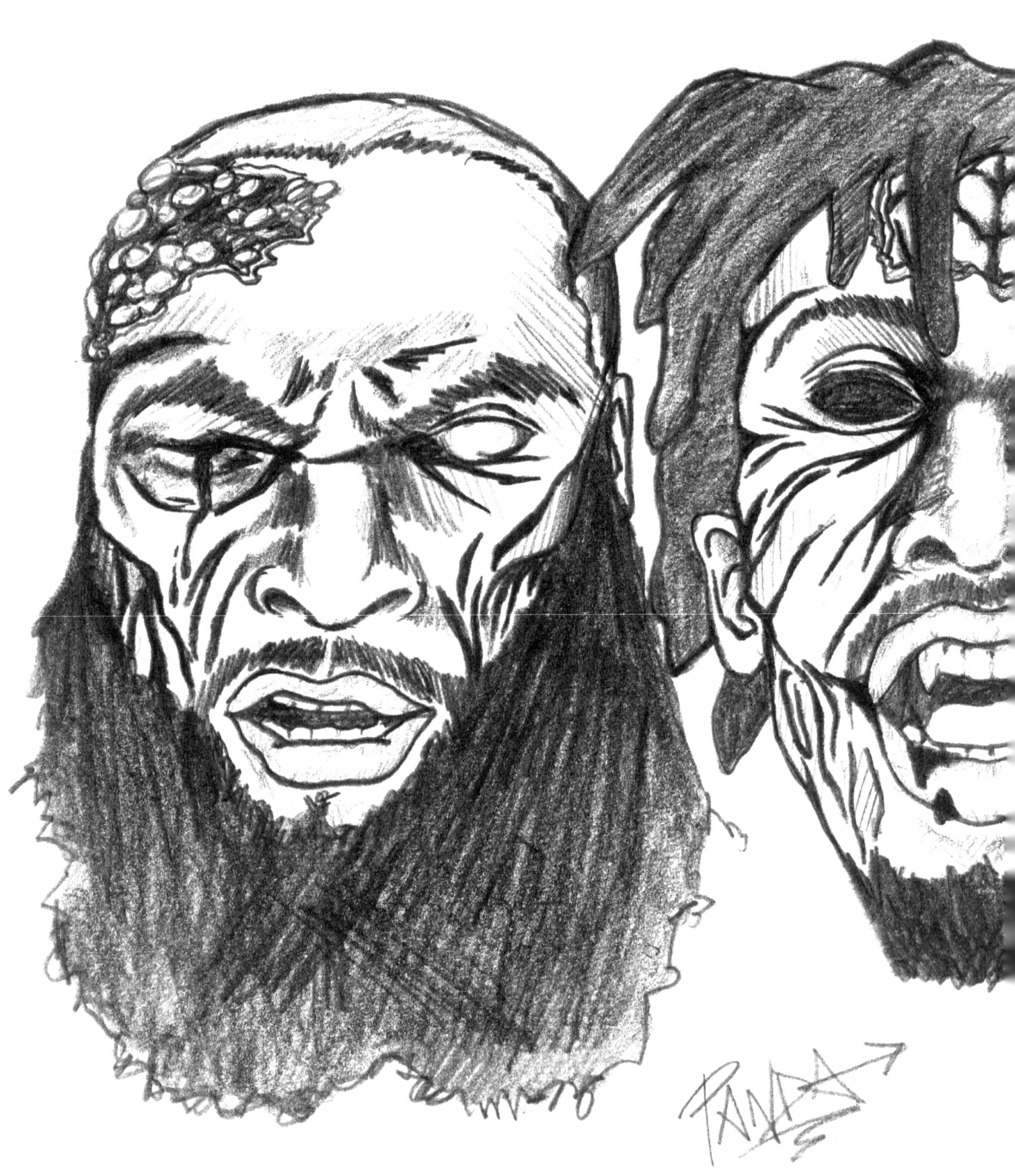

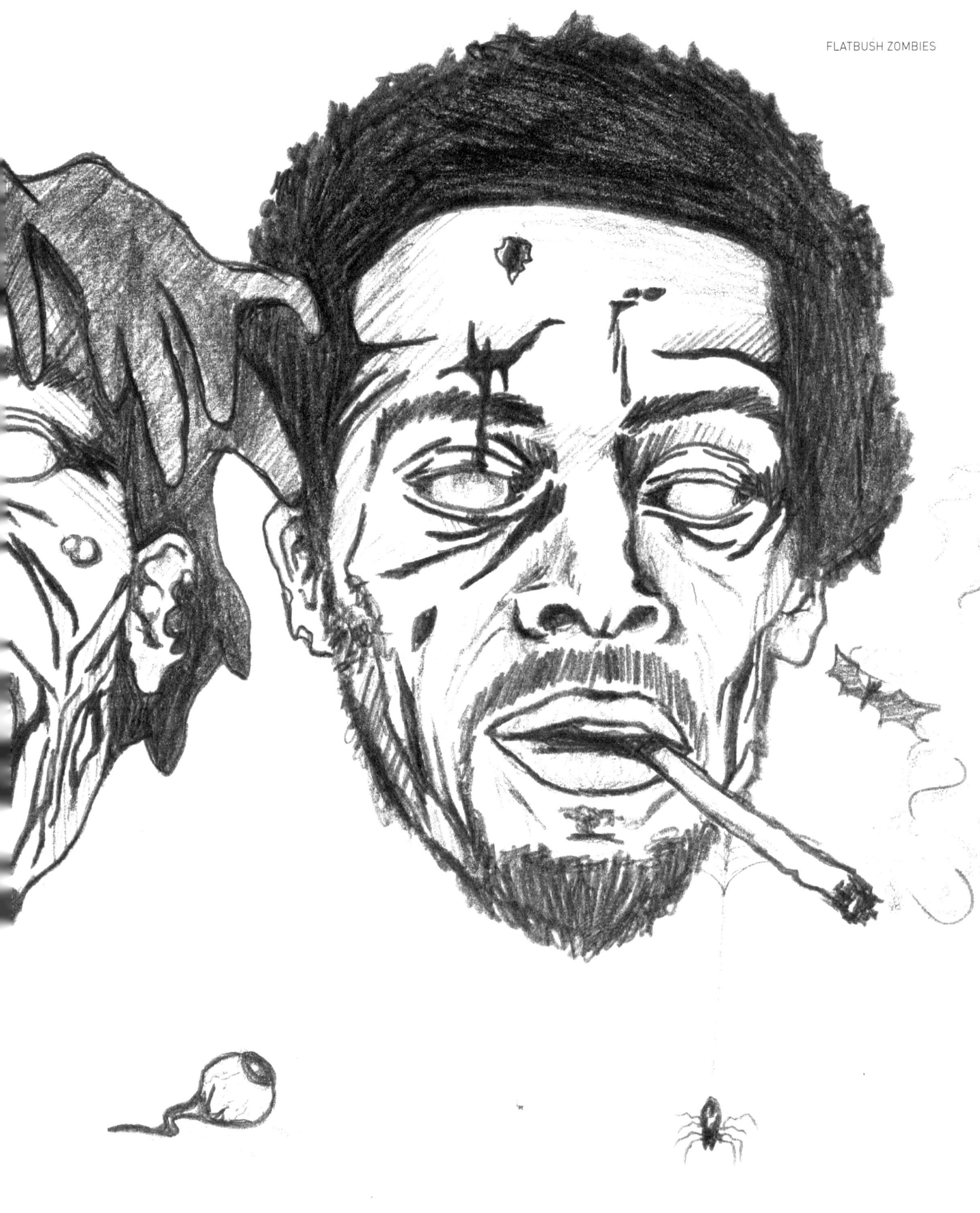

FLATBUSH ZOMBIES

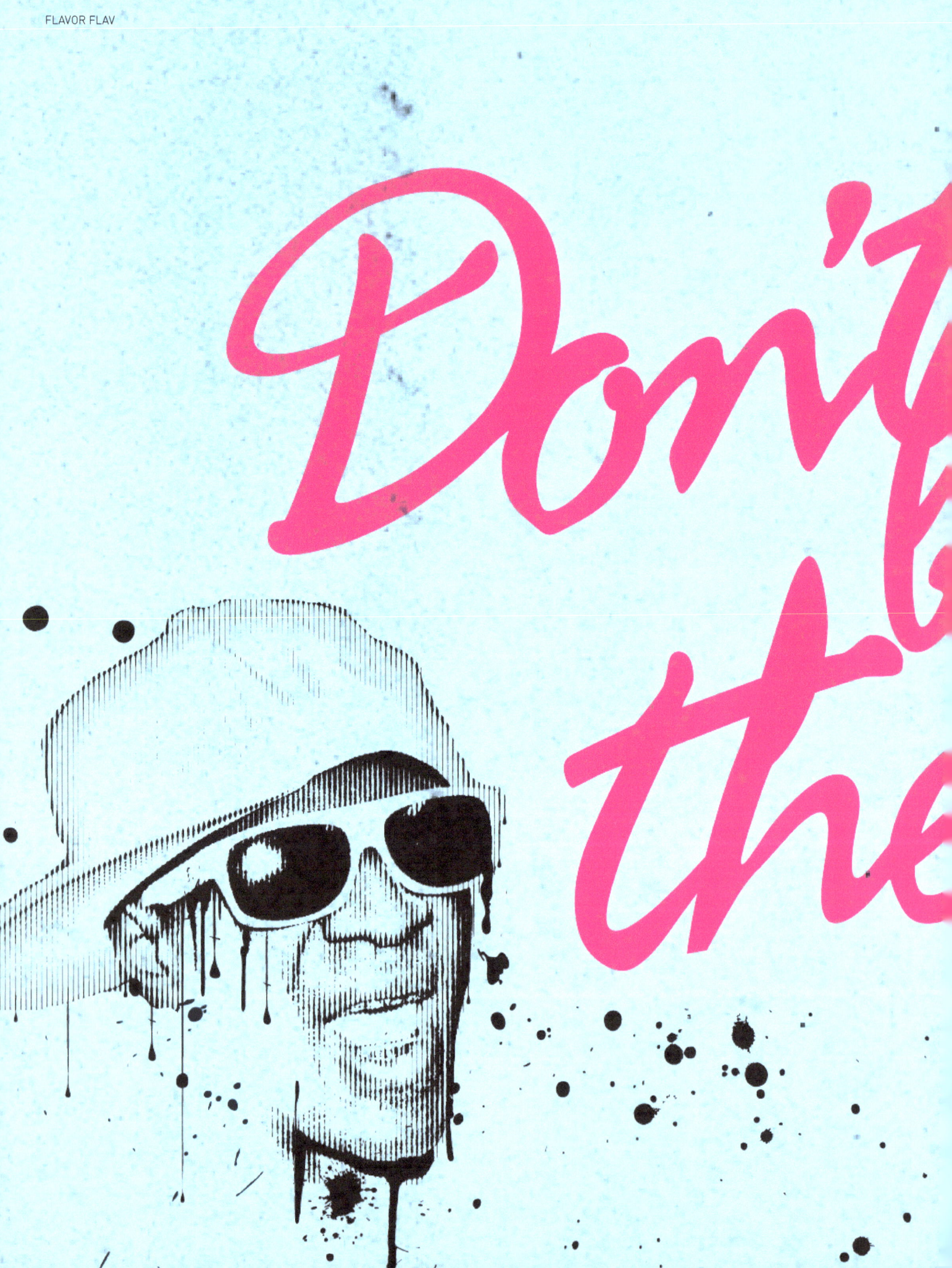

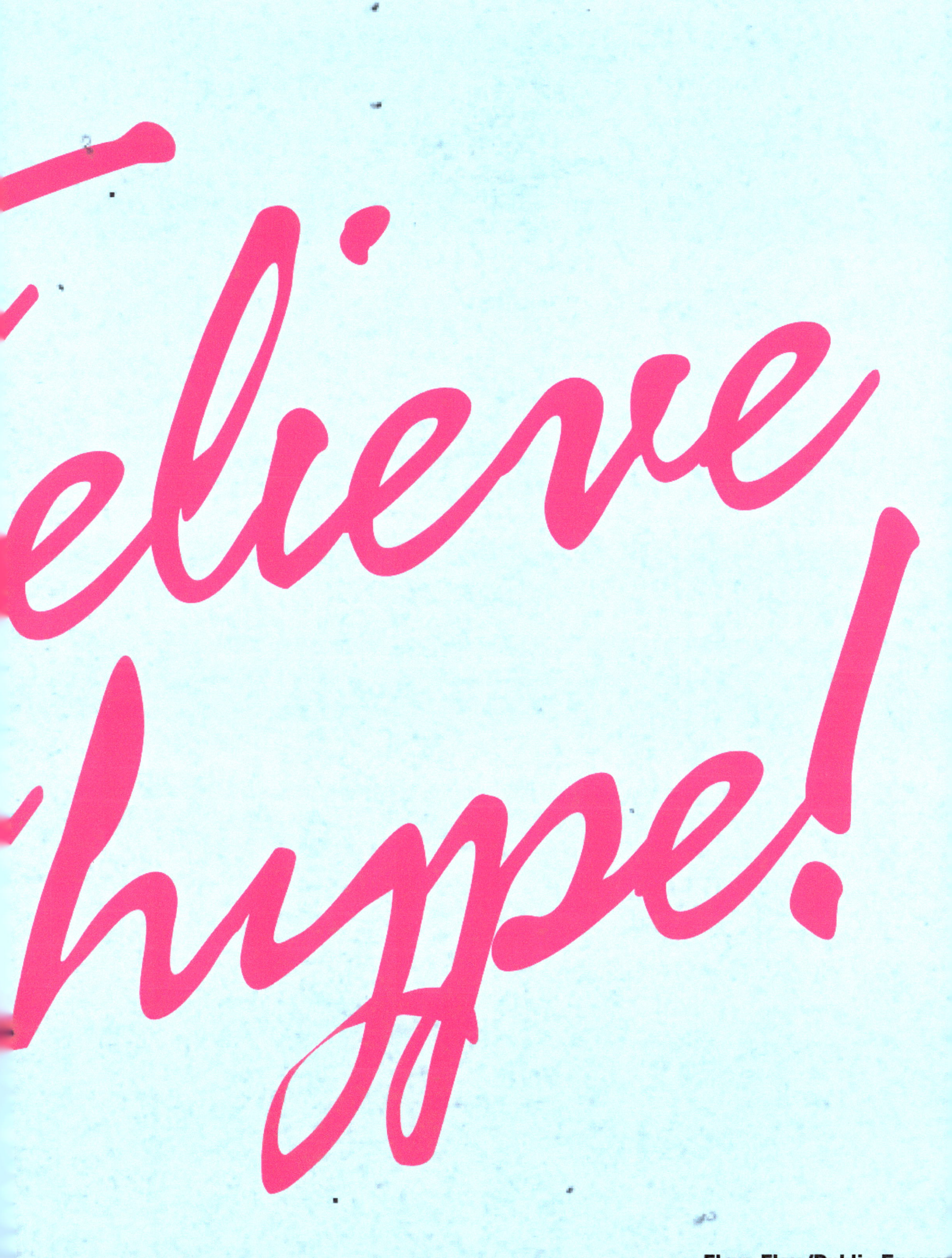

Flava Flav (Public Enemy)

FRANK OCEAN

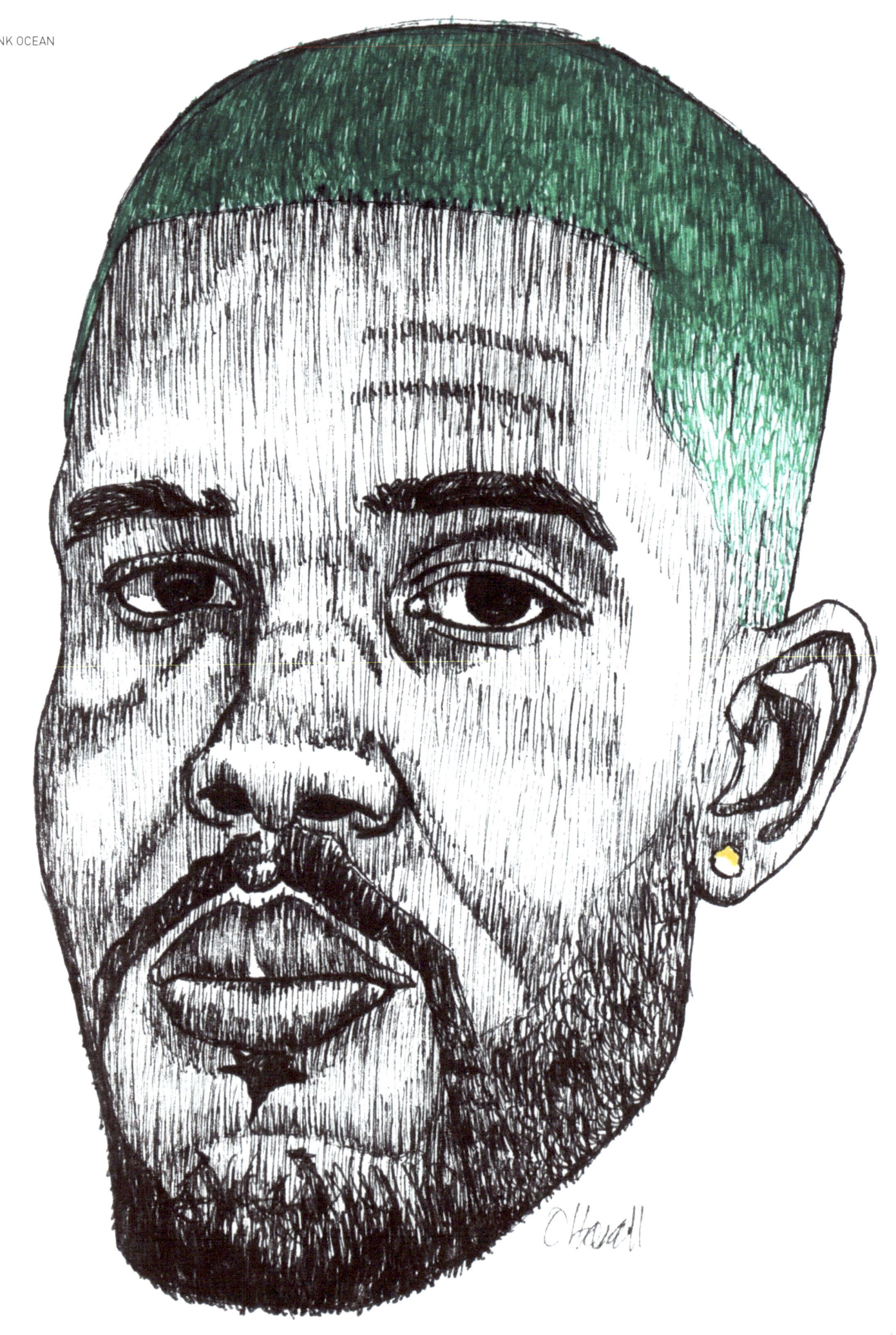

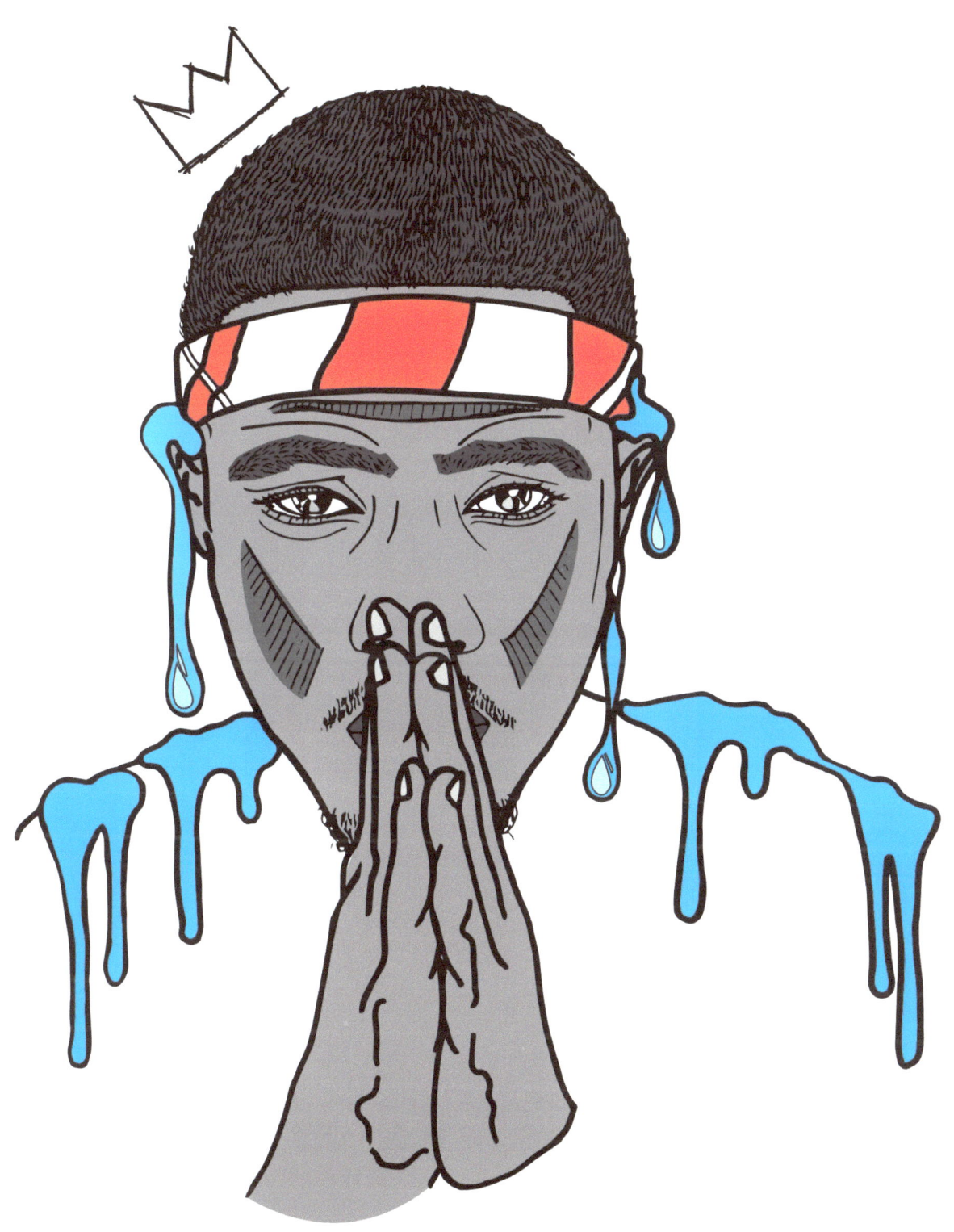

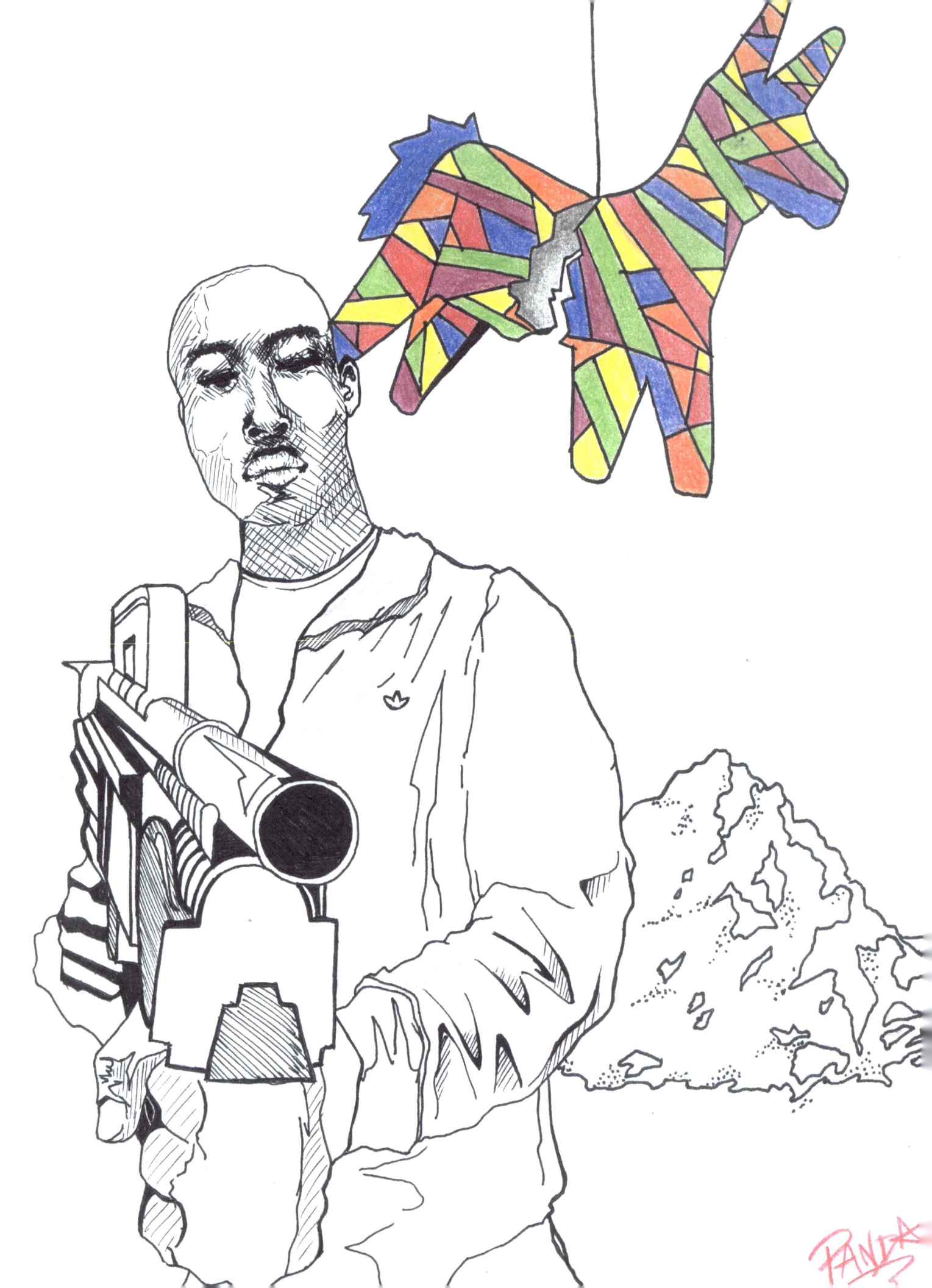

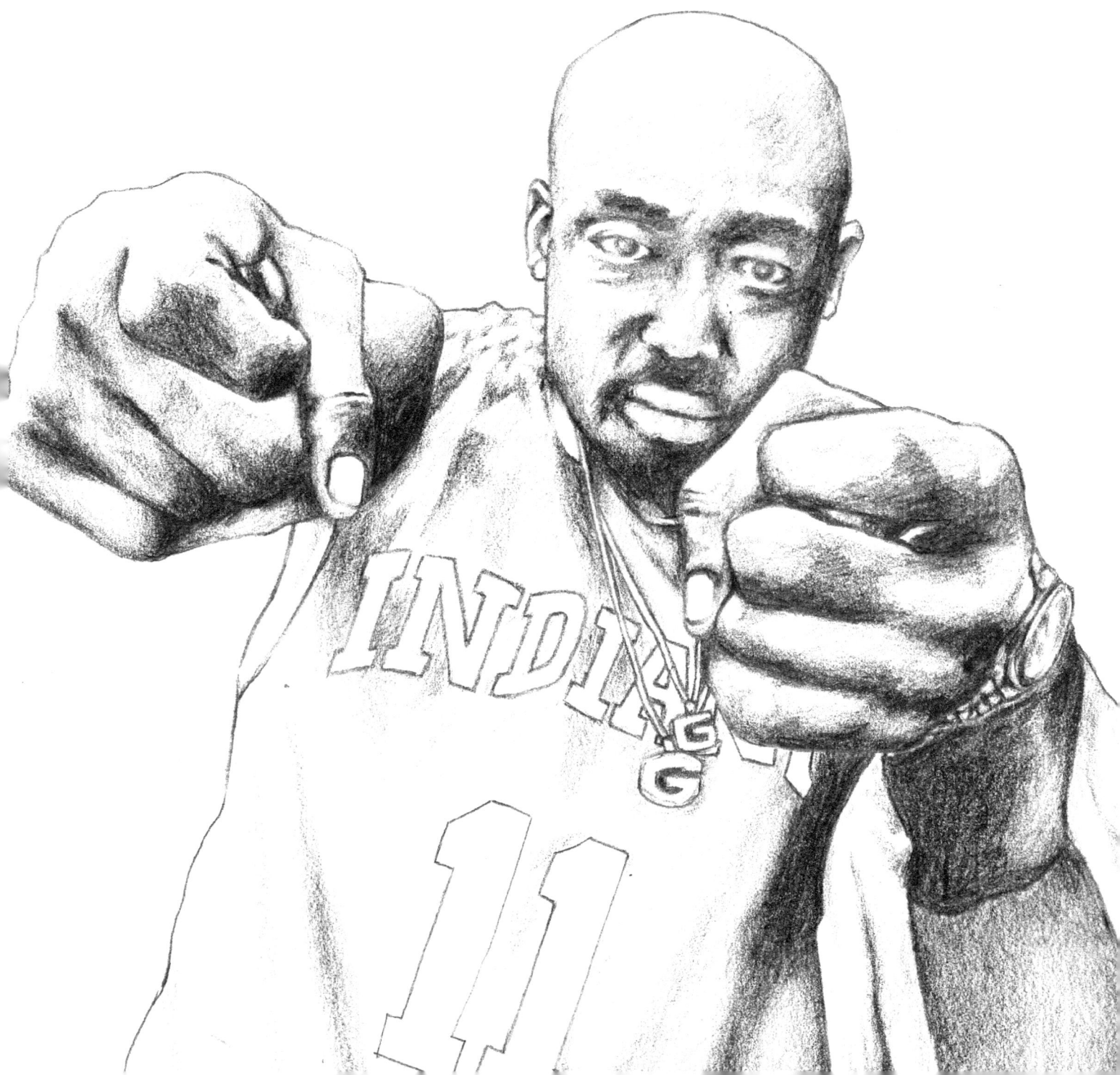

a-m

GHOSTFACE	LITTLE SIMZ
GORILLAZ	LL COOL J
ICE CUBE	LORD FINESSE
ISAIAH RASHAD	MASTA ACE
J COLE	MAXO CREAM
JAY ROCK	METHOD MAN
JAY Z	MF DOOM
JOEY FATTS ASTON MATTHEWS	MISSY ELLIOT
KANYE WEST	M.O.P.
KENDRICK LAMAR	MOS DEF
KID N PLAY	
KRS1	
LARGE PROFESSOR	
LE$	
LIL JON	
LIL UZI VERT	
LIL YACHTY	
LITTLE HALF DEAD	

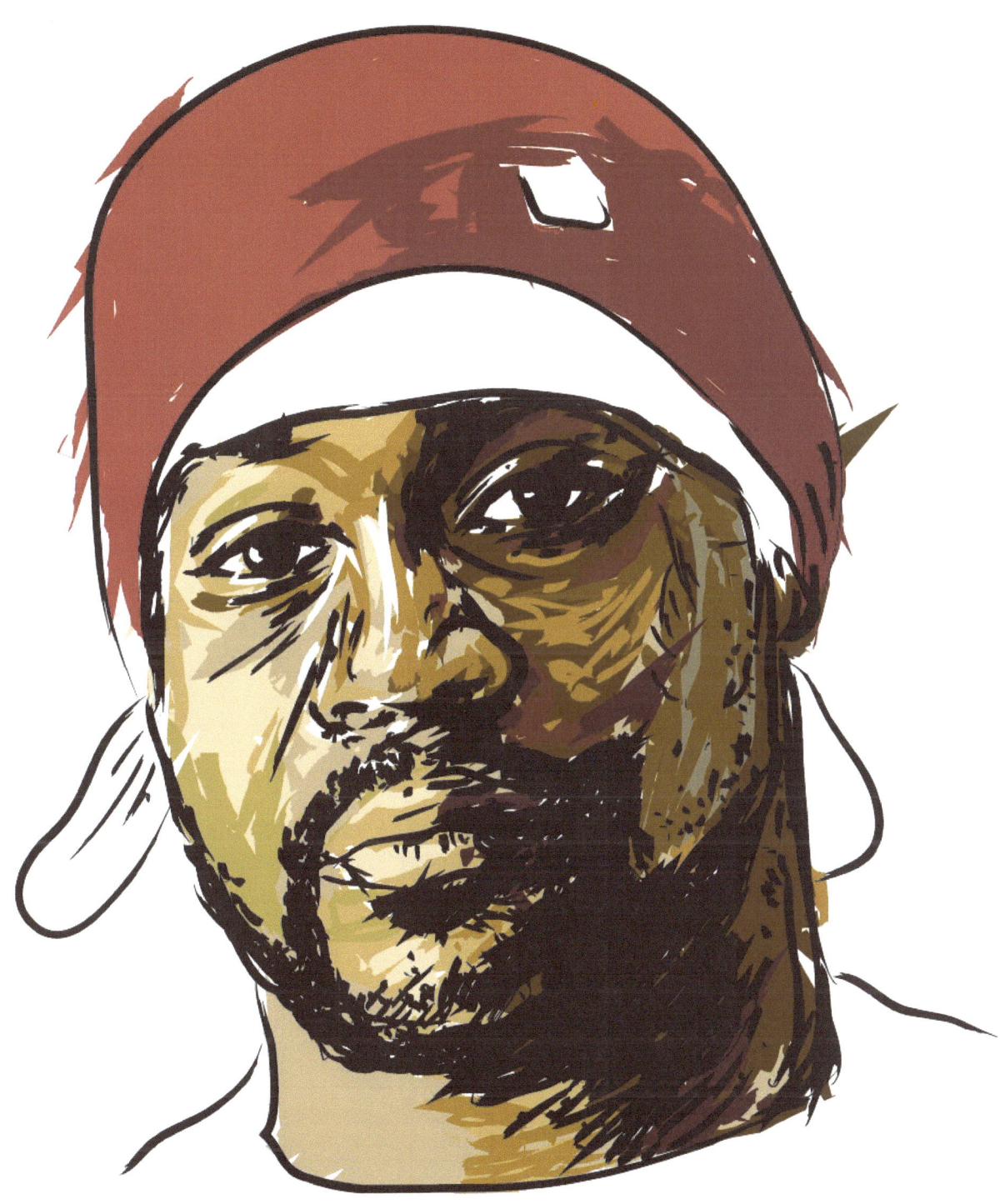

GHOSTFACE

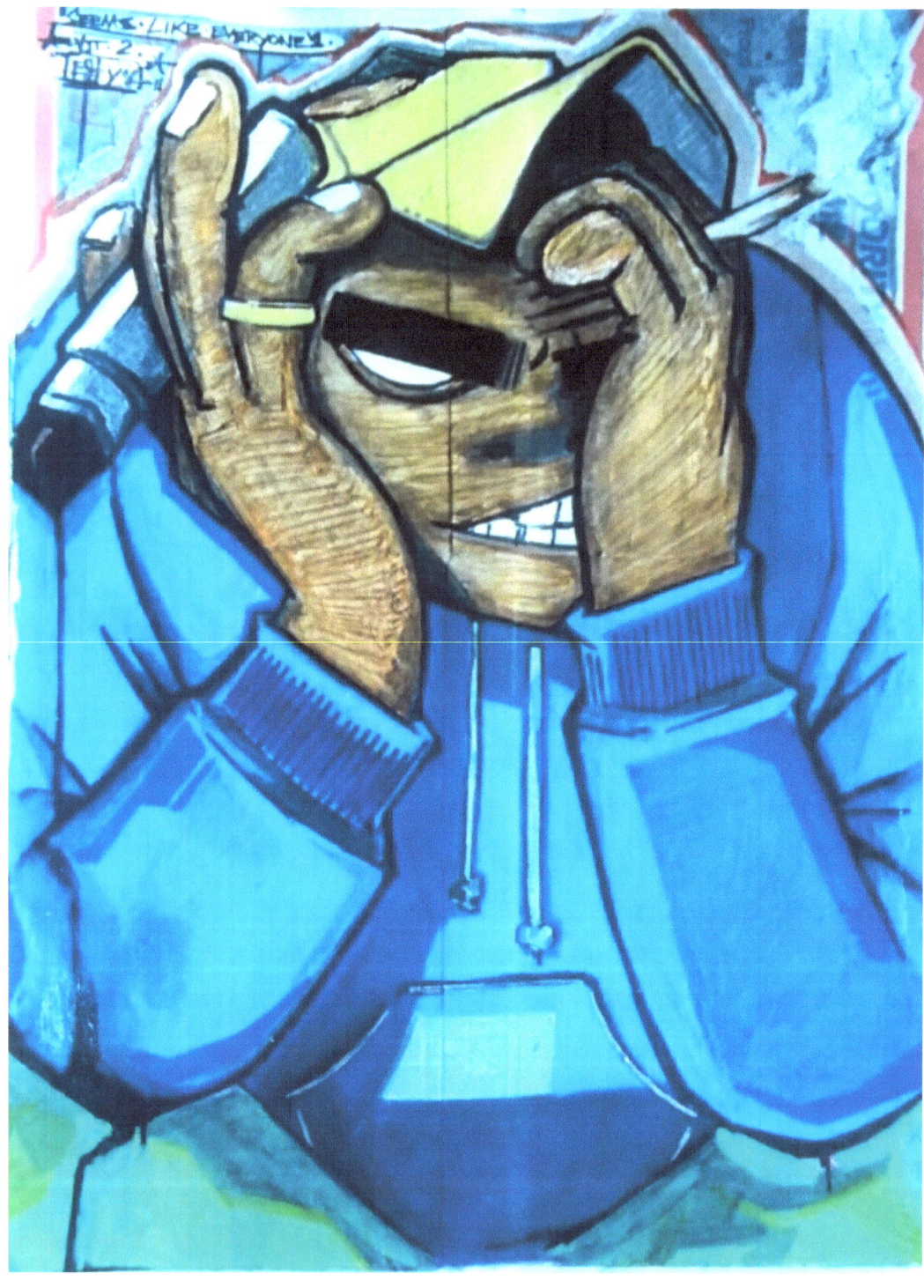

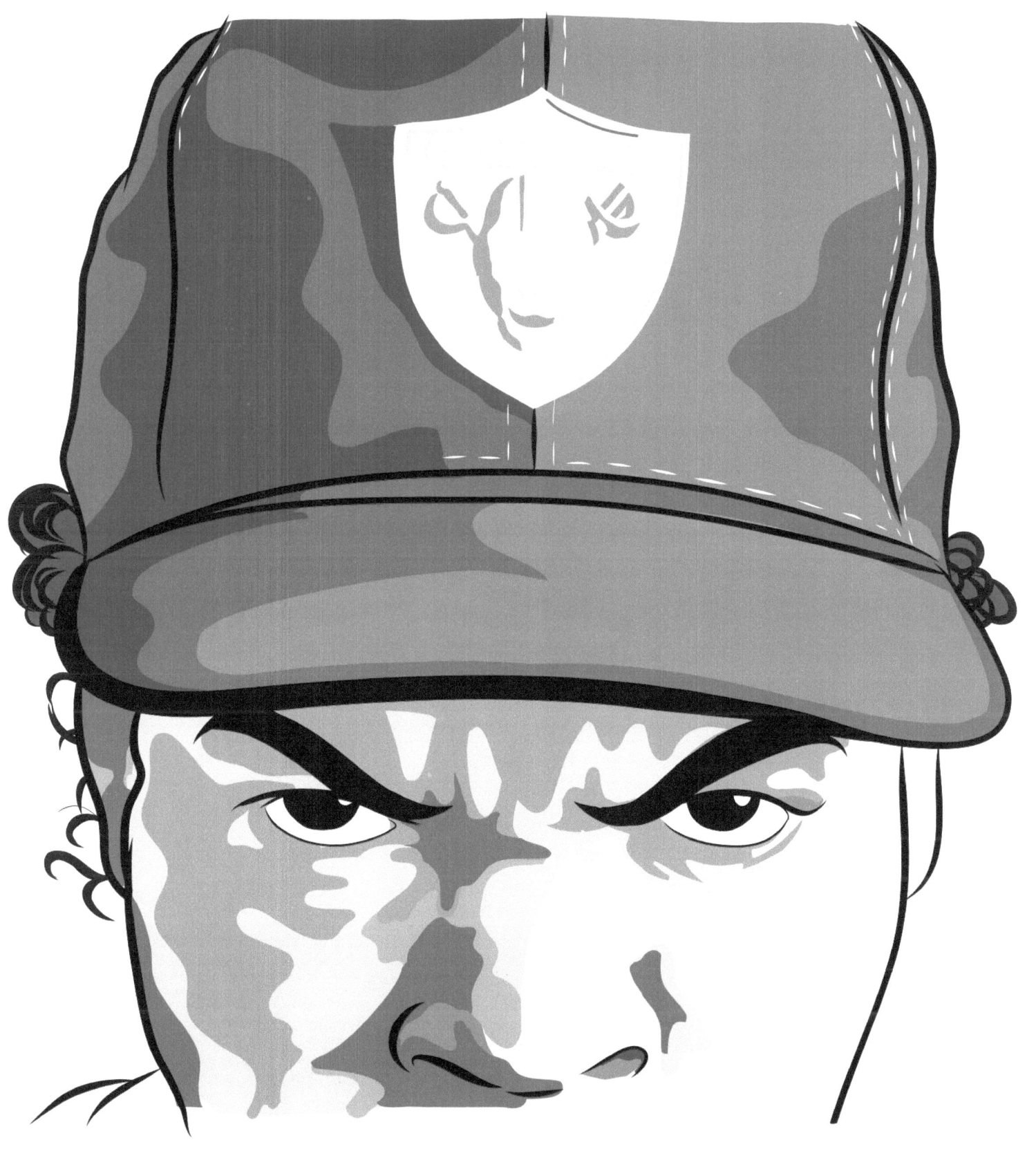

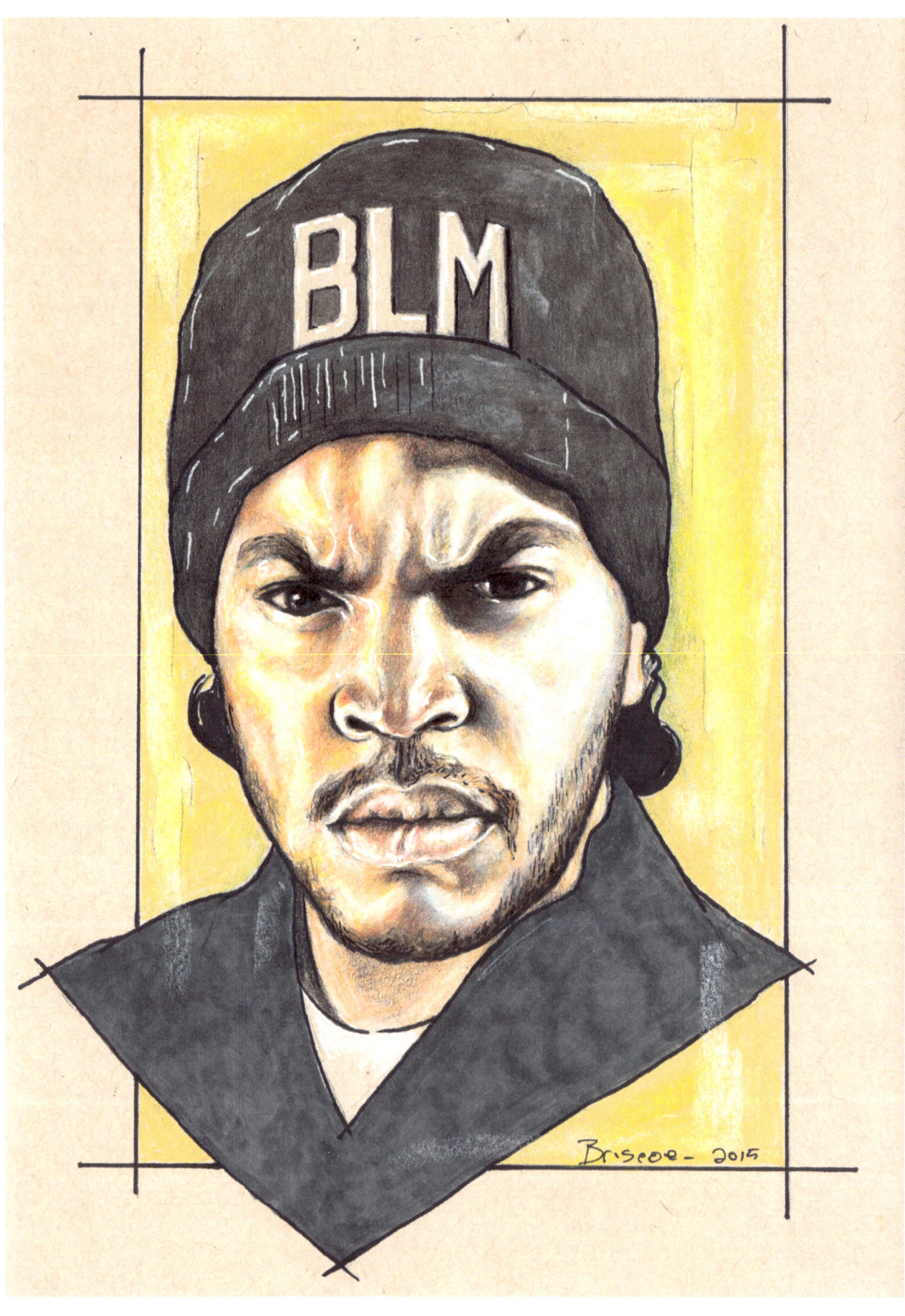

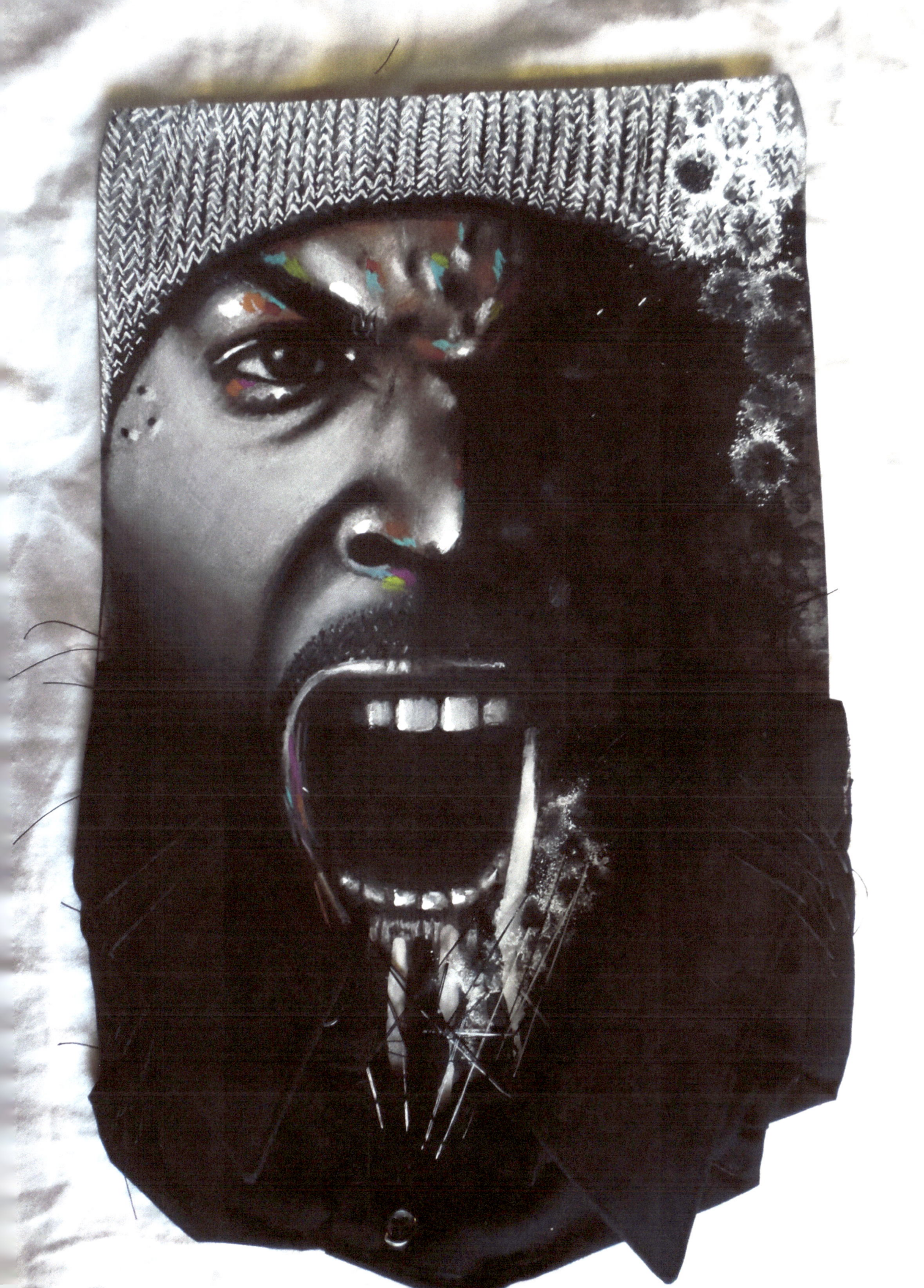

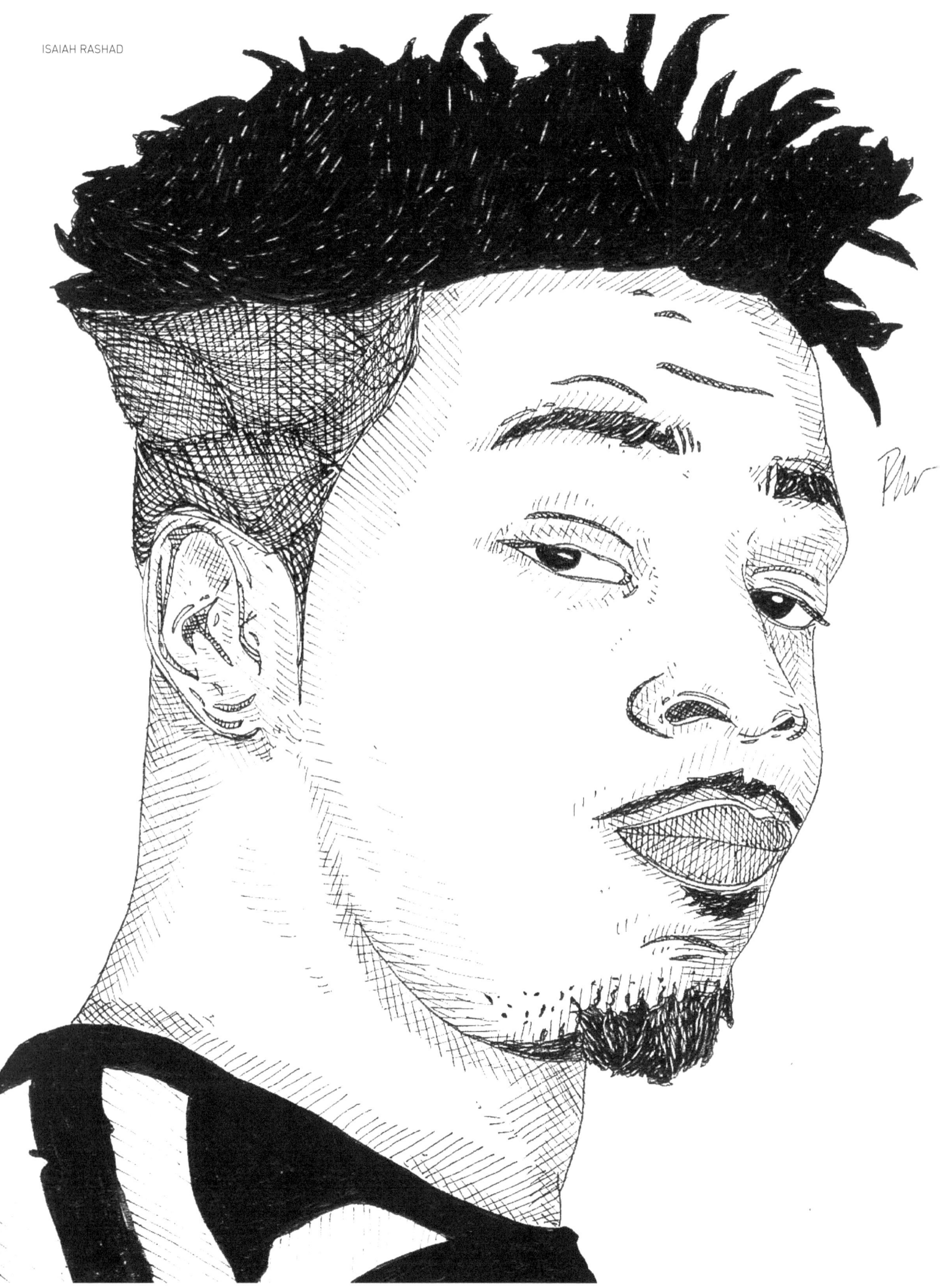

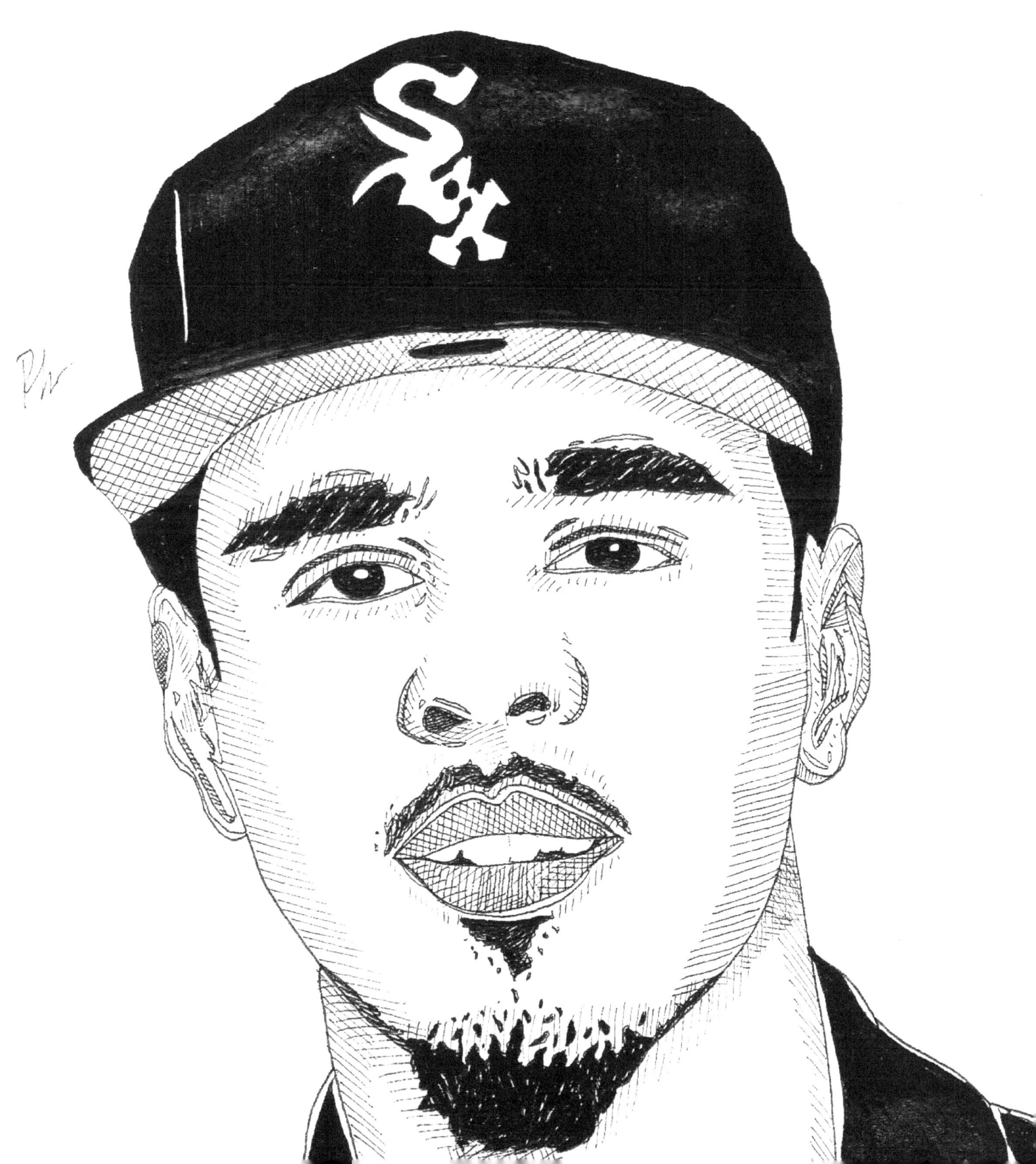

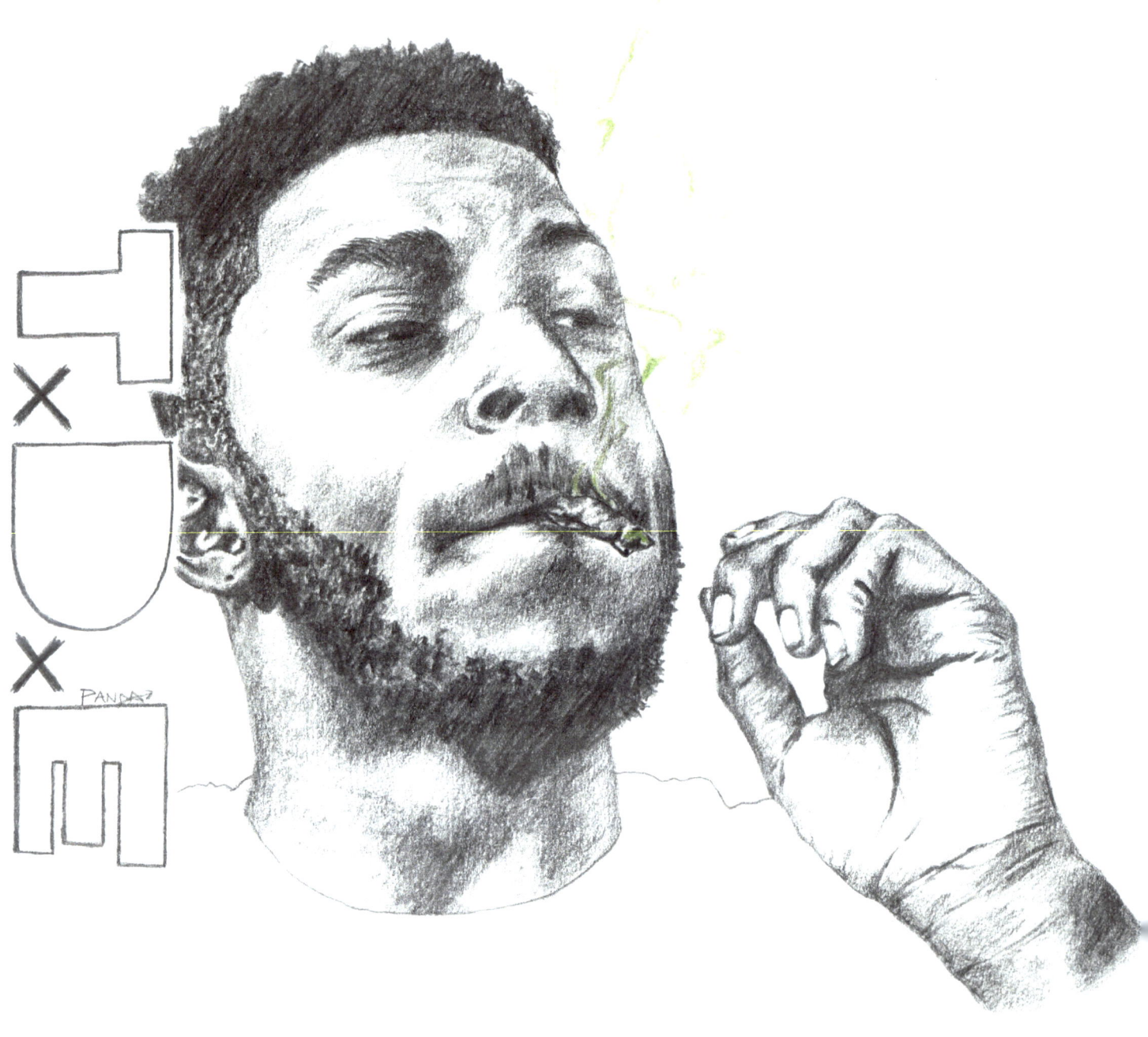

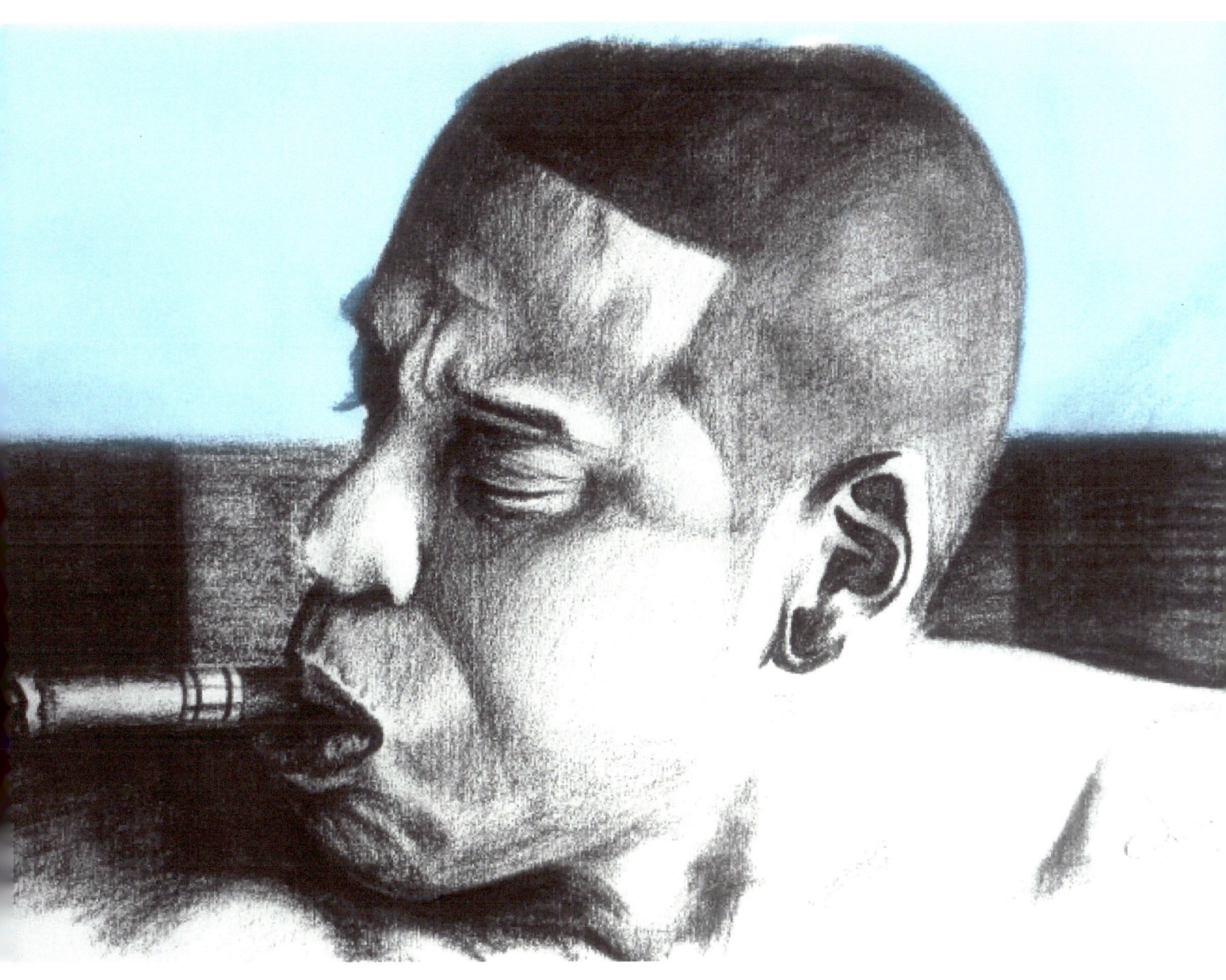

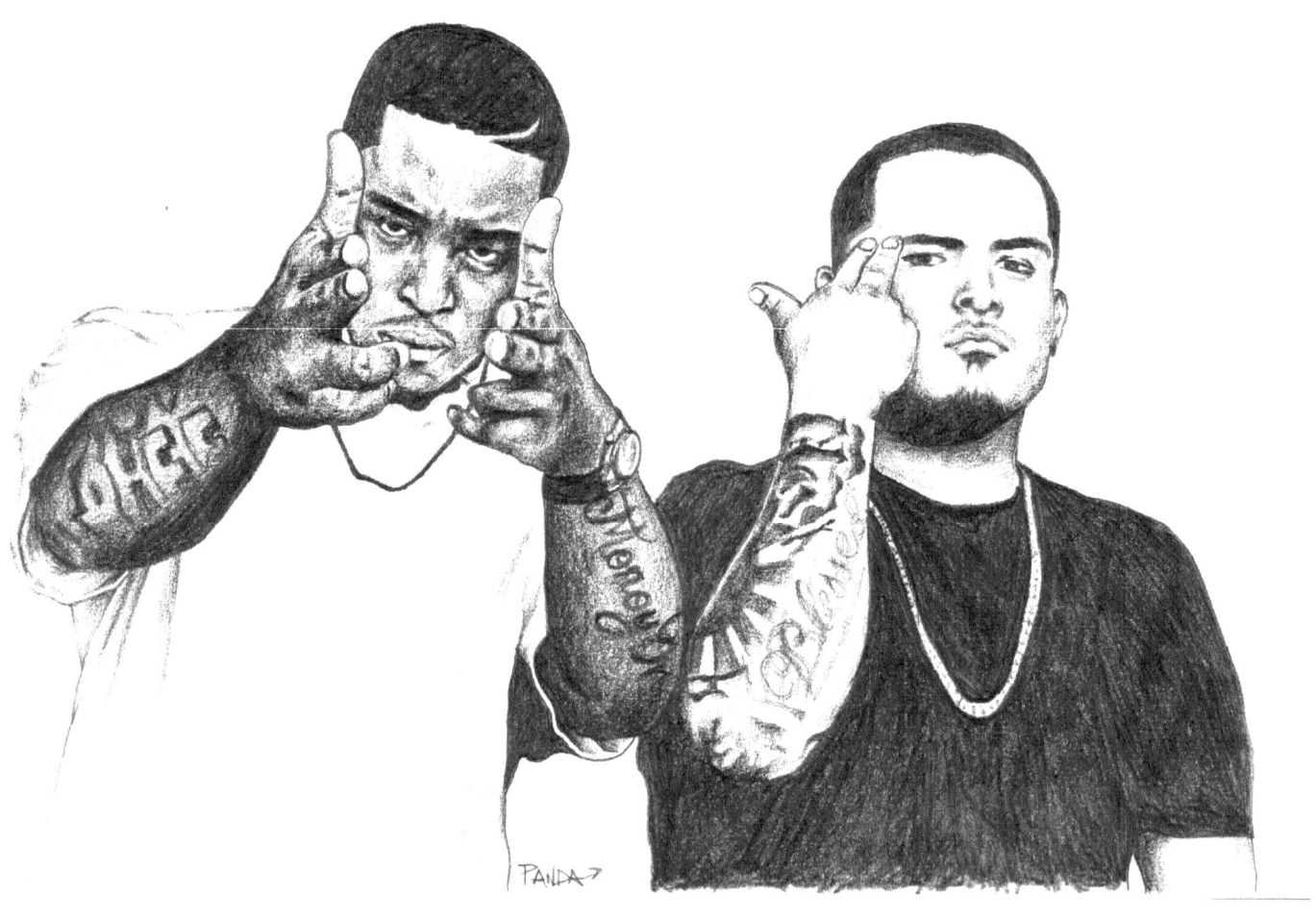

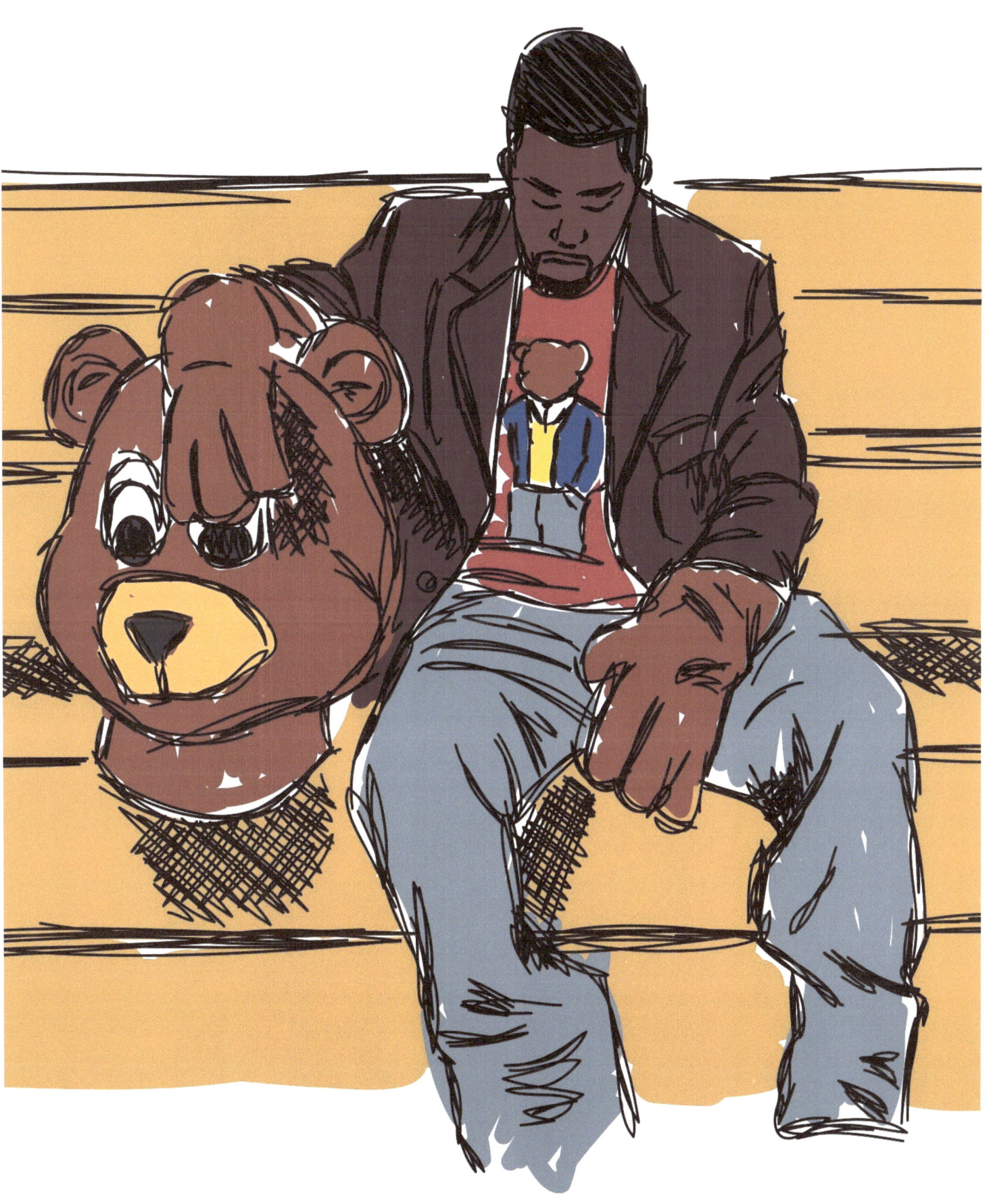

KANYE WEST

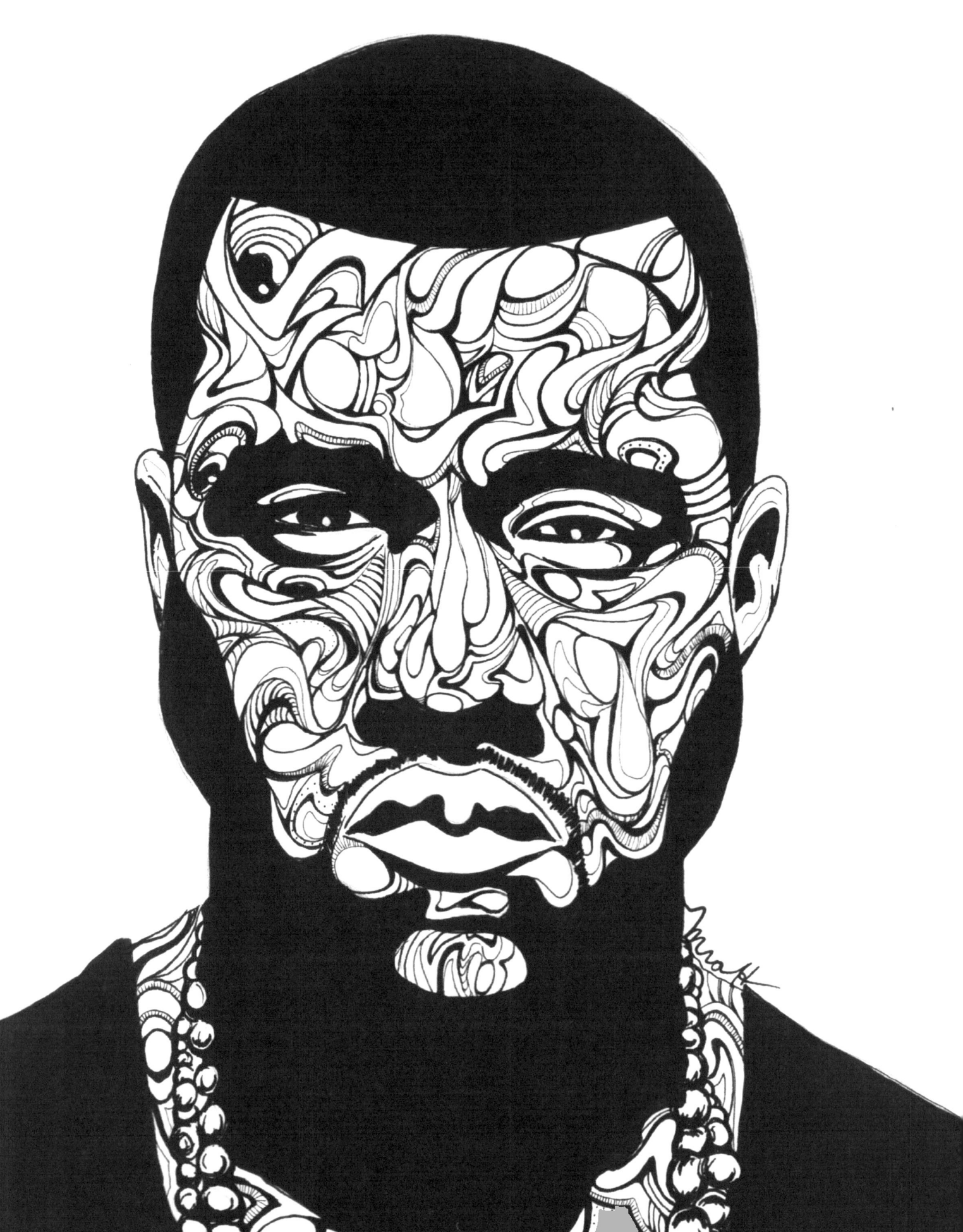

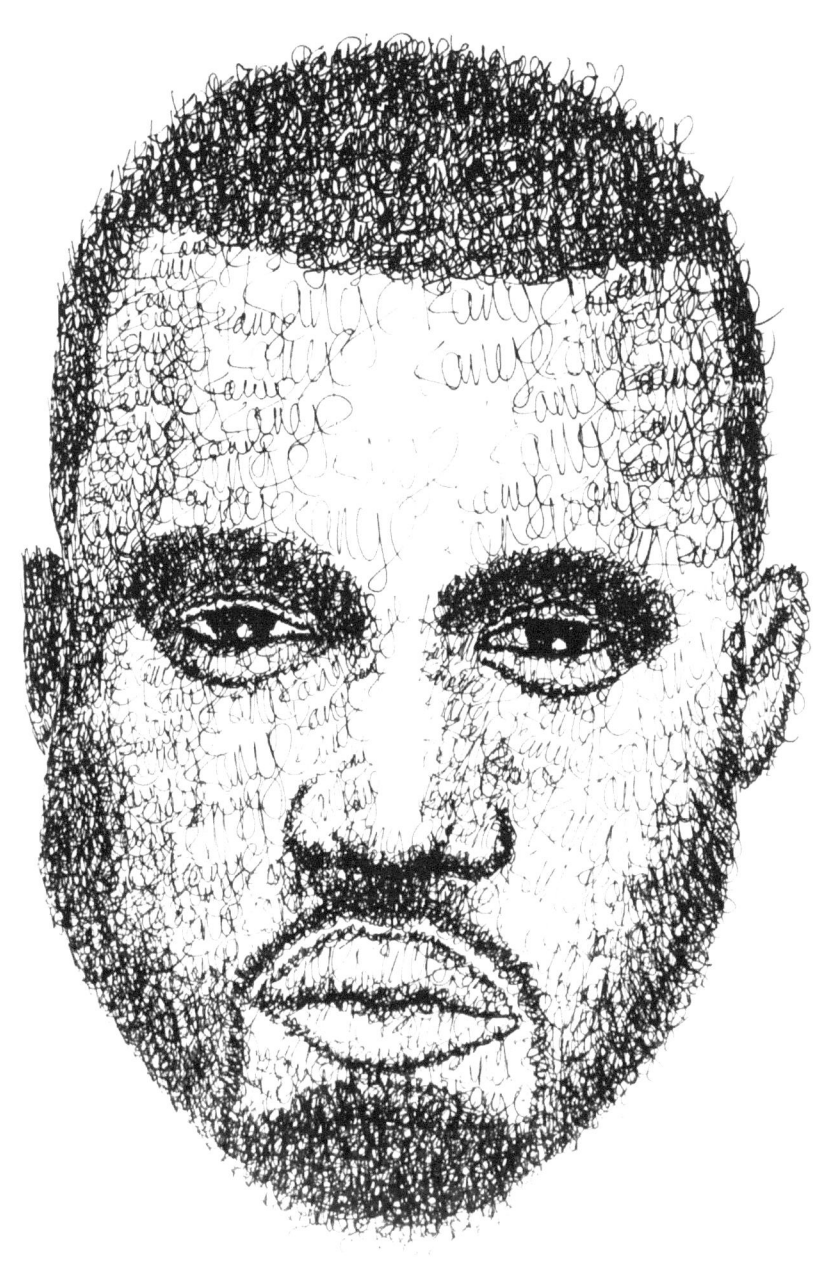

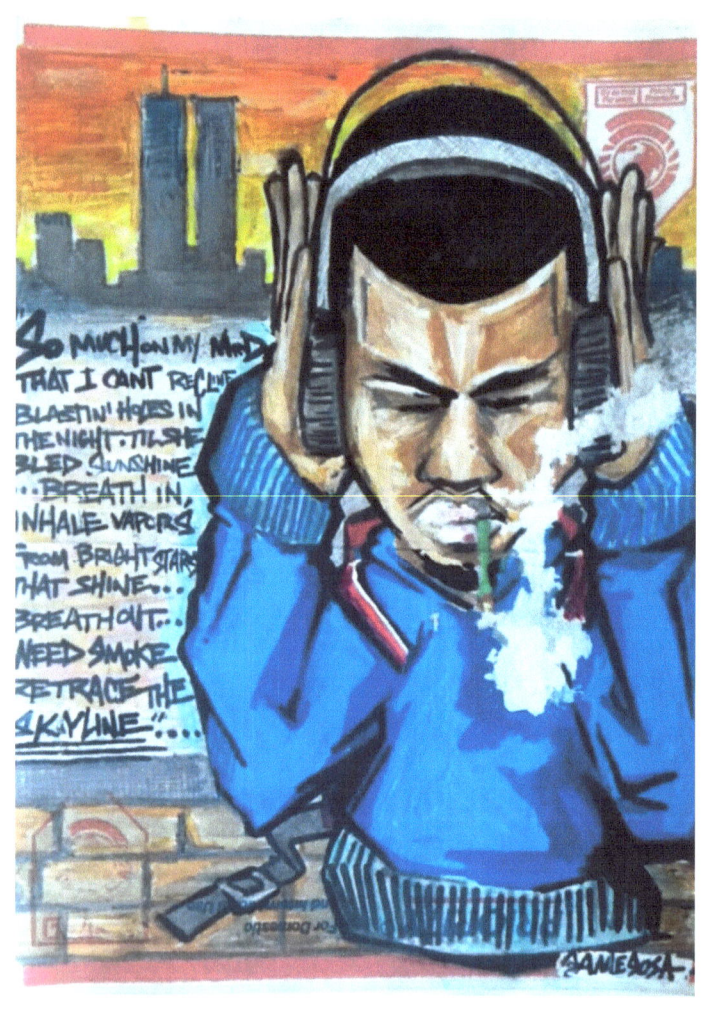
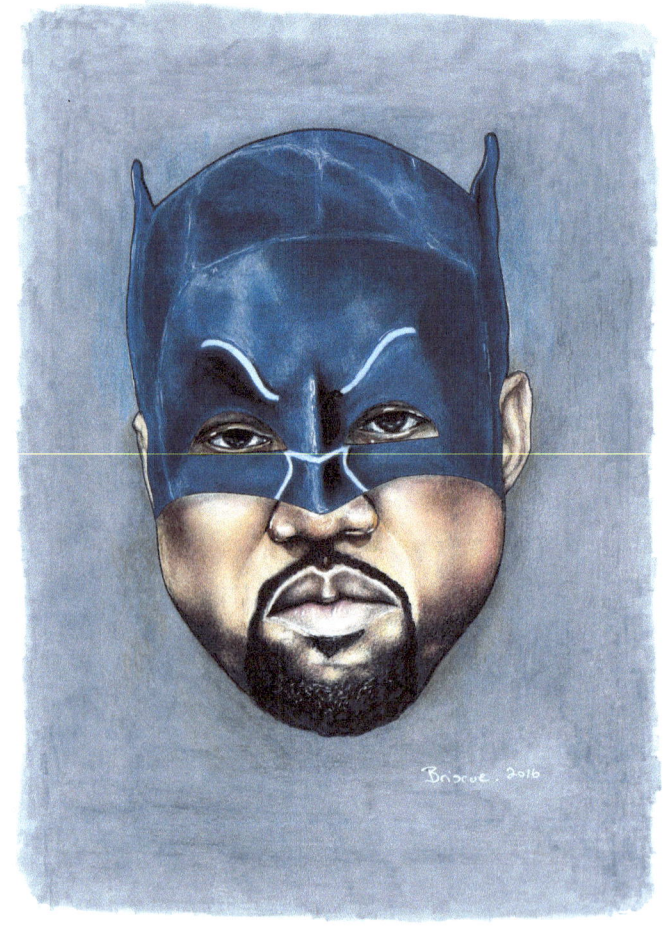

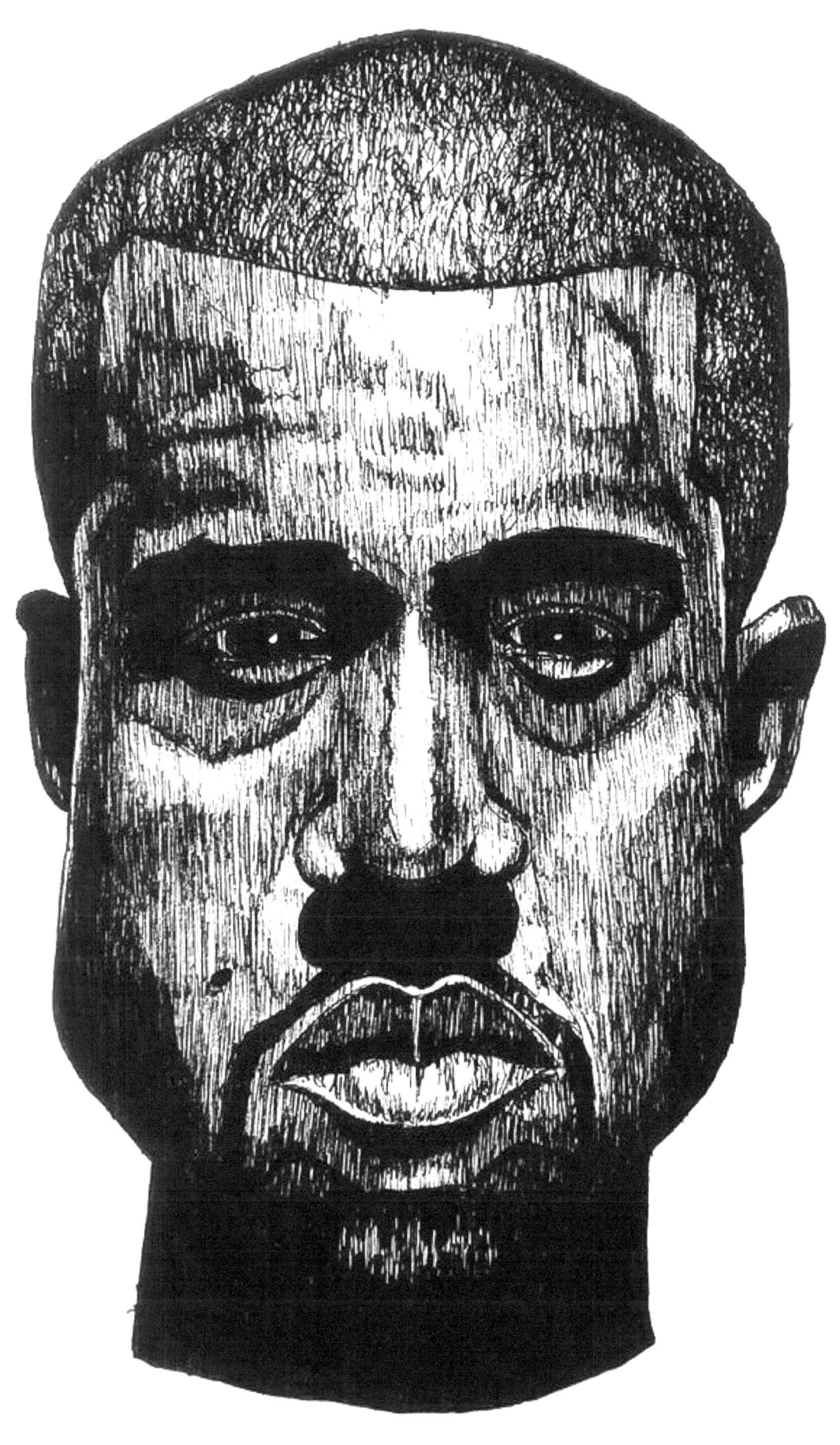

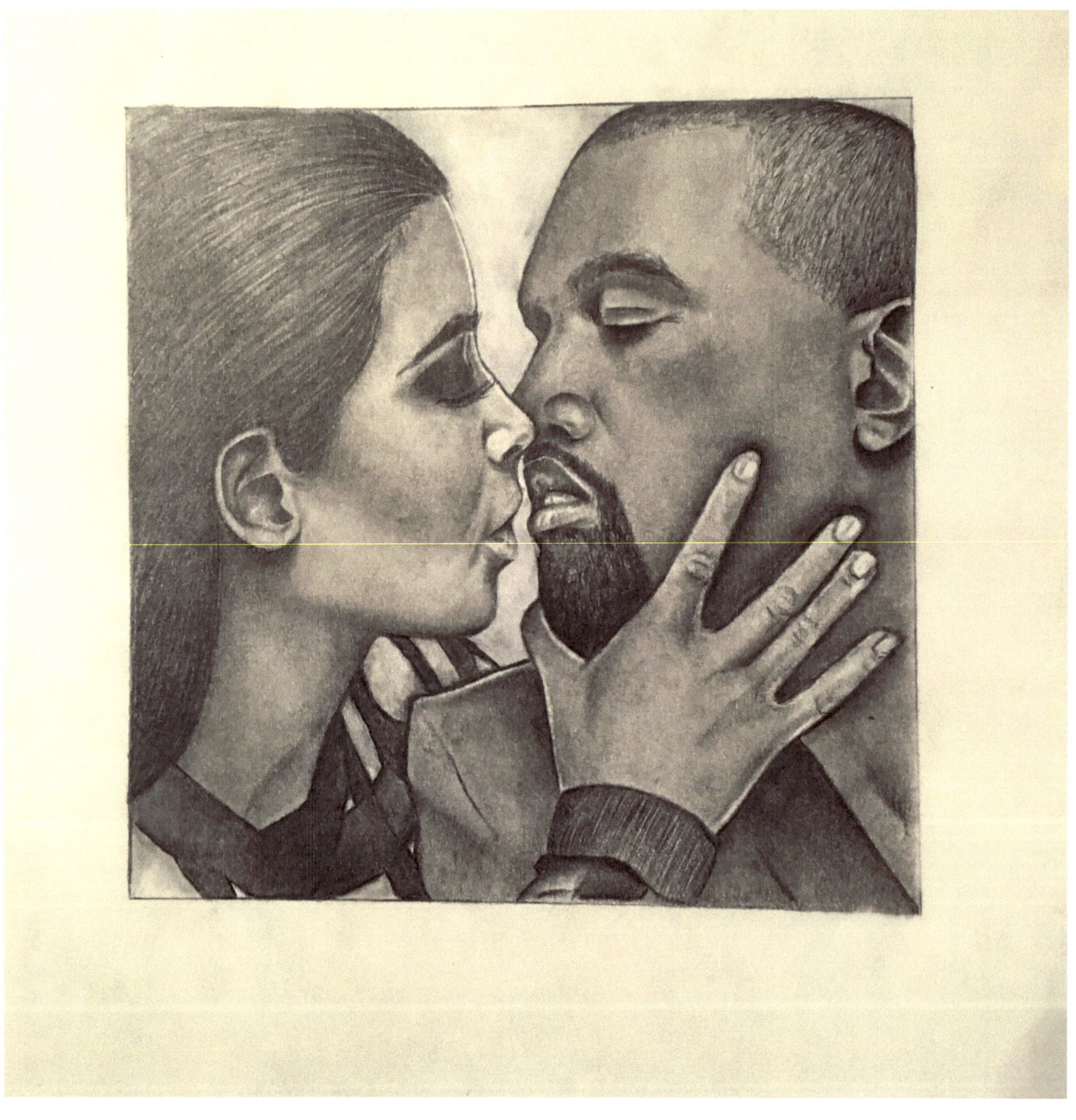

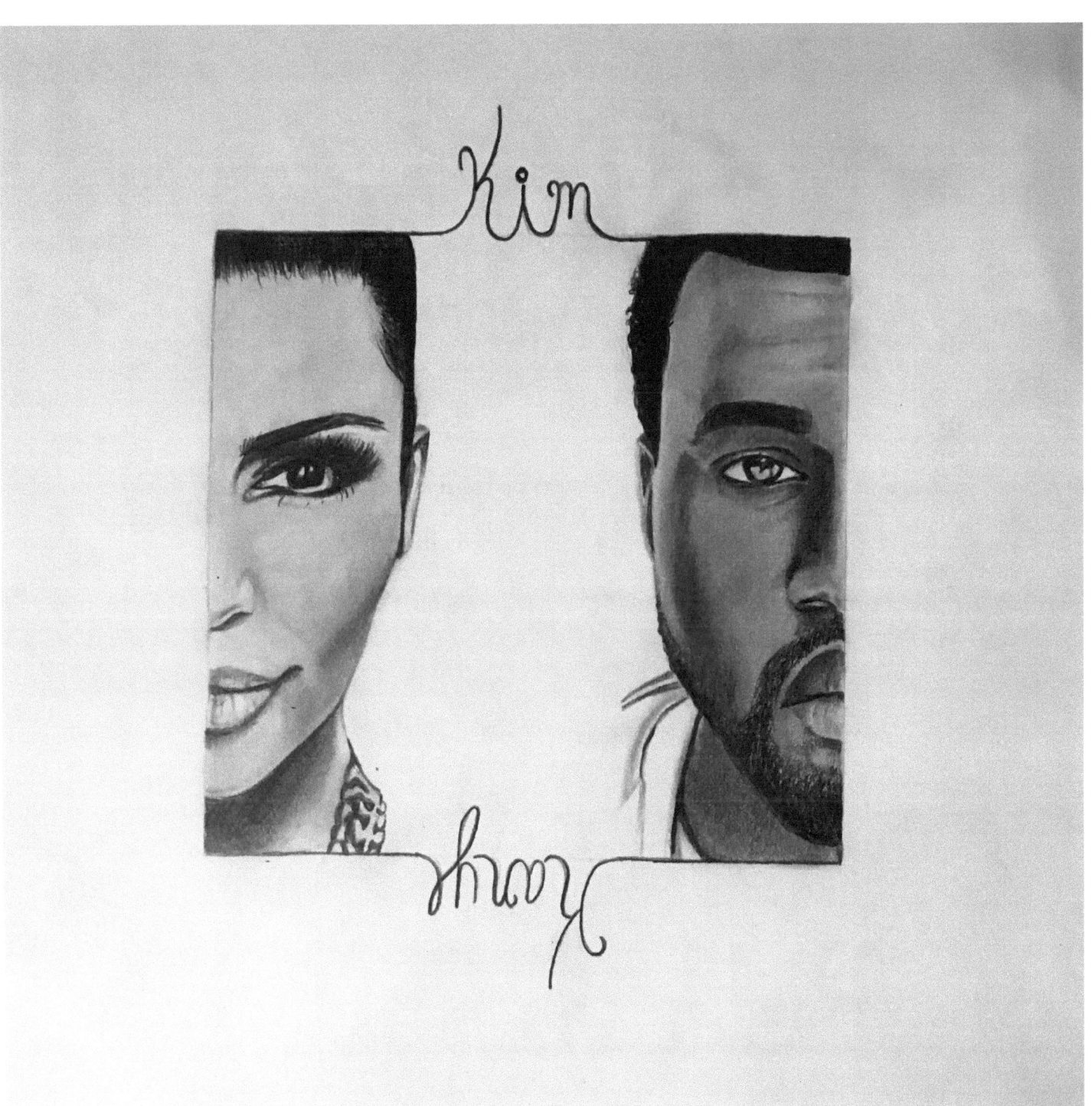

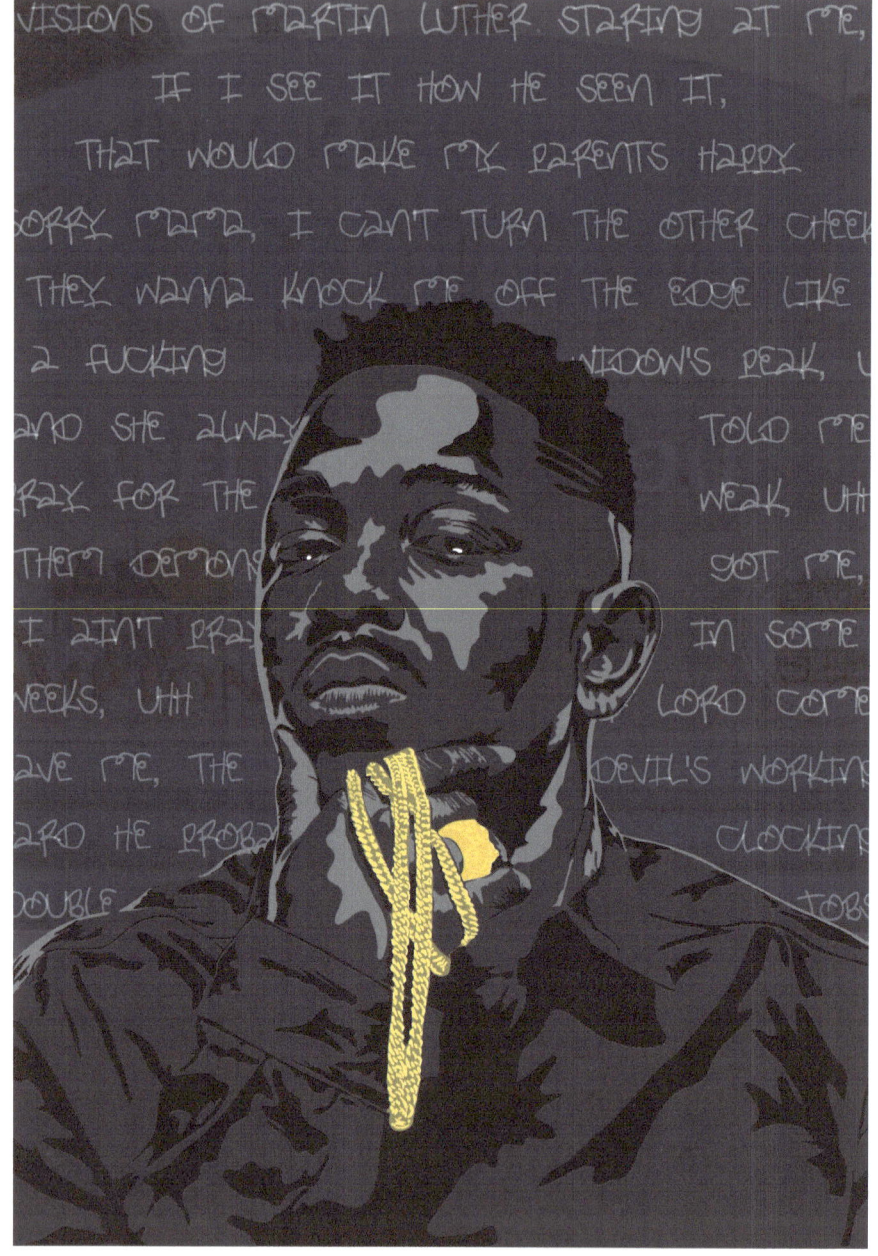

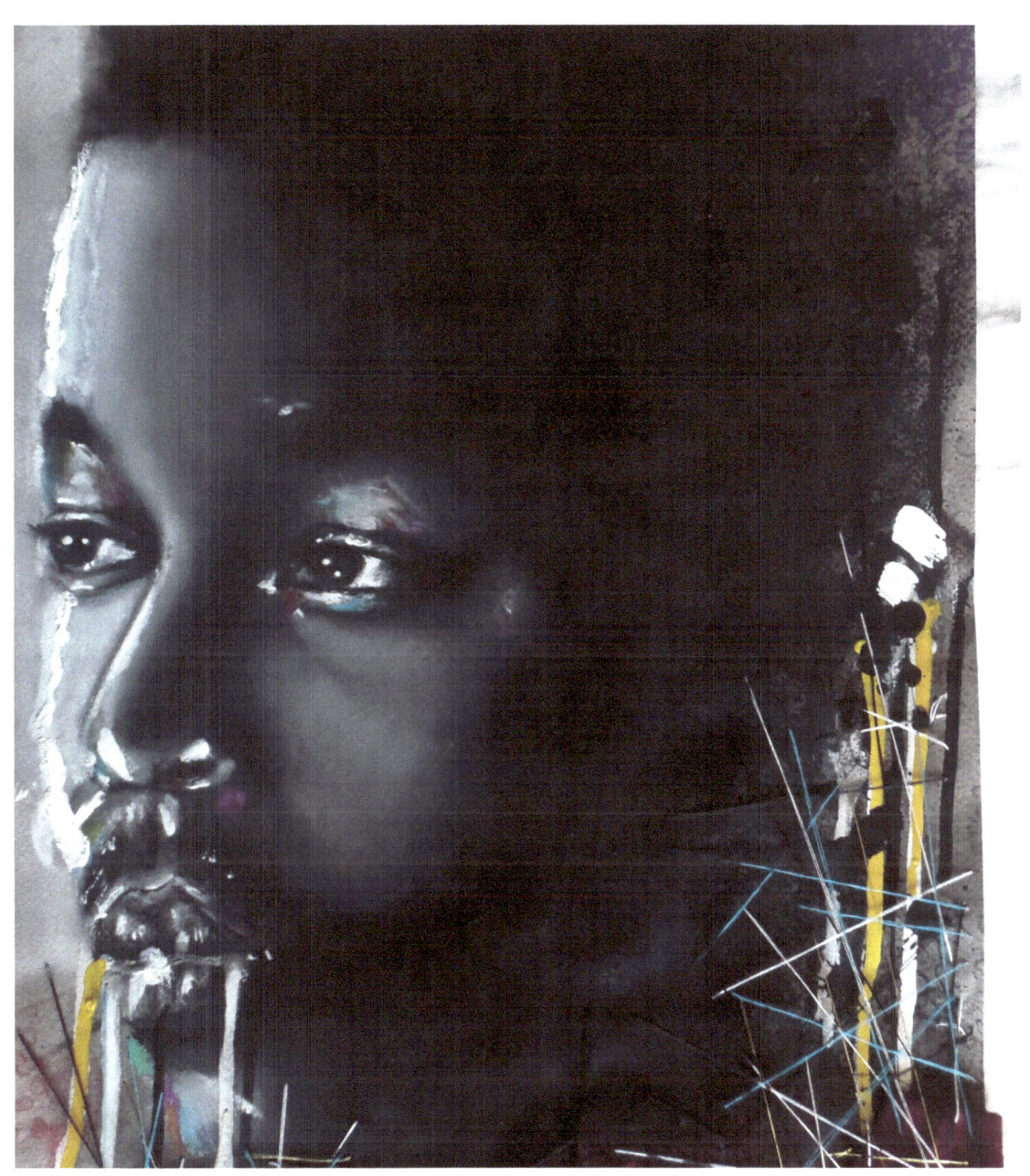

KENDRICK LAMAR

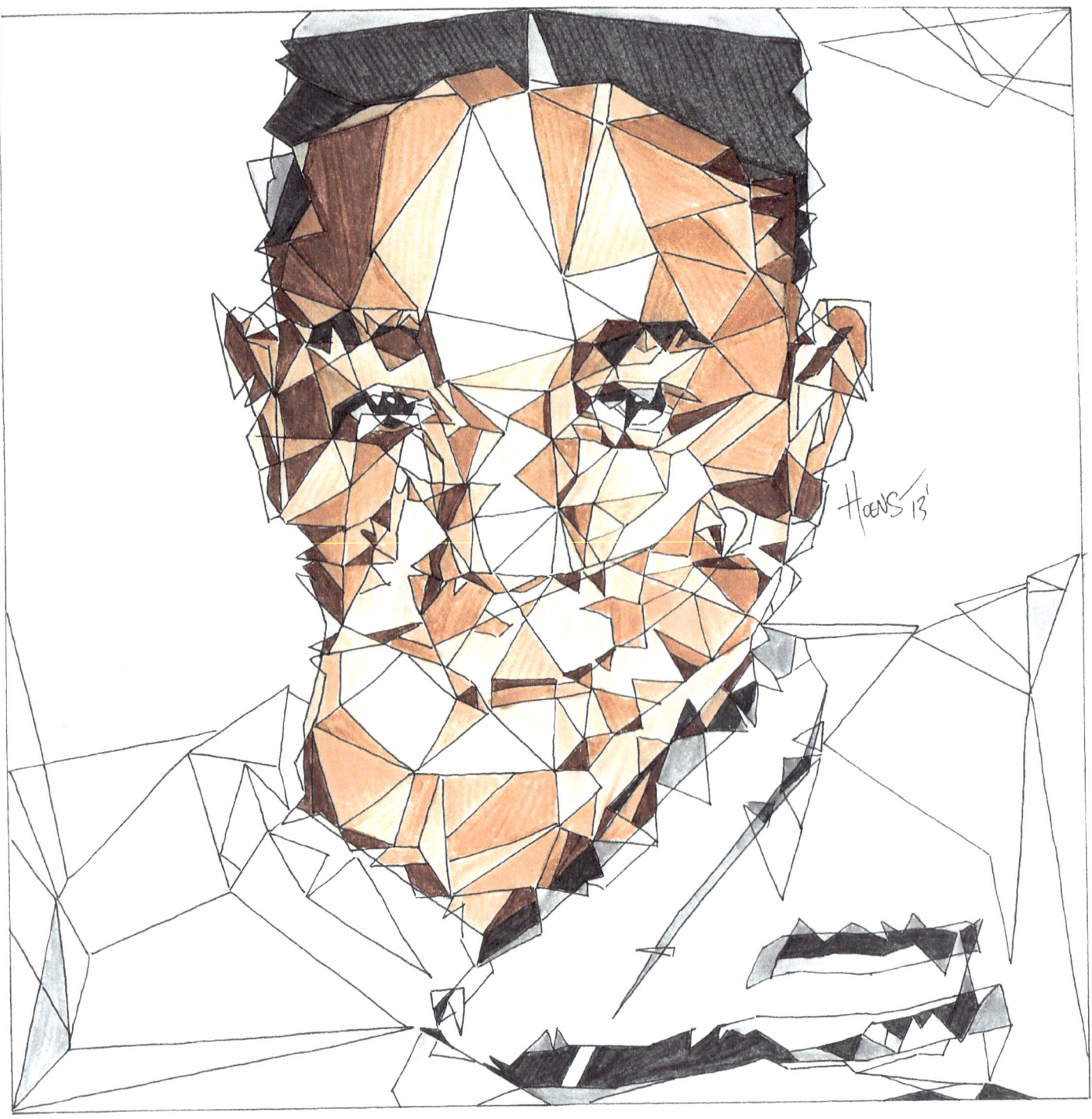

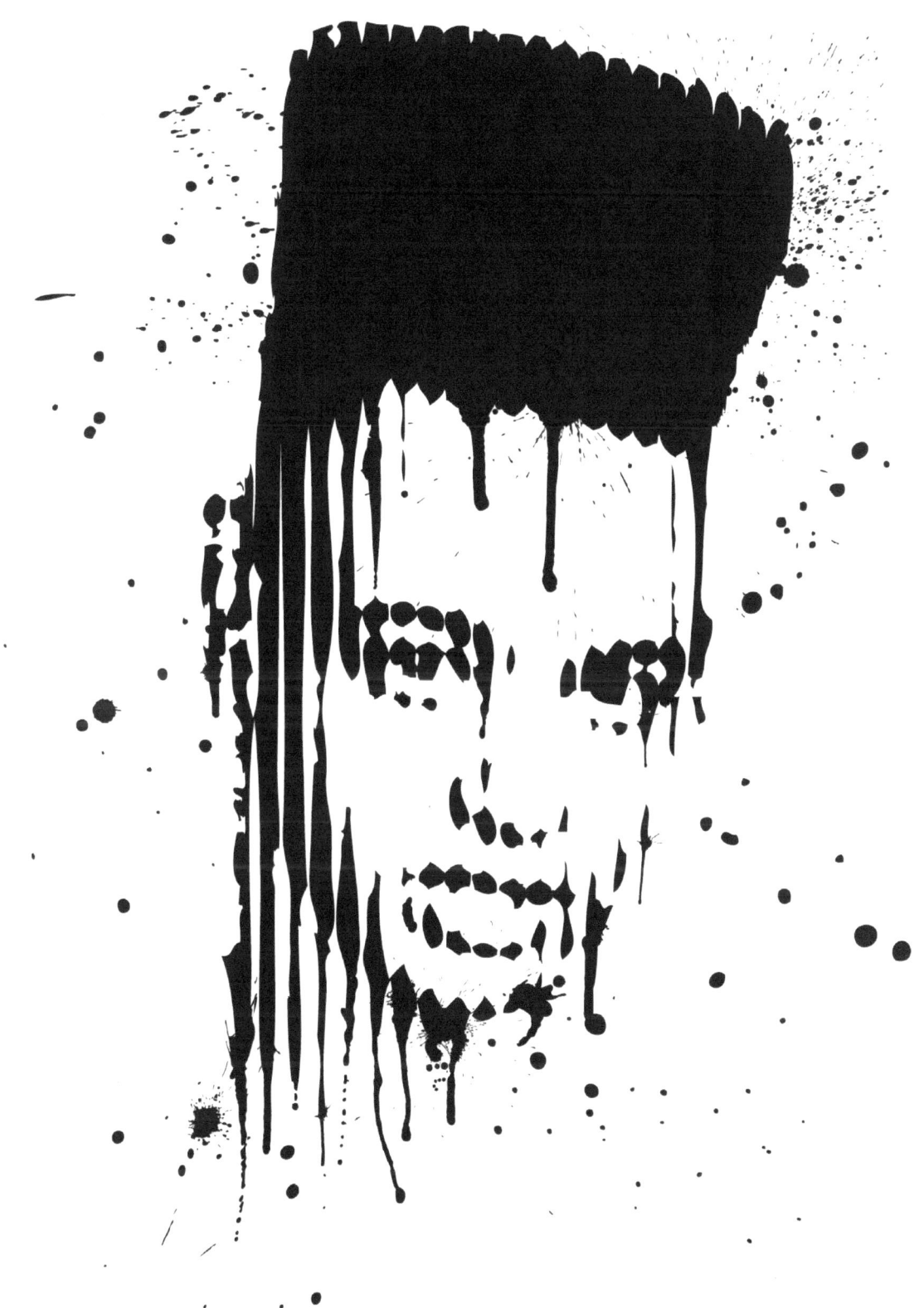

KRS ONE

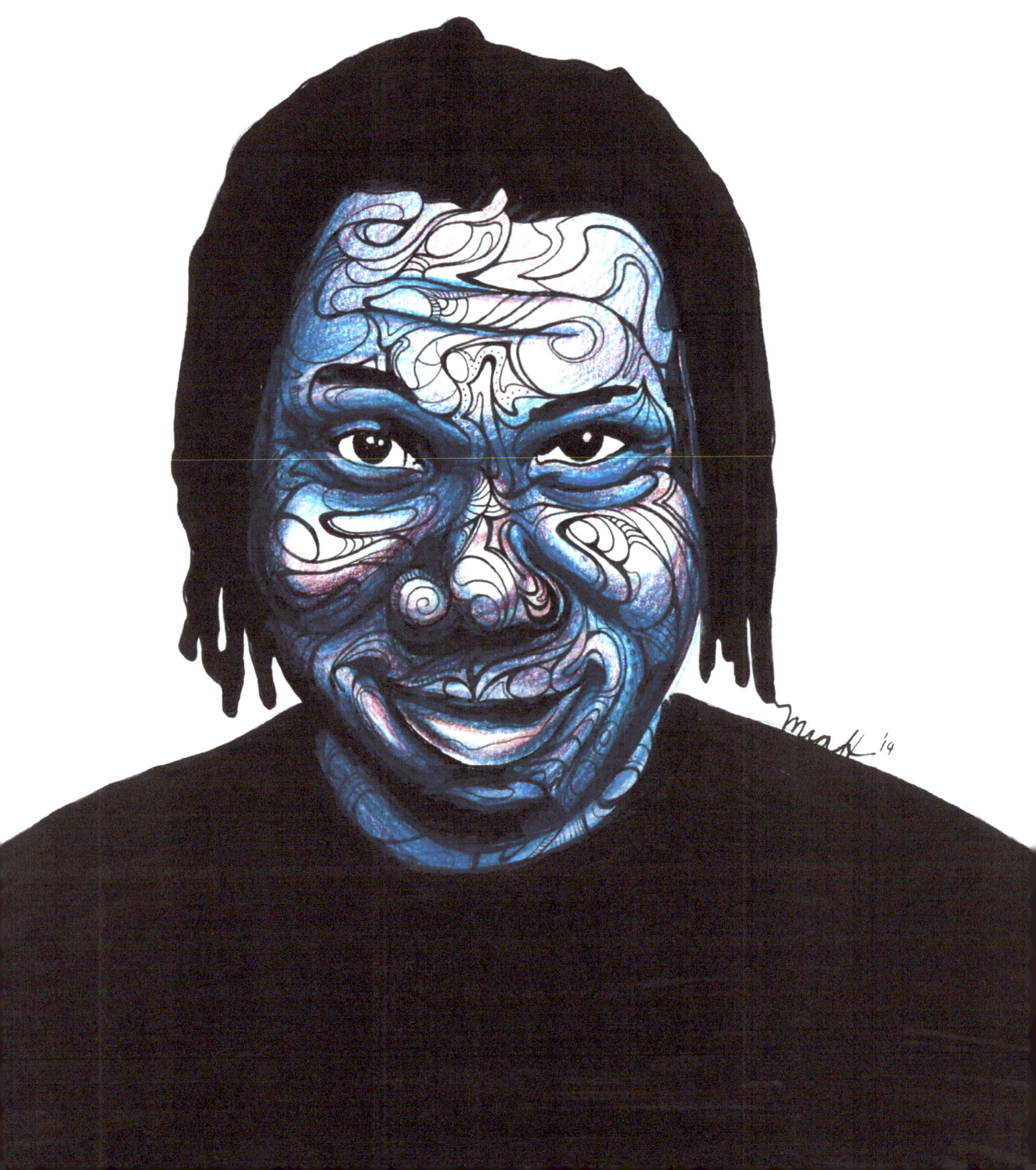

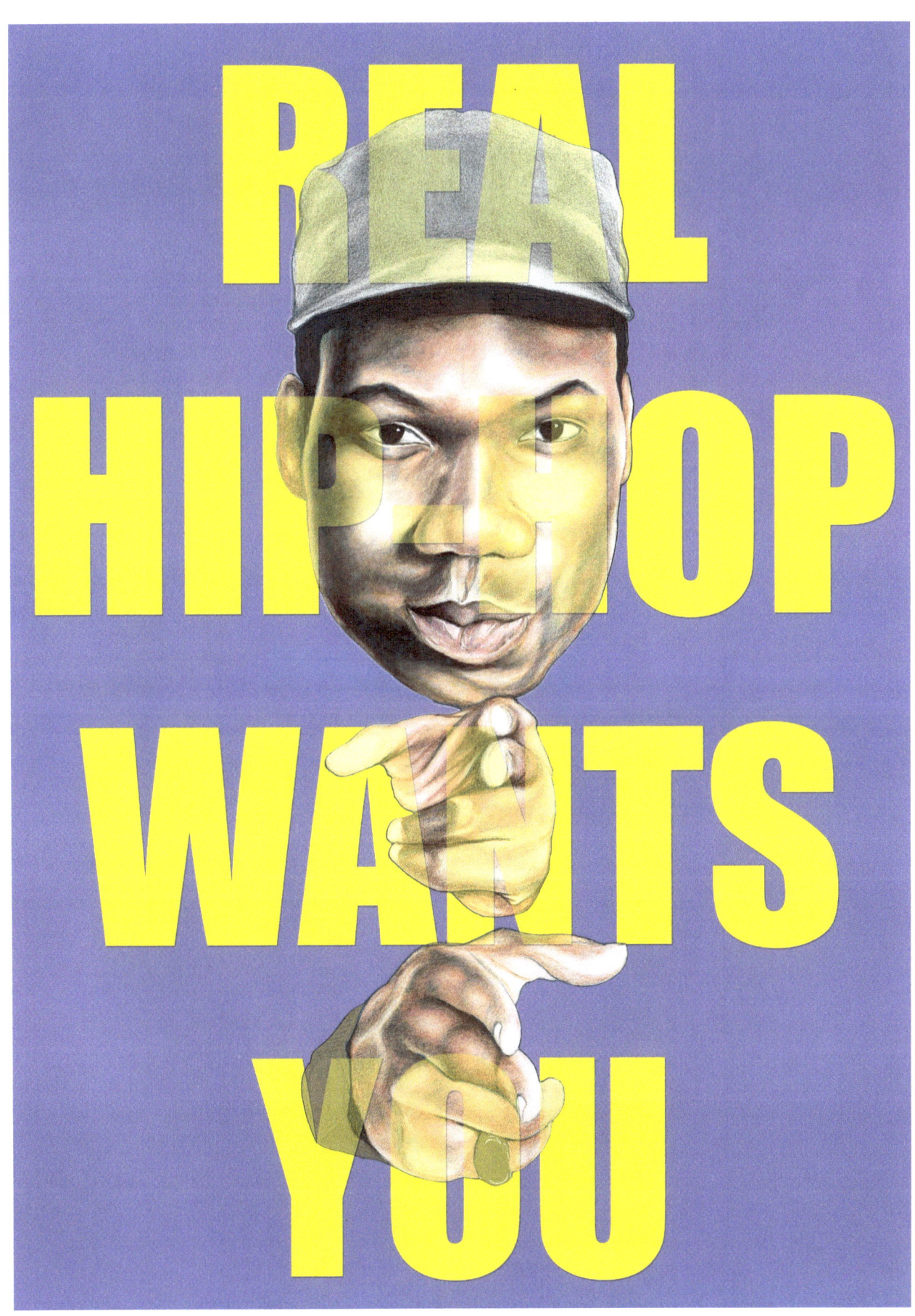

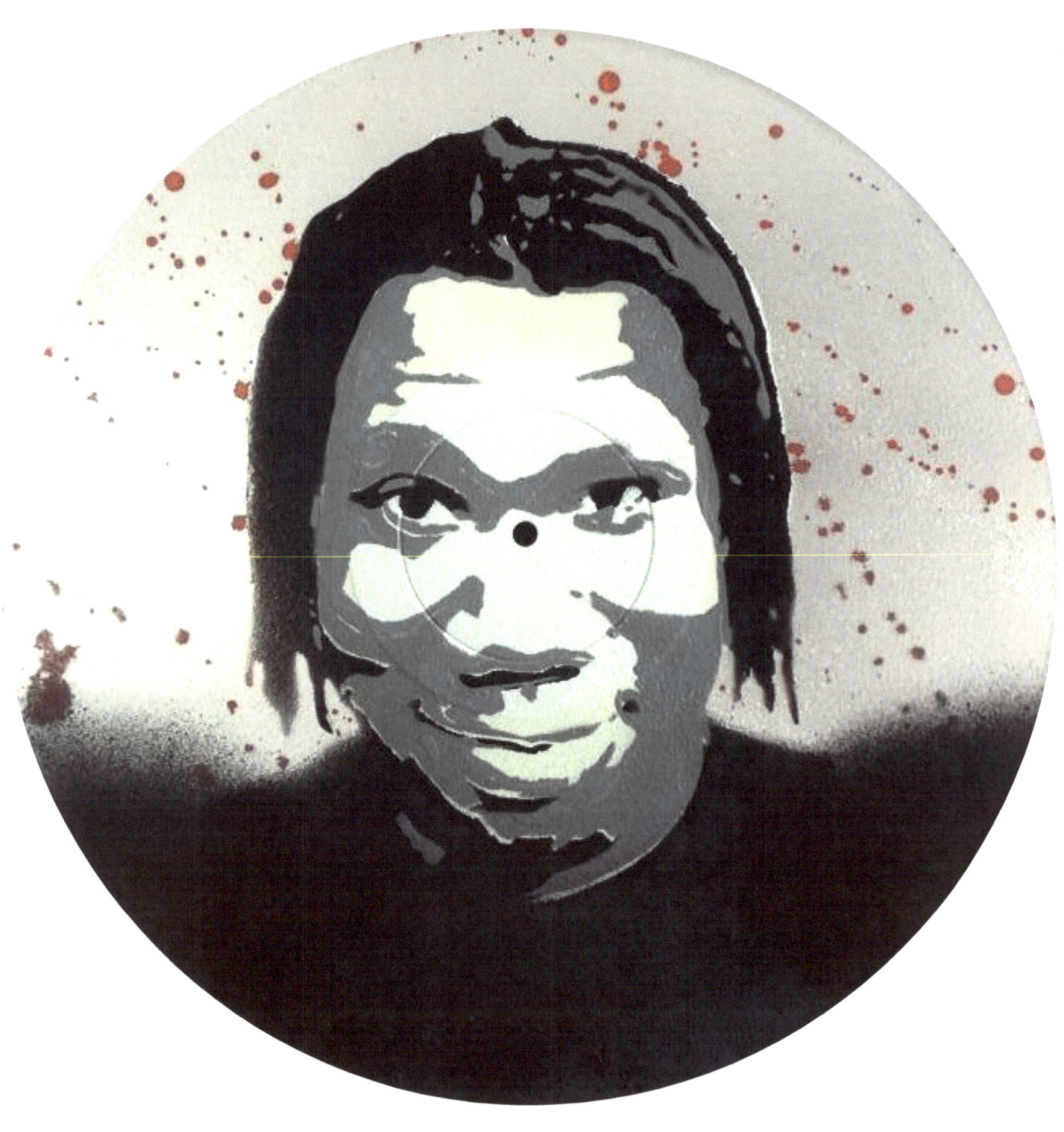

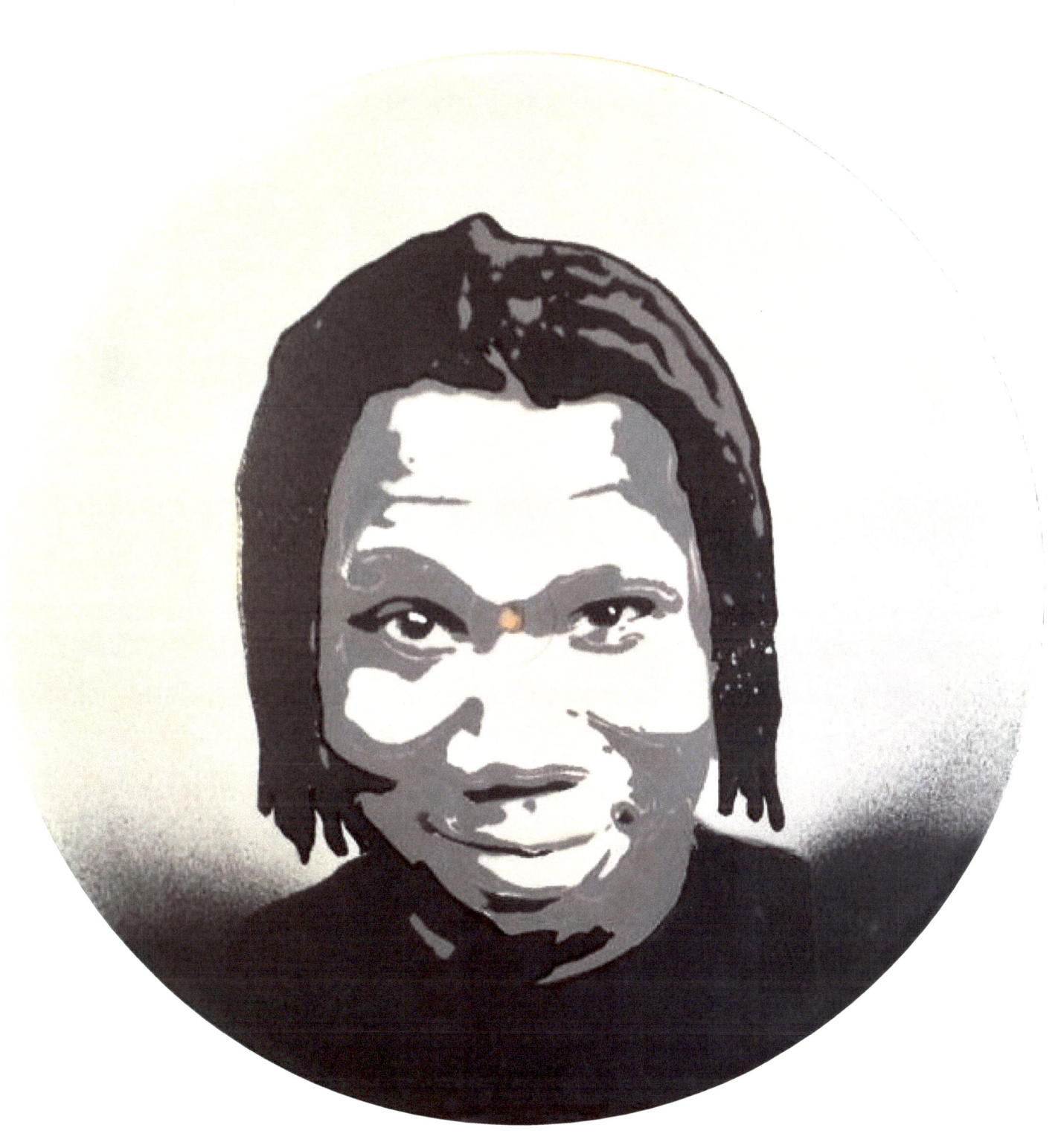

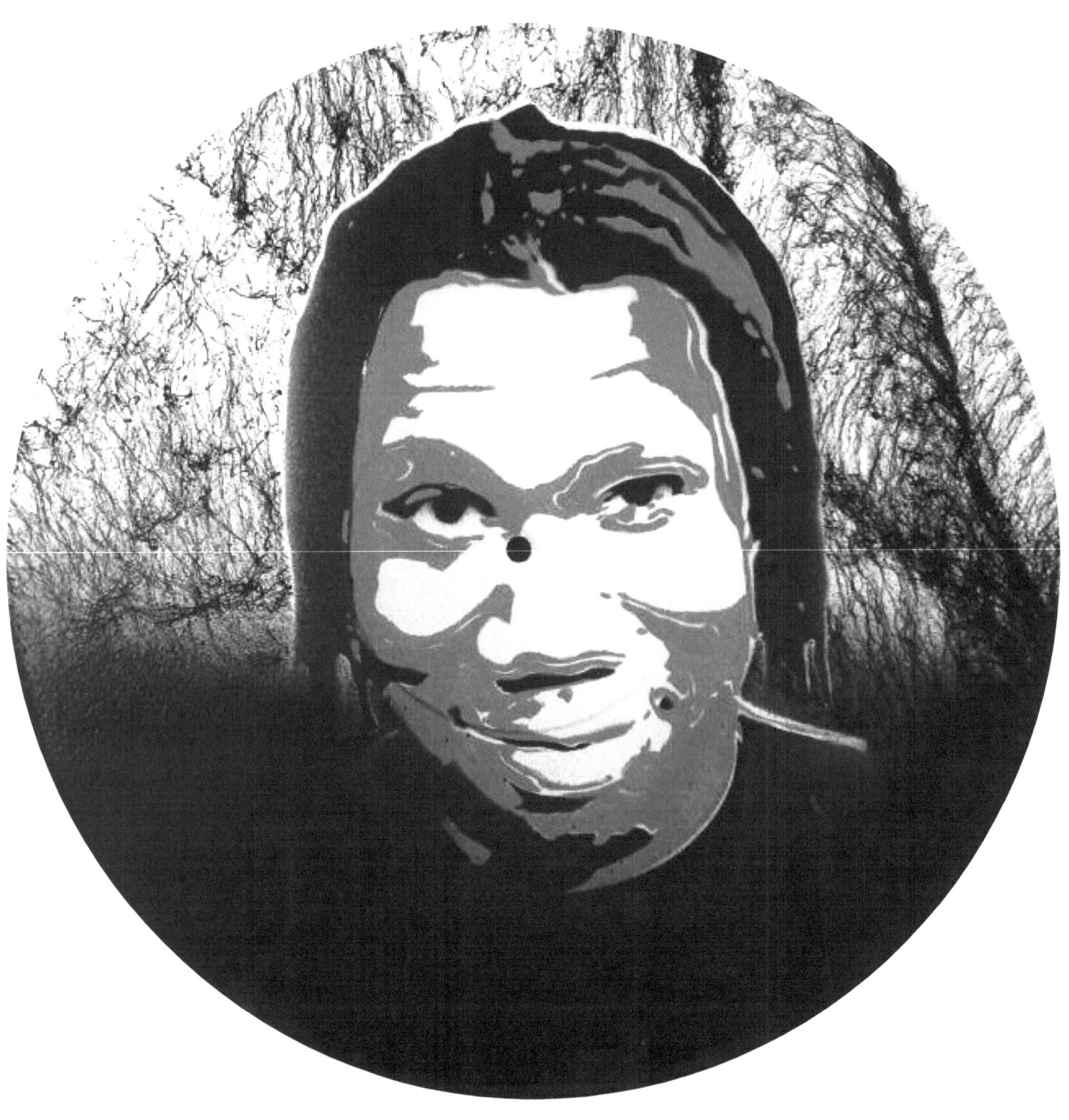

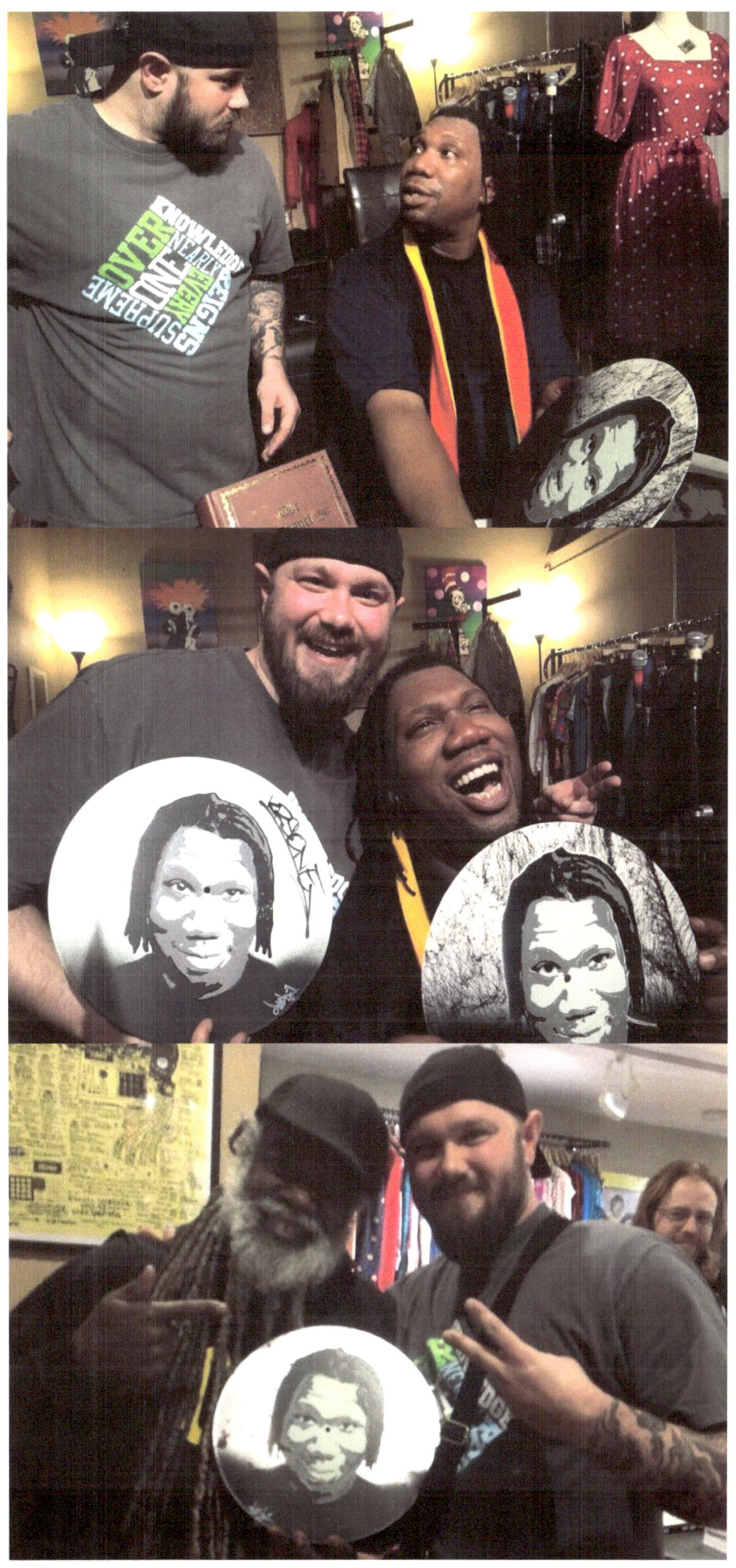

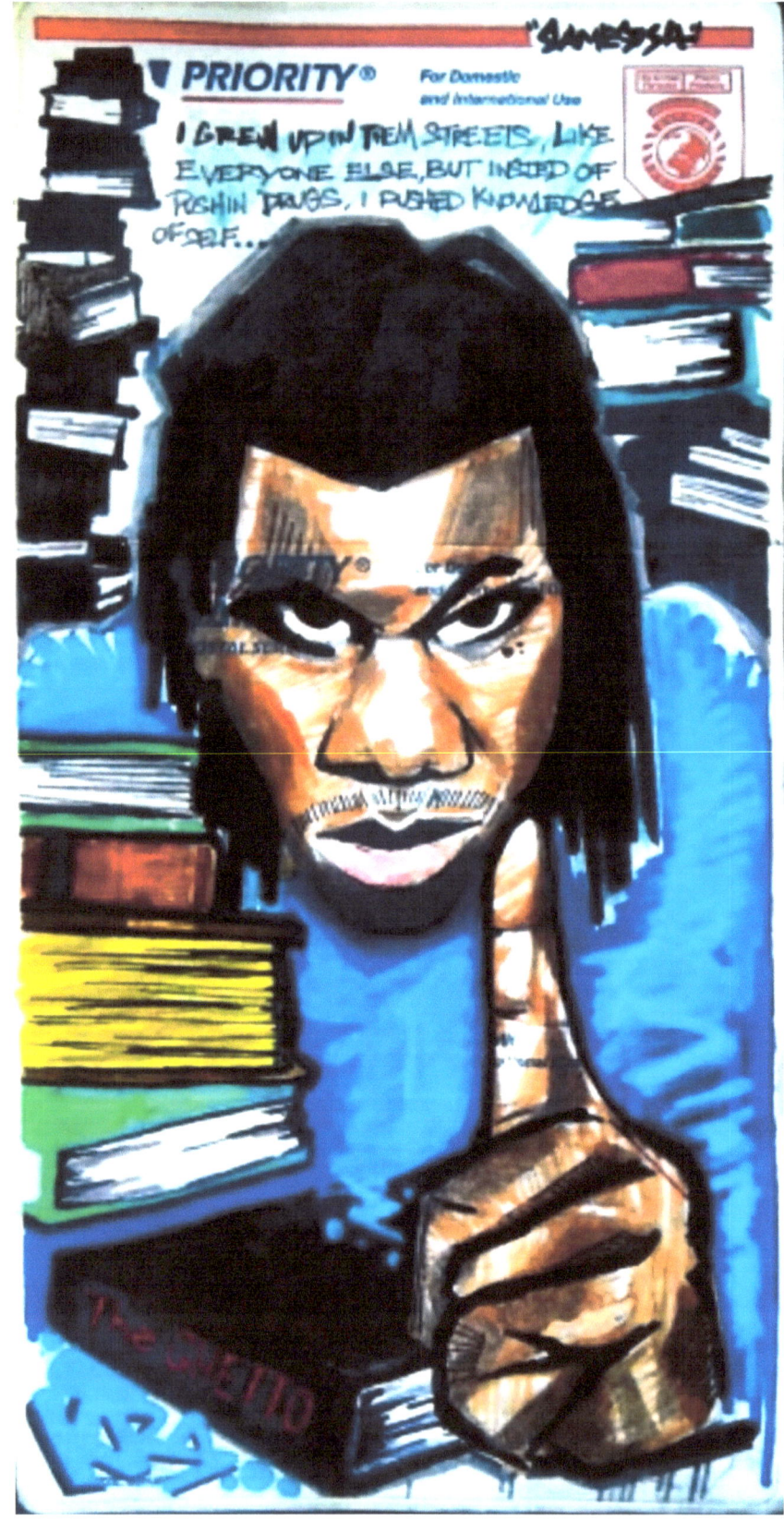

LARGE PROFESSOR

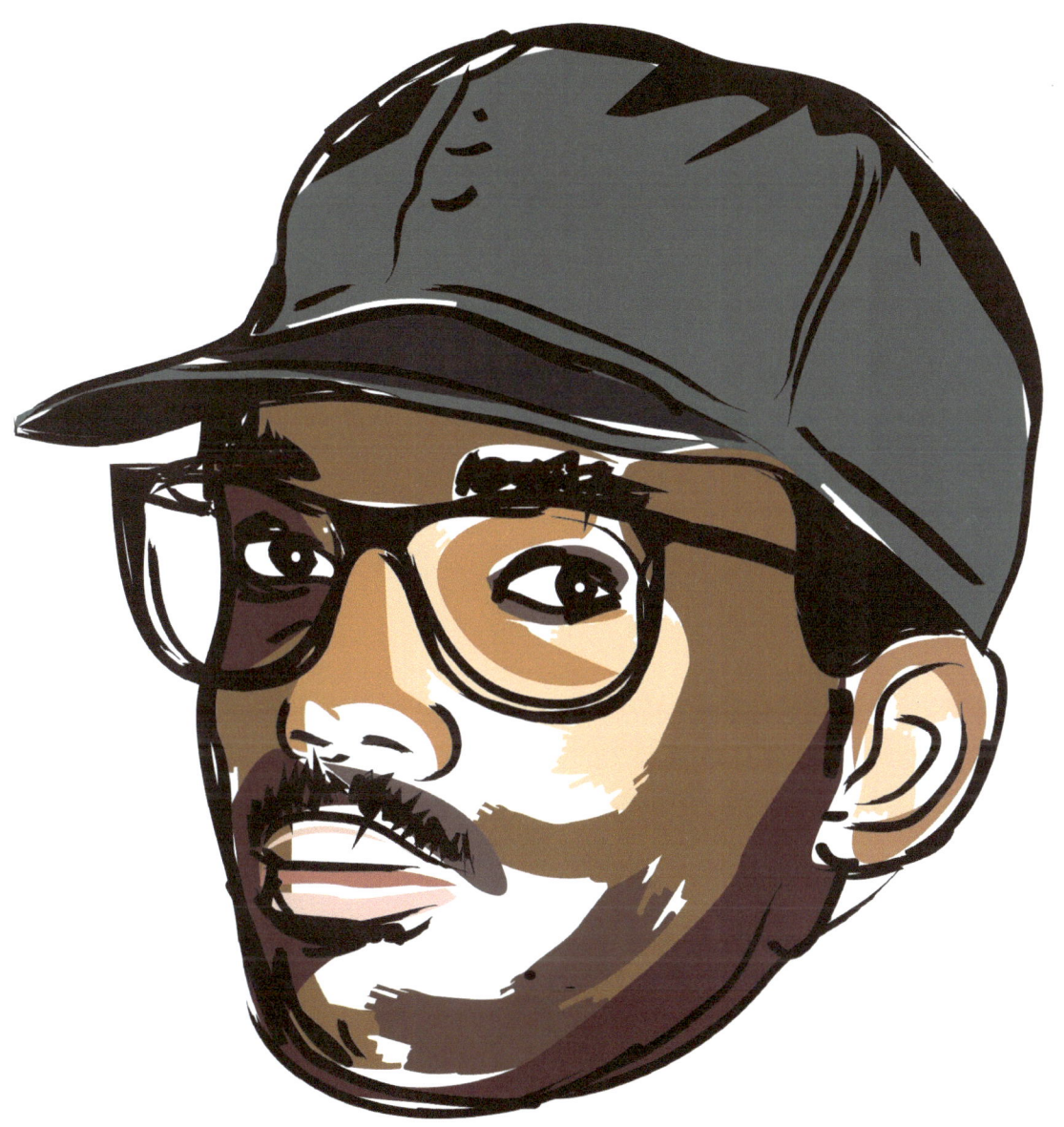

LE$

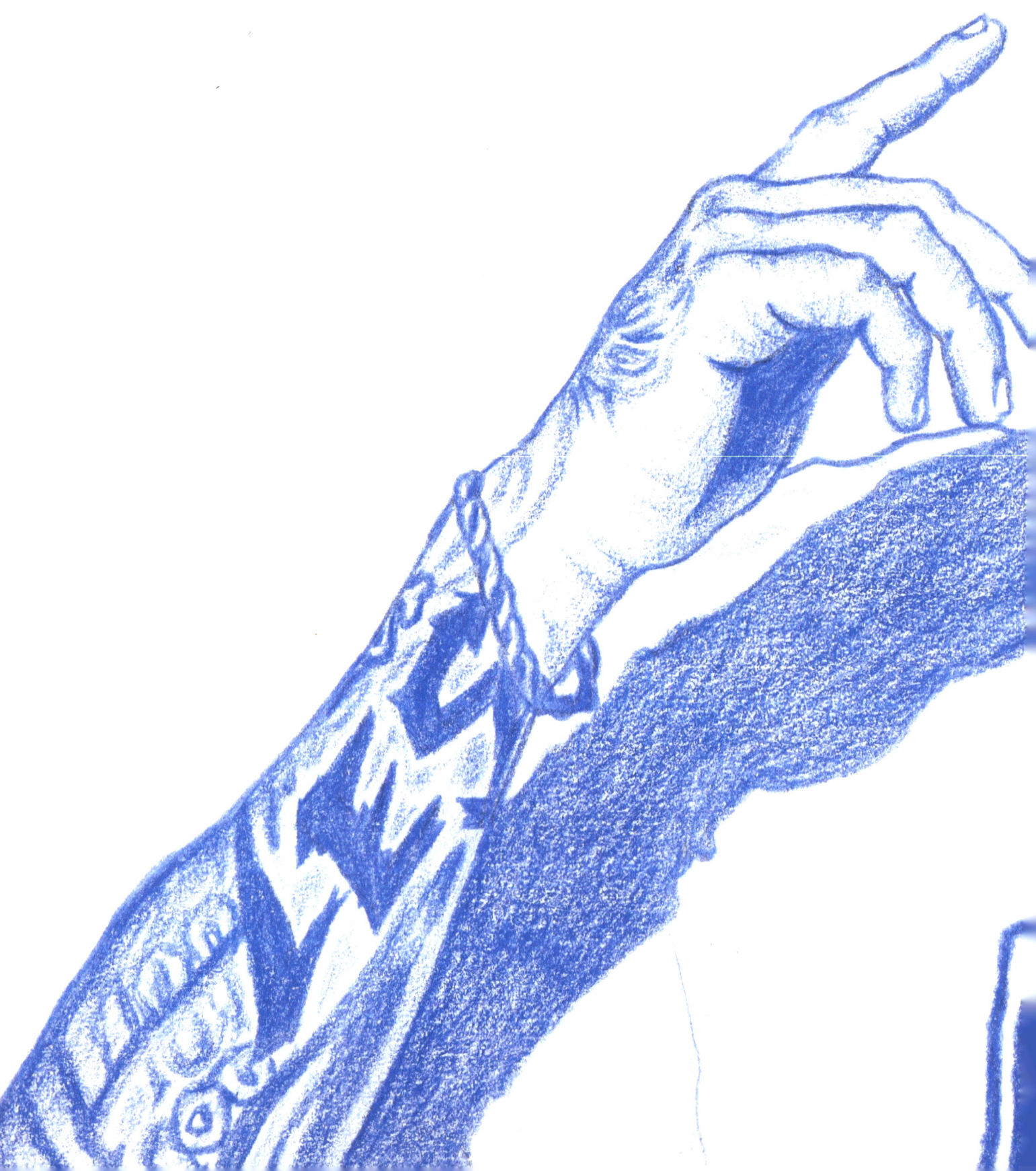

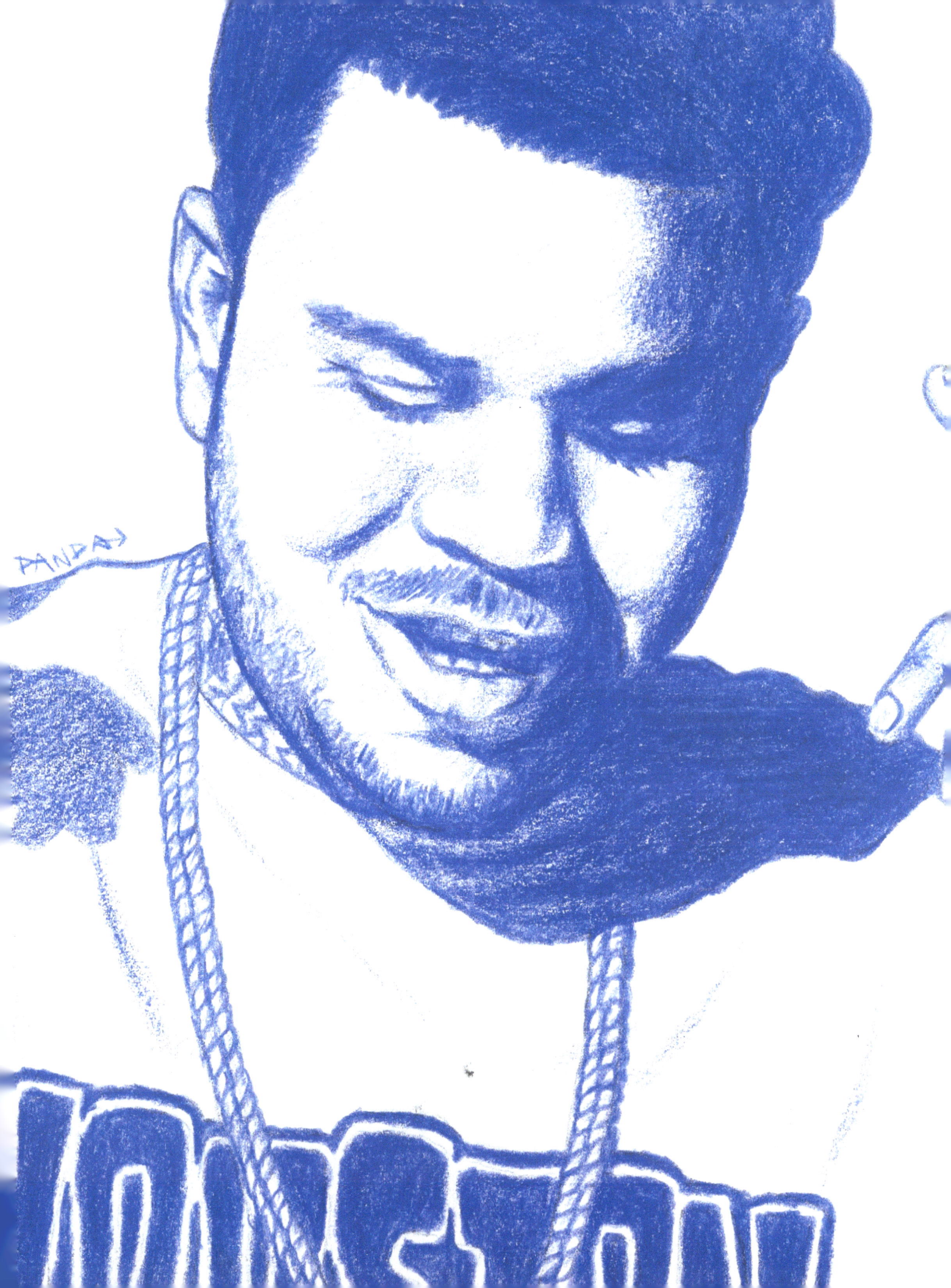

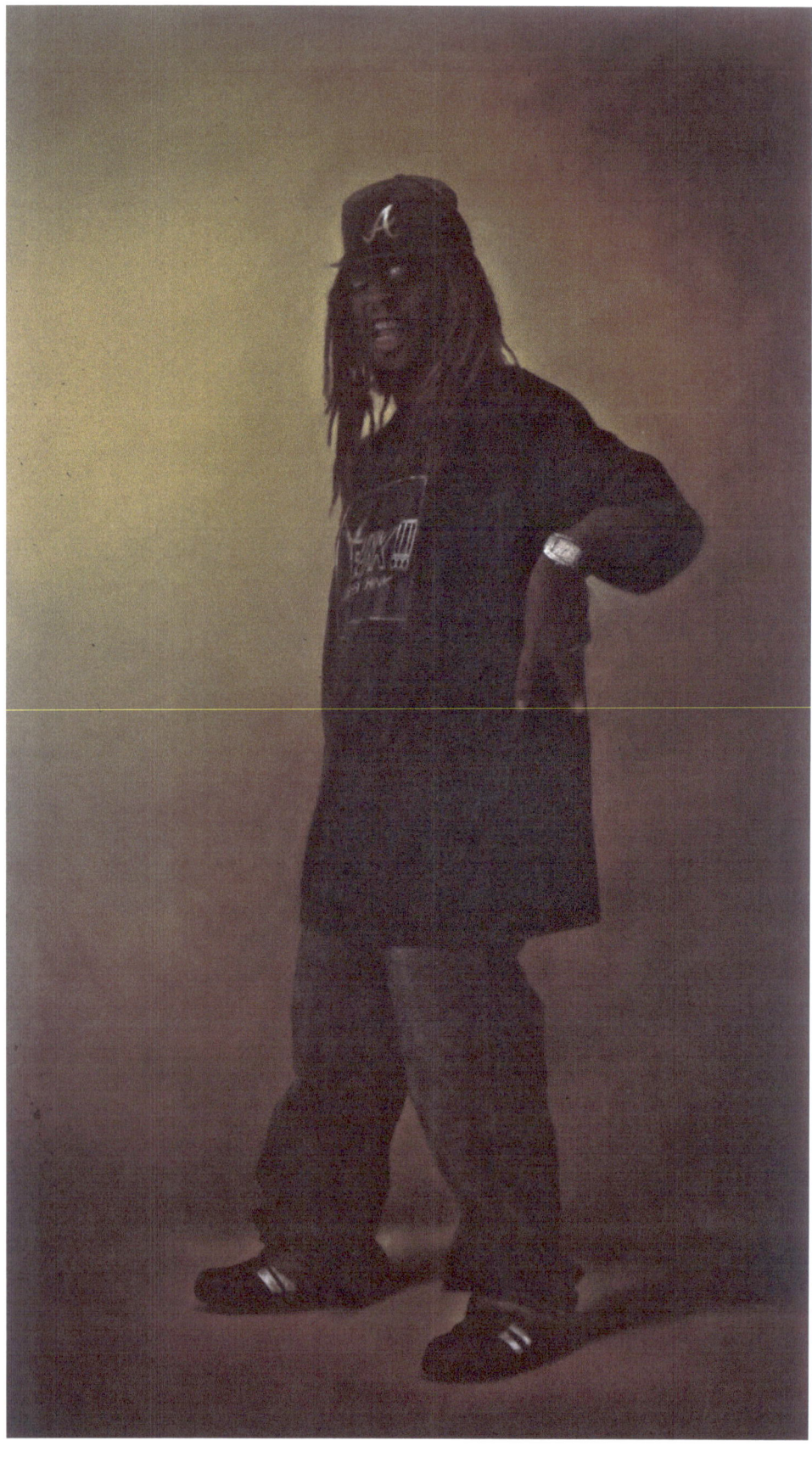

LIL UZI VERT
LIL YACHTY

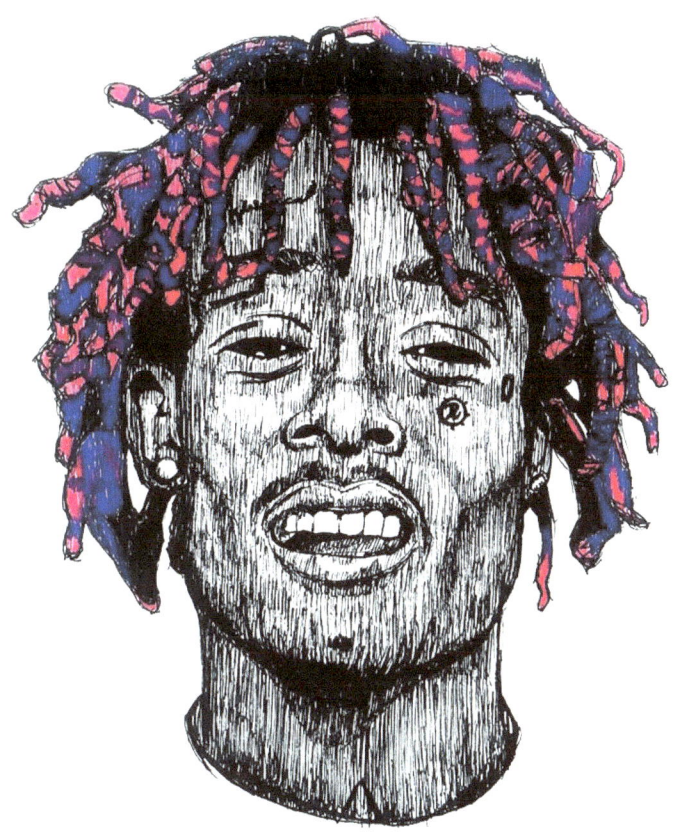

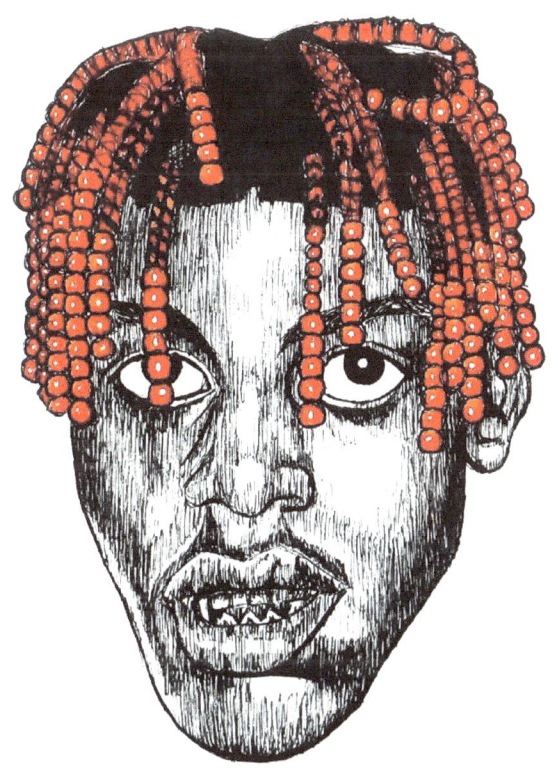

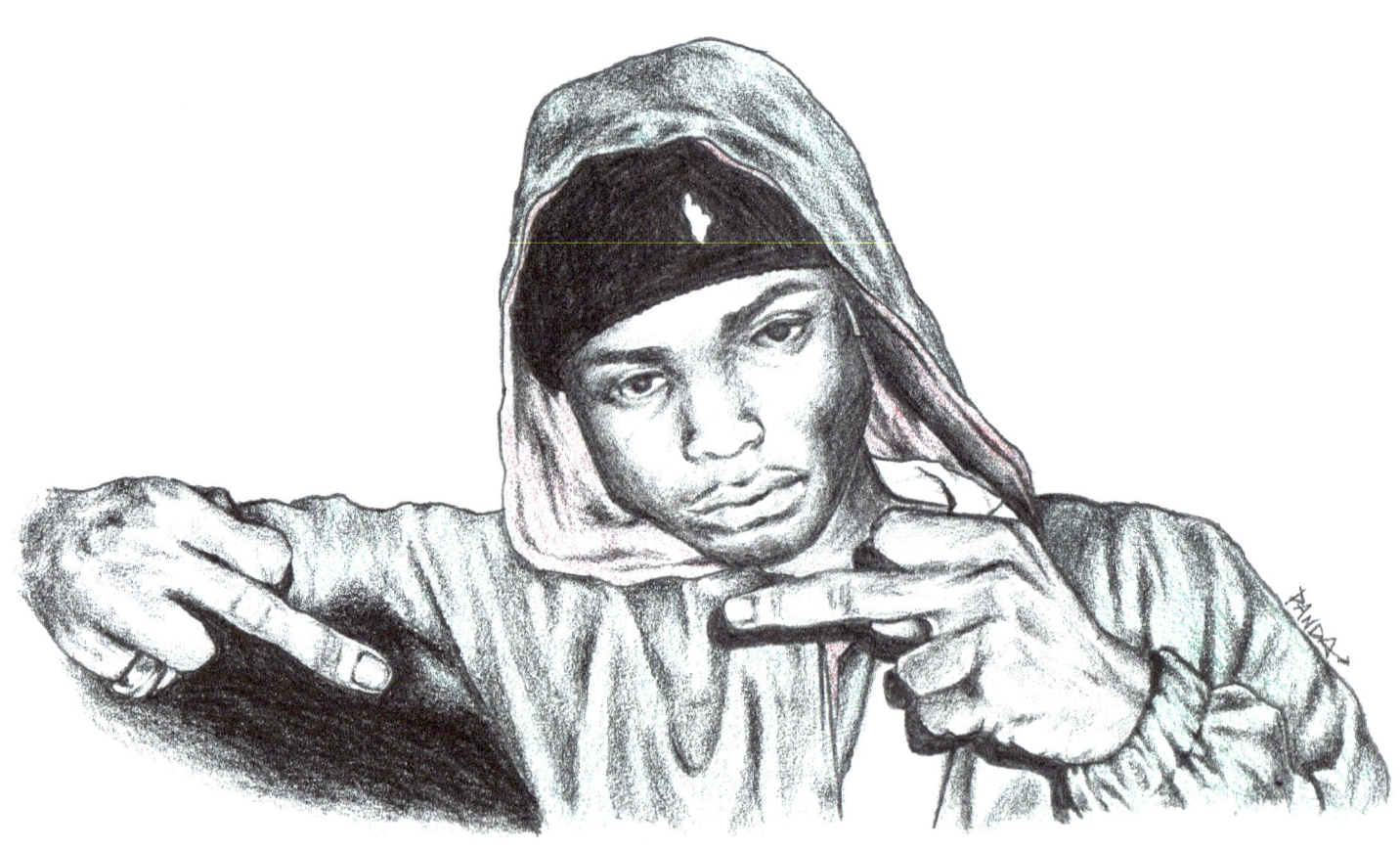

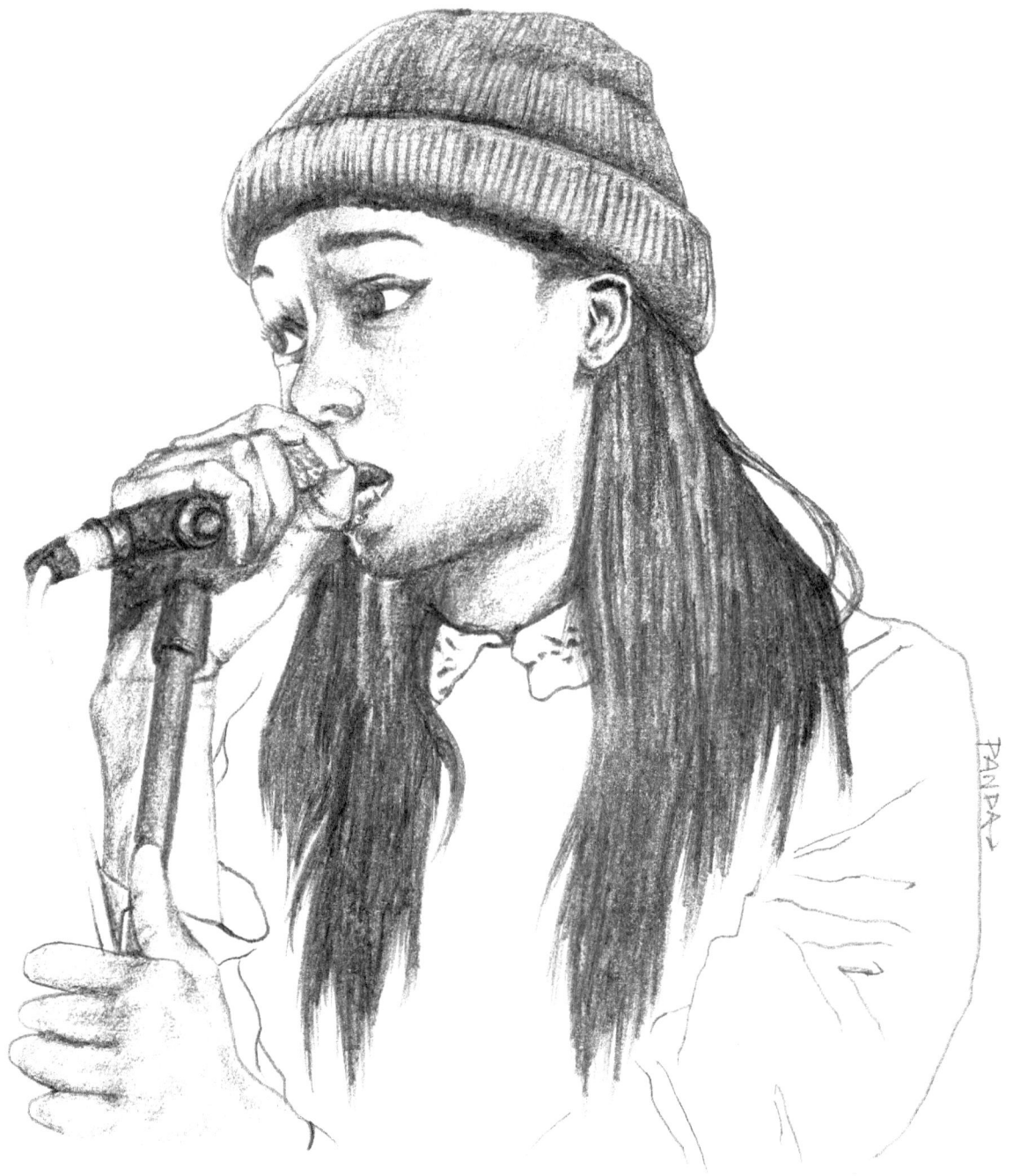

LL COOL J

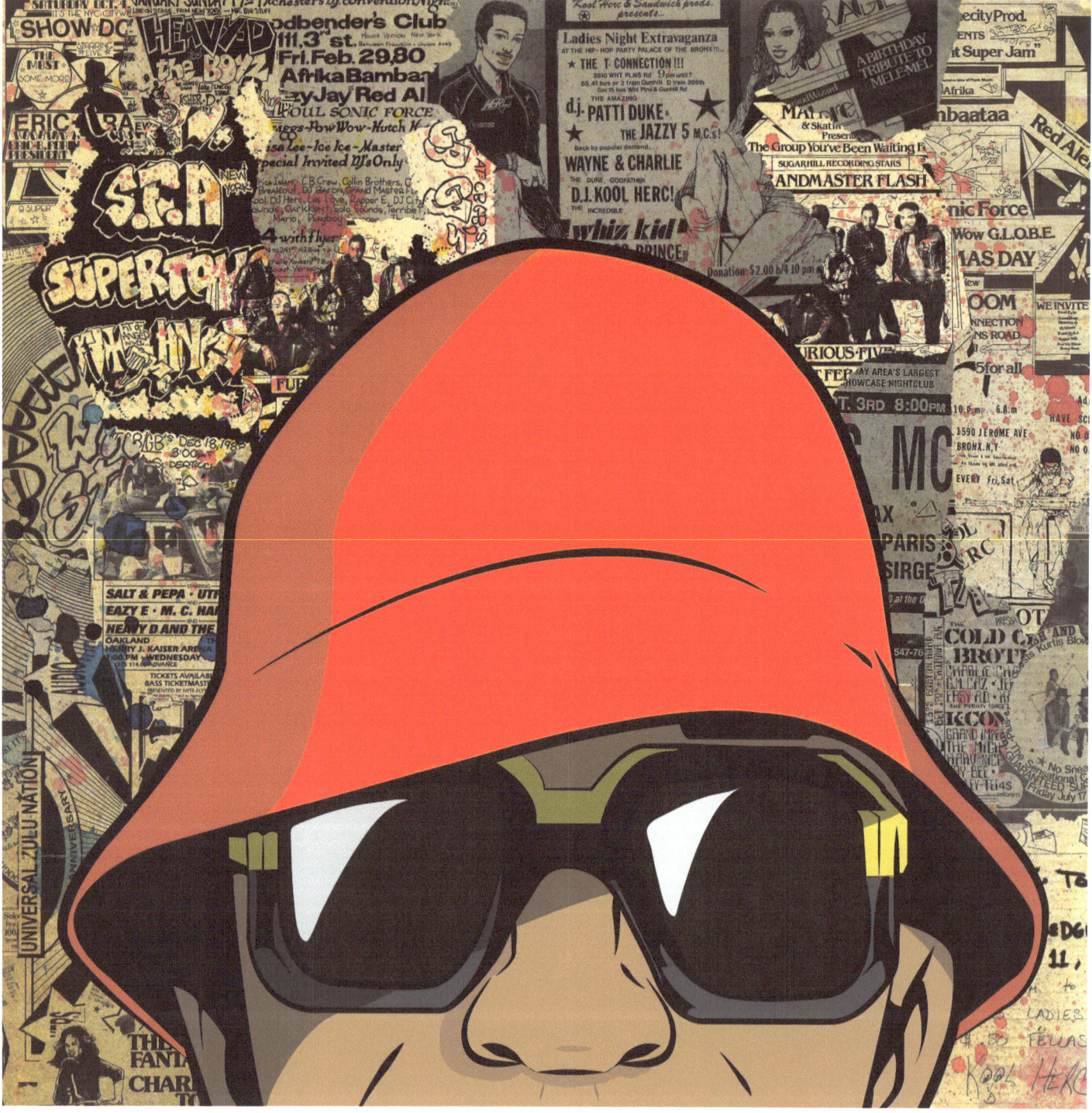

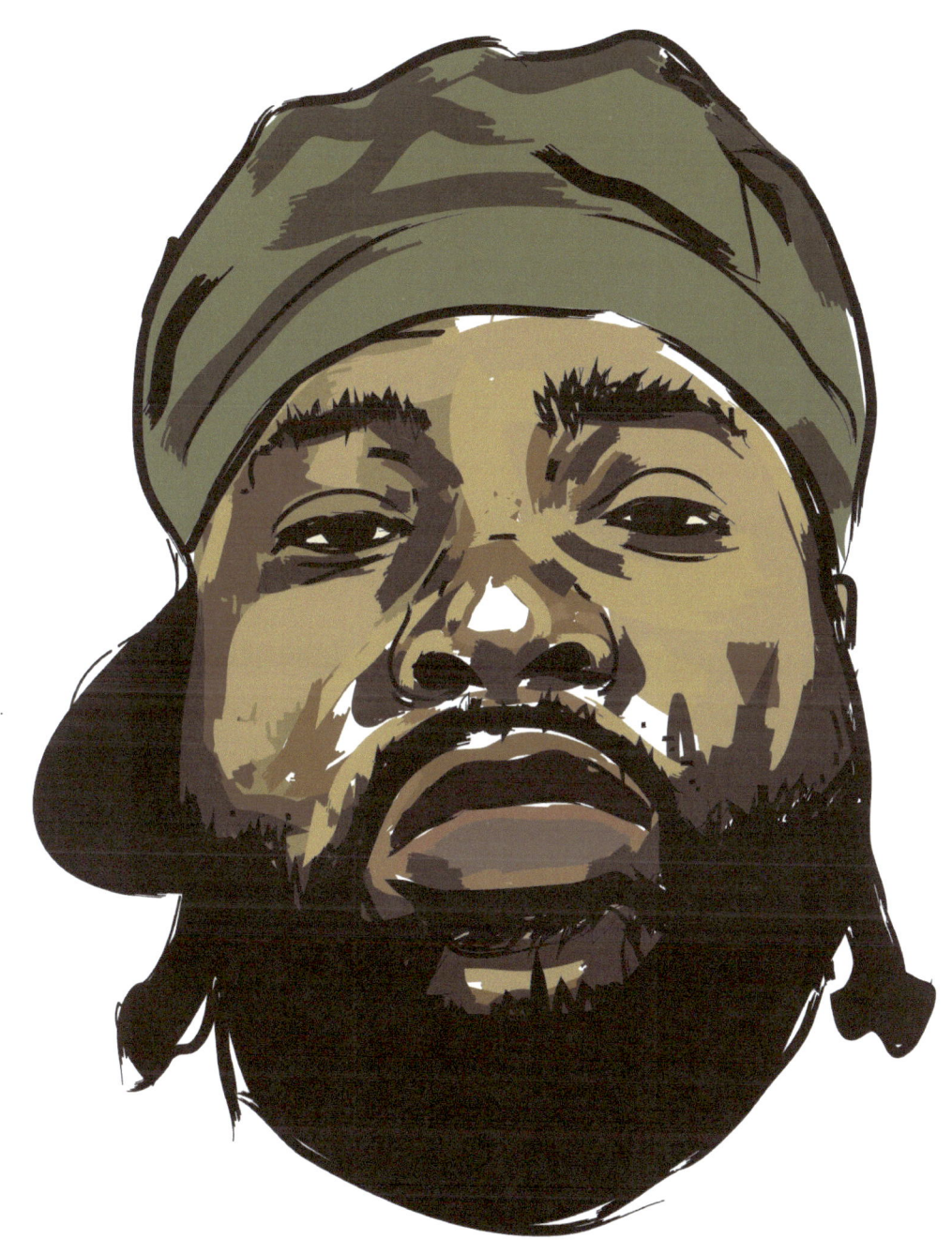

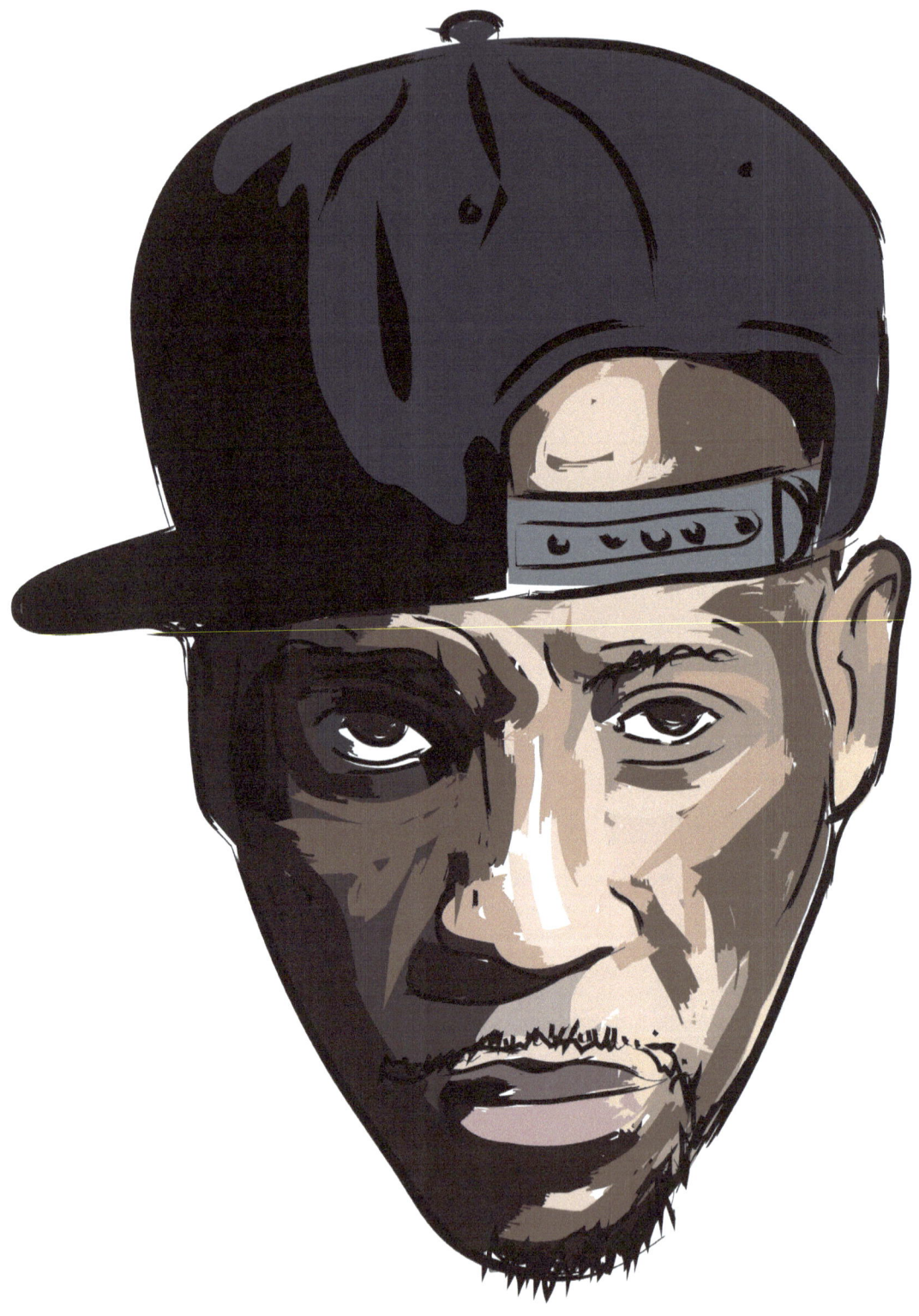

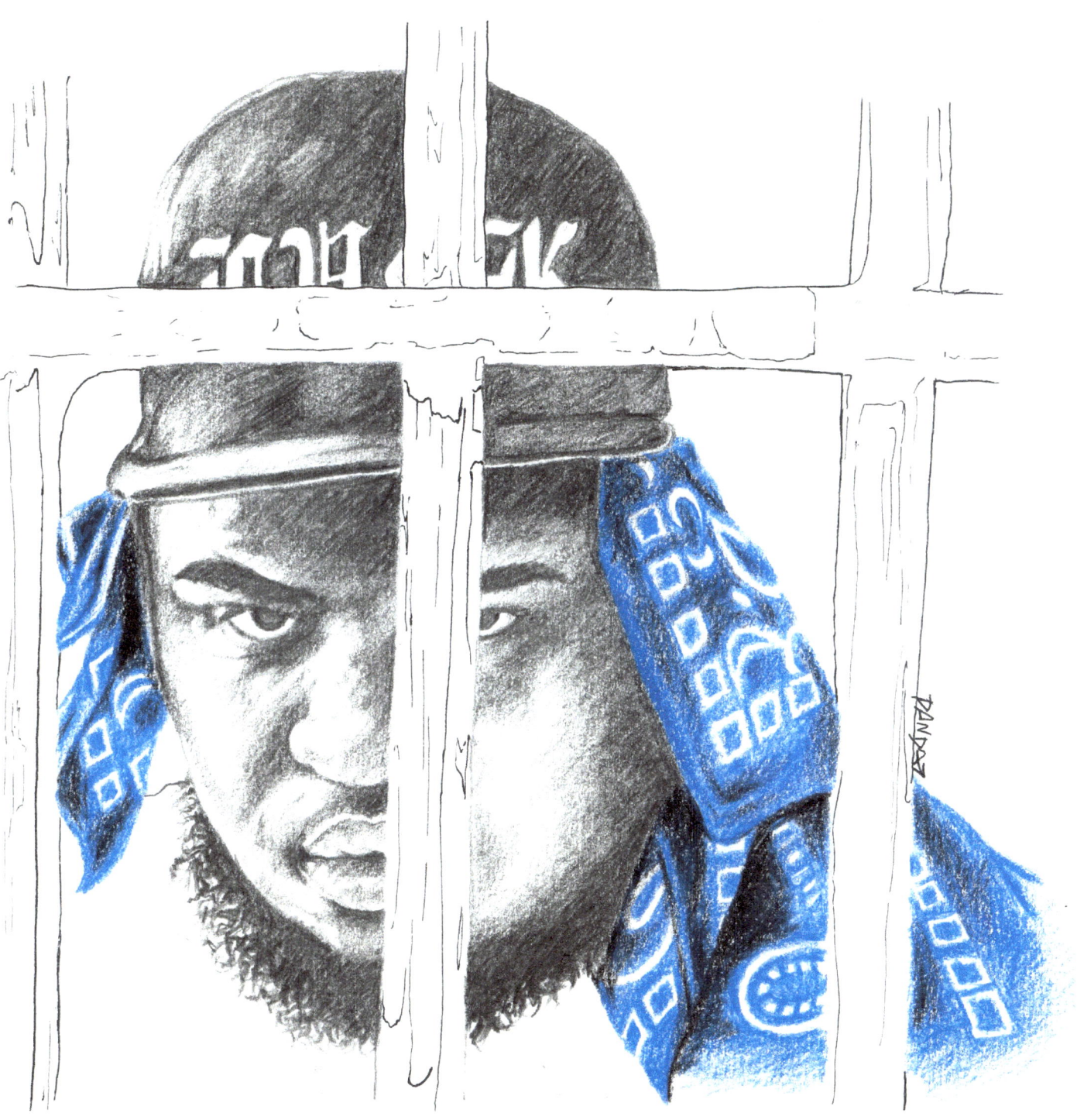

METHOD MAN

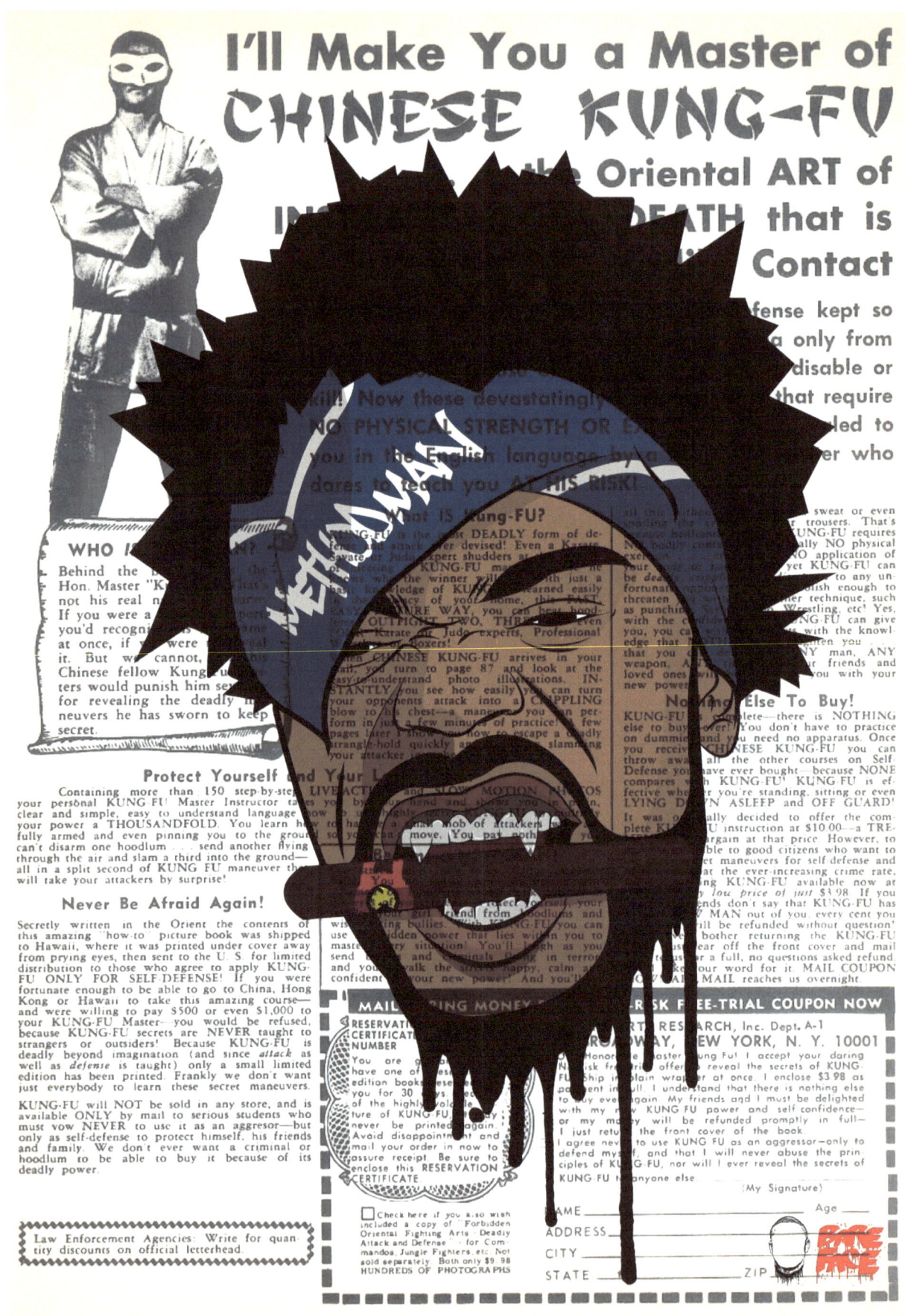

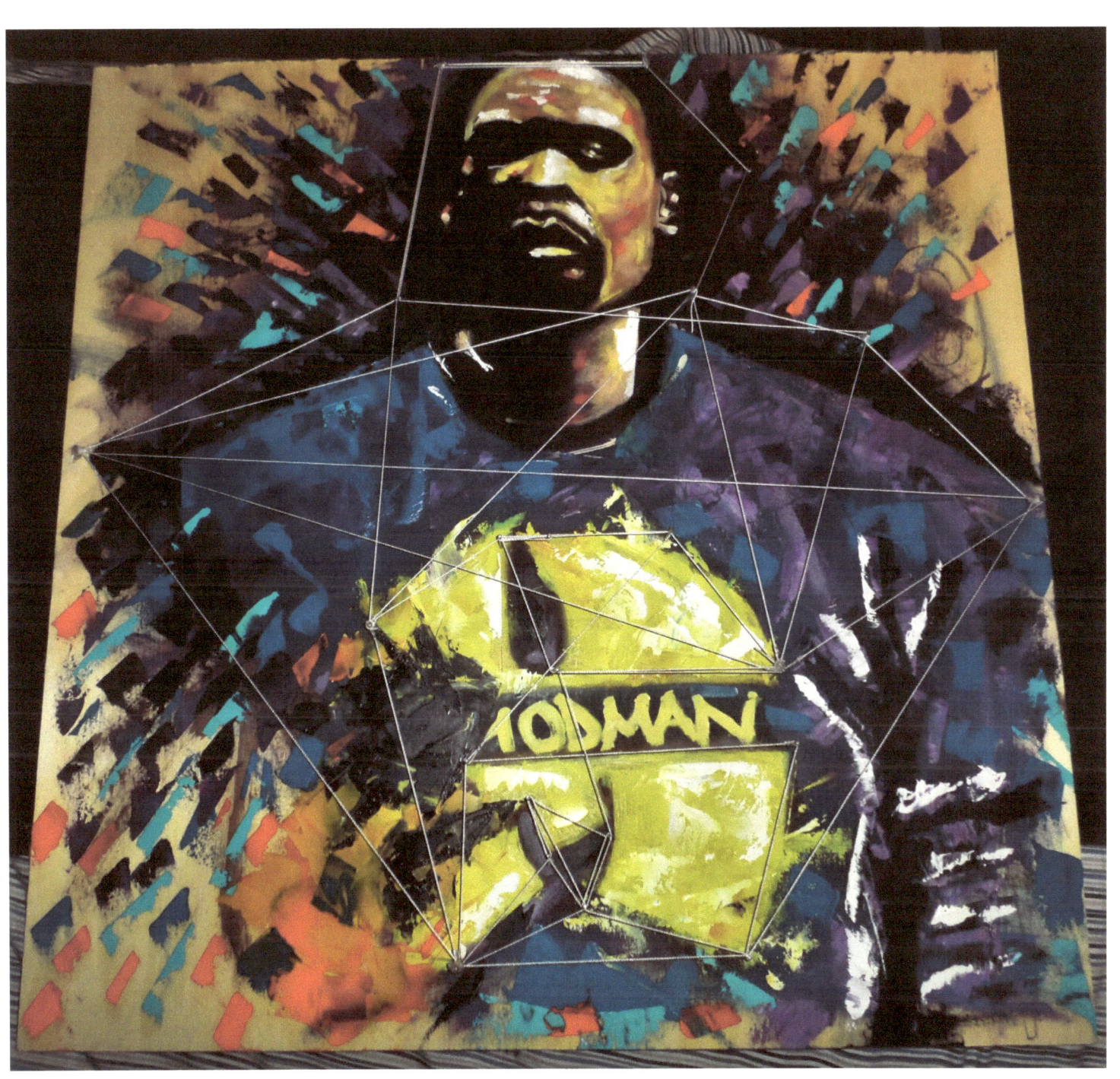

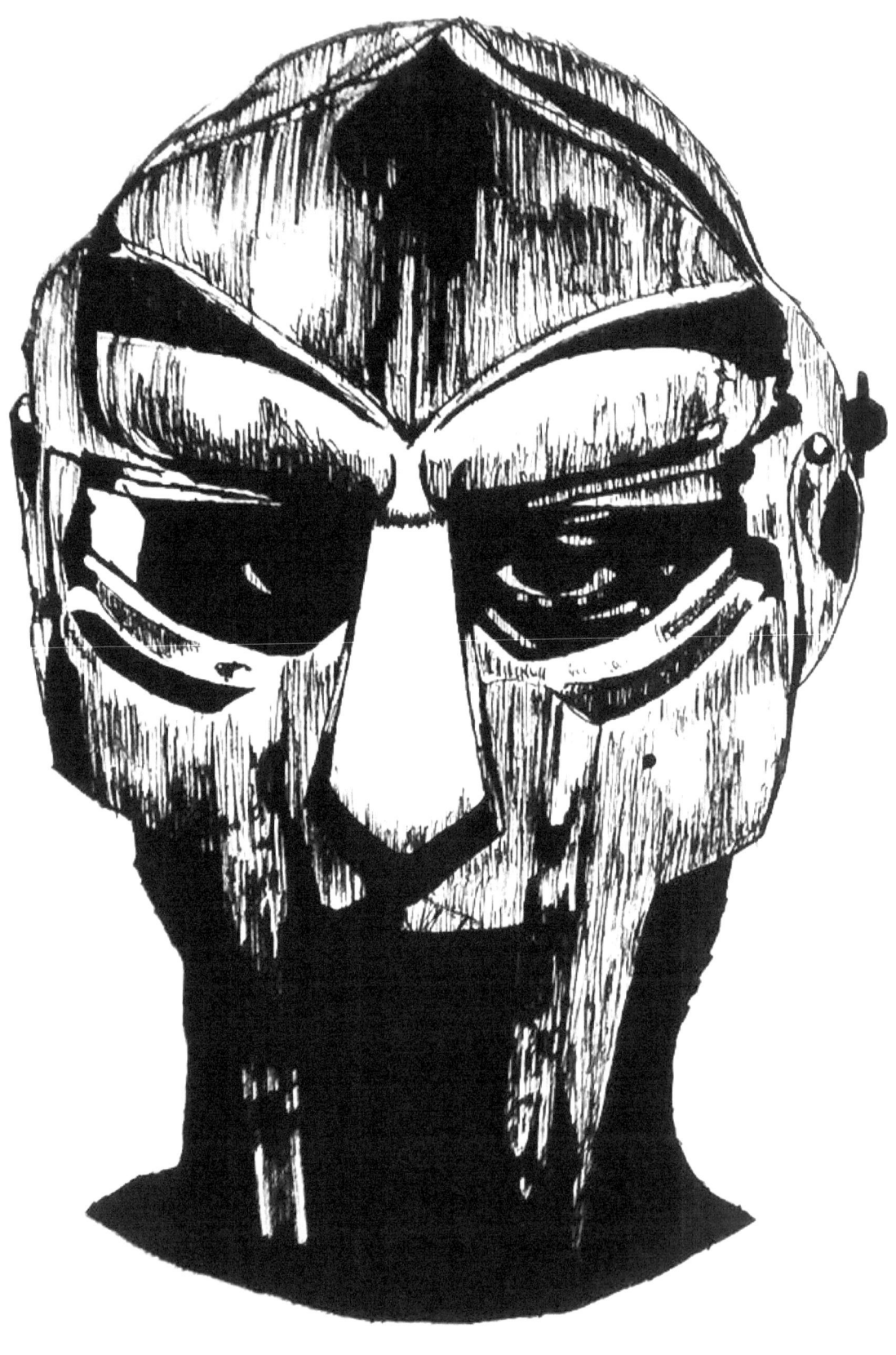

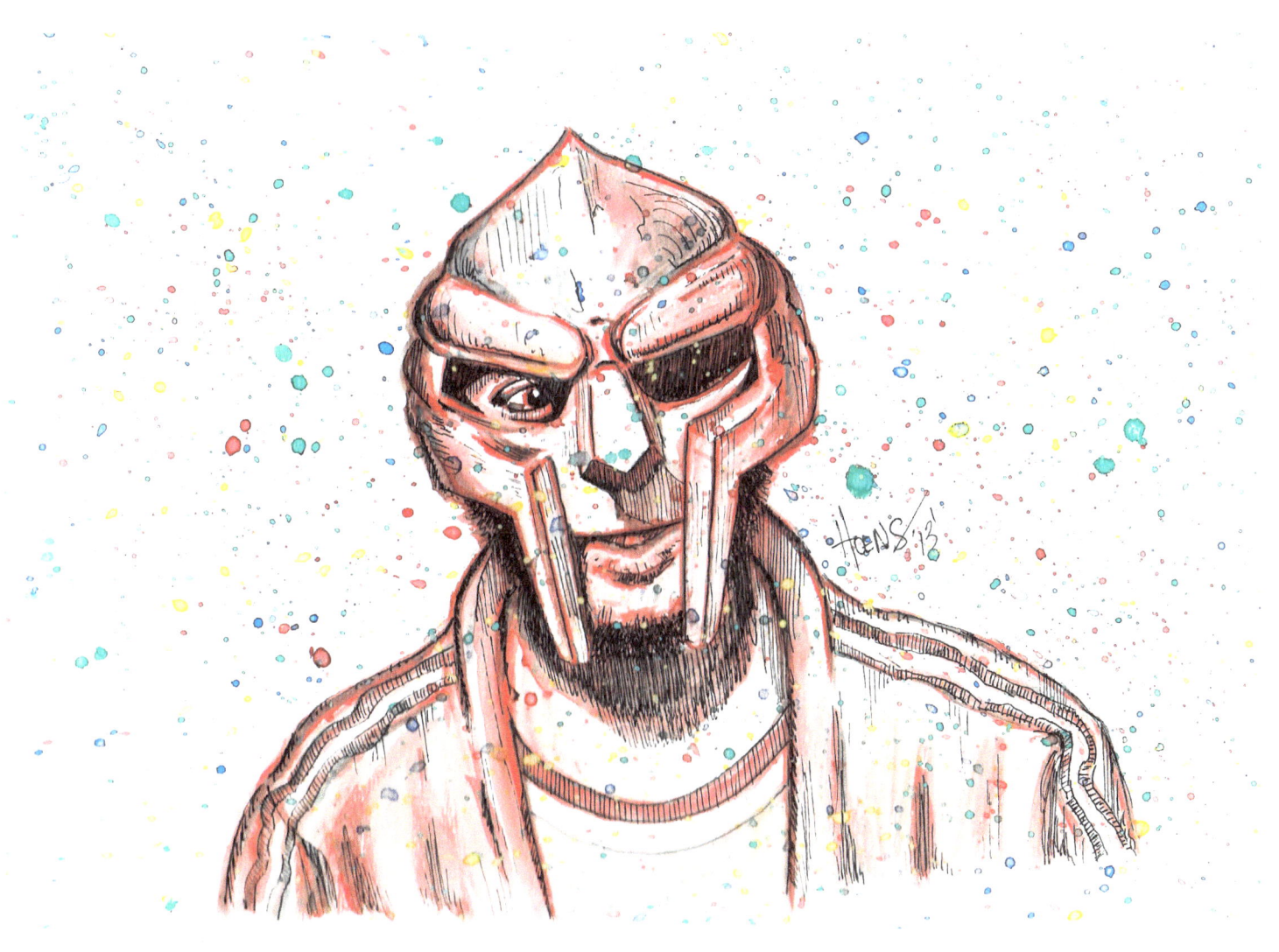

MISSY ELLIOT

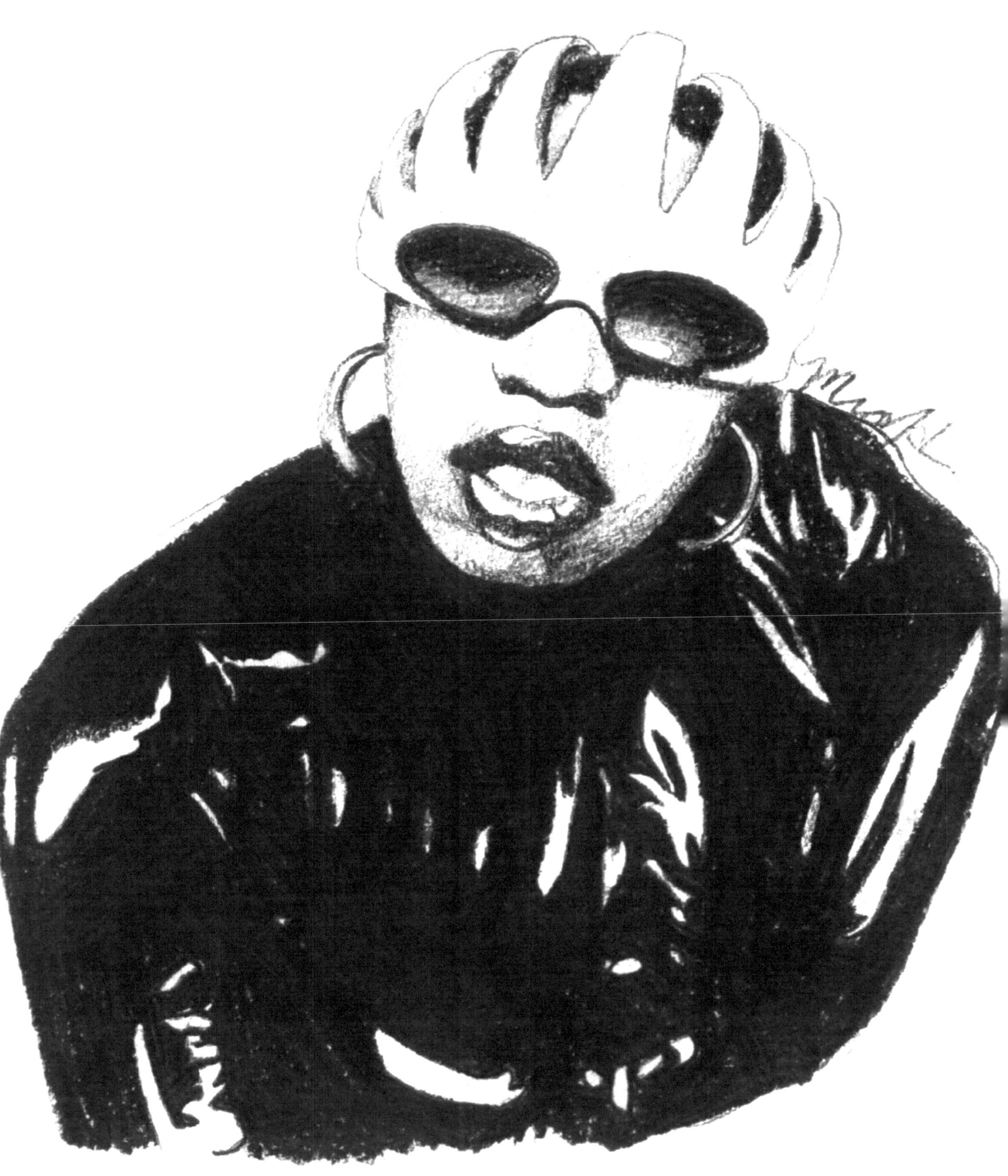

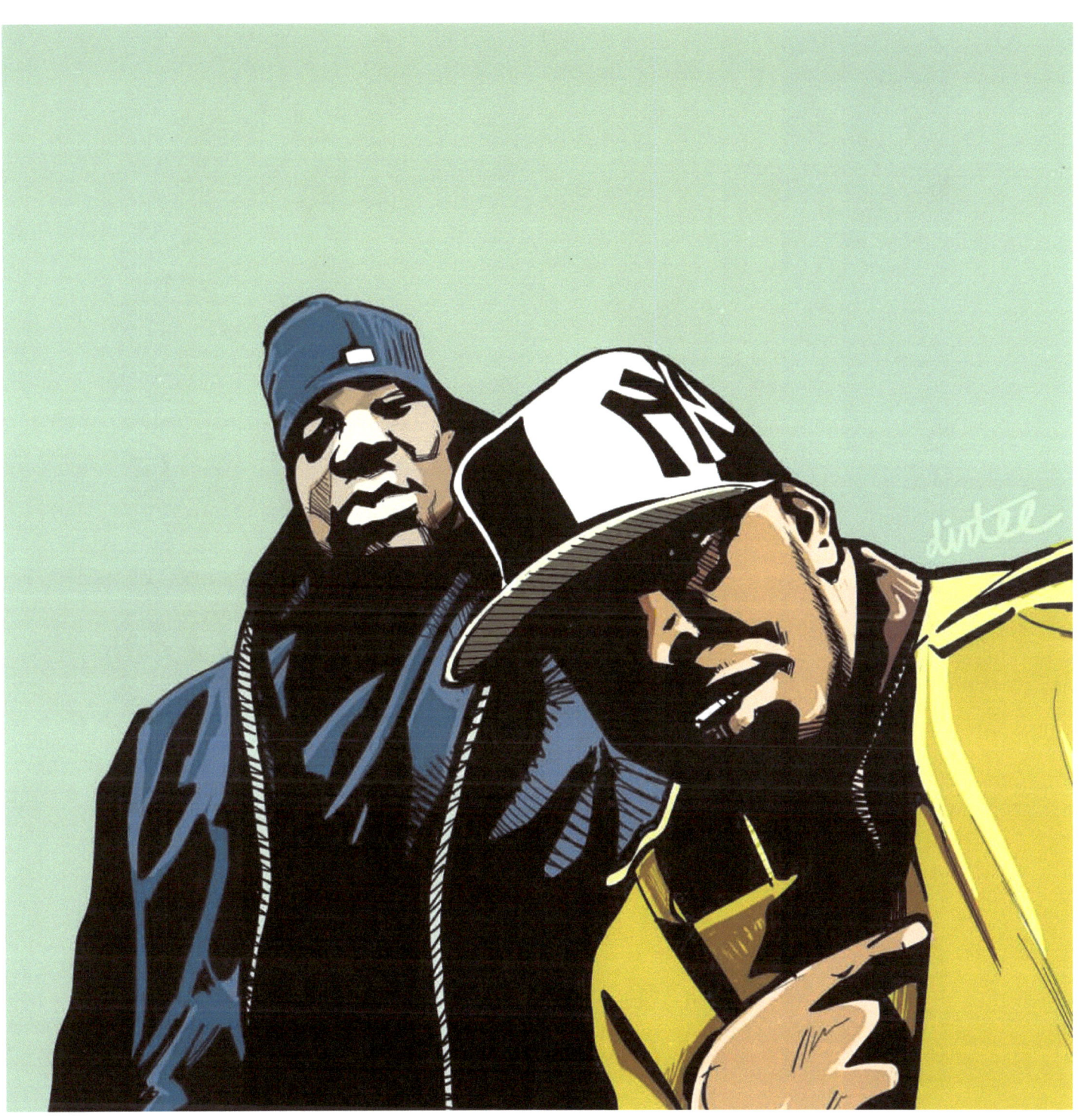

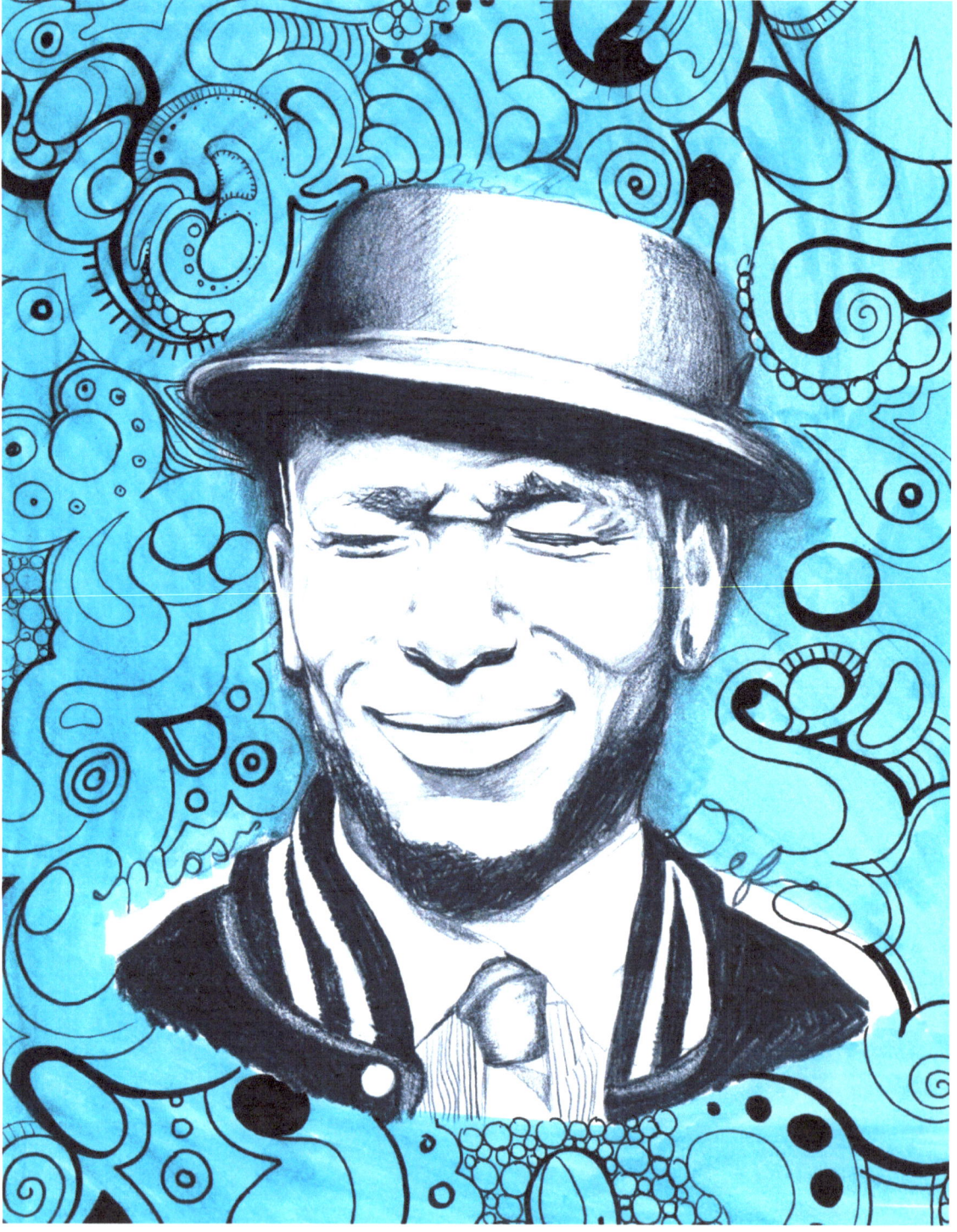

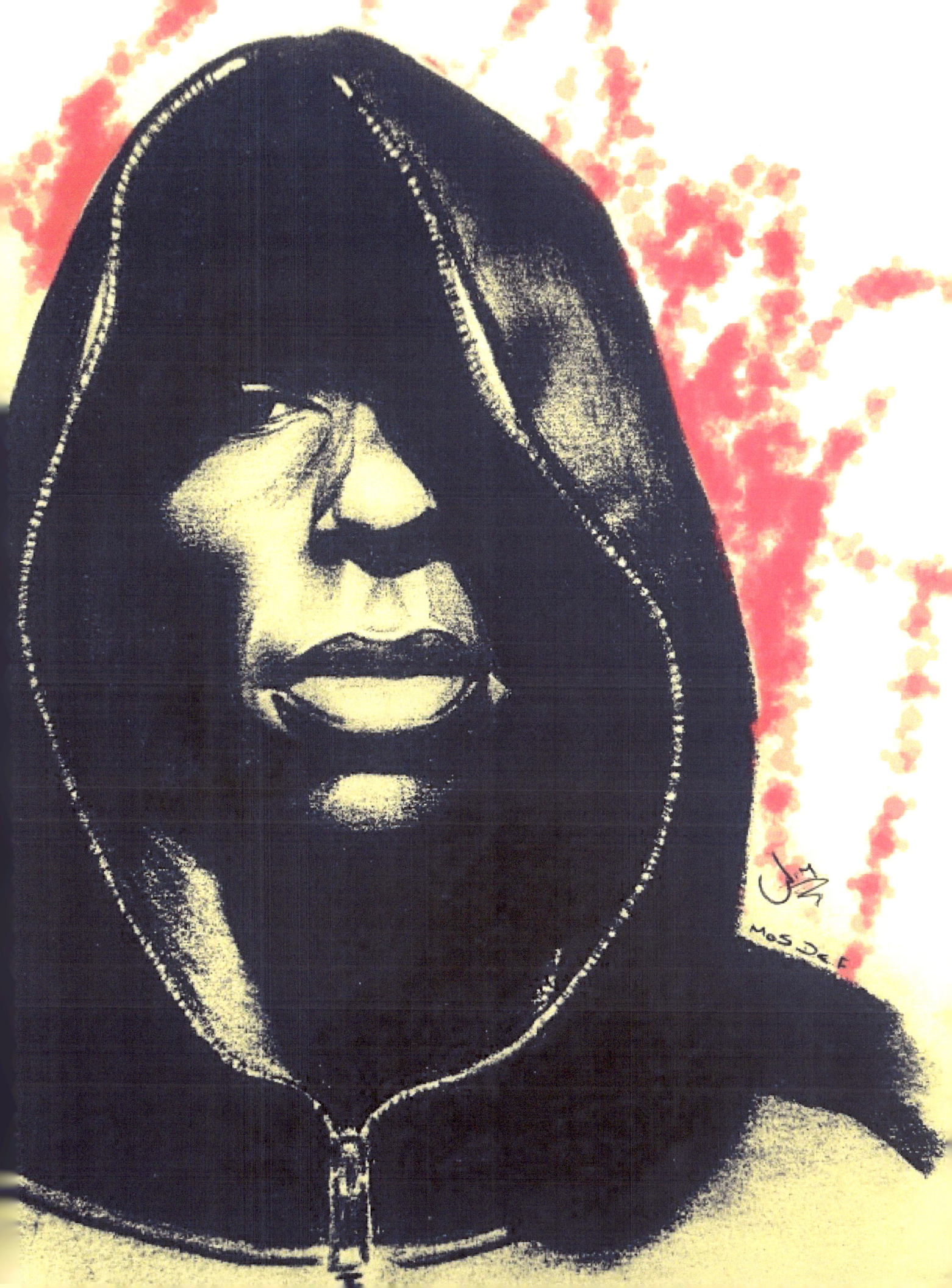

N-Z

NAS	SLUG
OL DIRTY BASTARD	SMOKE DZA
PETE ROCK	SNOOP DOGG
PHIFE DAWG	SZA
PUBLIC ENEMY	TALIB KWELI
PUSHA T	THE GAME
Q TIP	THE WKND
QUASI DOOM	TI
RAKIM	TRAVIS SCOTT
REDMAN	TUPAC
REVERAND RUN	TYGA
RICK ROSS	TYLER THE CREATOR
RUSSELL SIMMONS	WIZ KHALIFA
RZA	WU TANG CLAN
SADE	YOUNG THUG
SCHOOL BOY Q	
SEAN PRICE	
SIR MICHAEL ROCKS	
SLICK RICK	

NAS

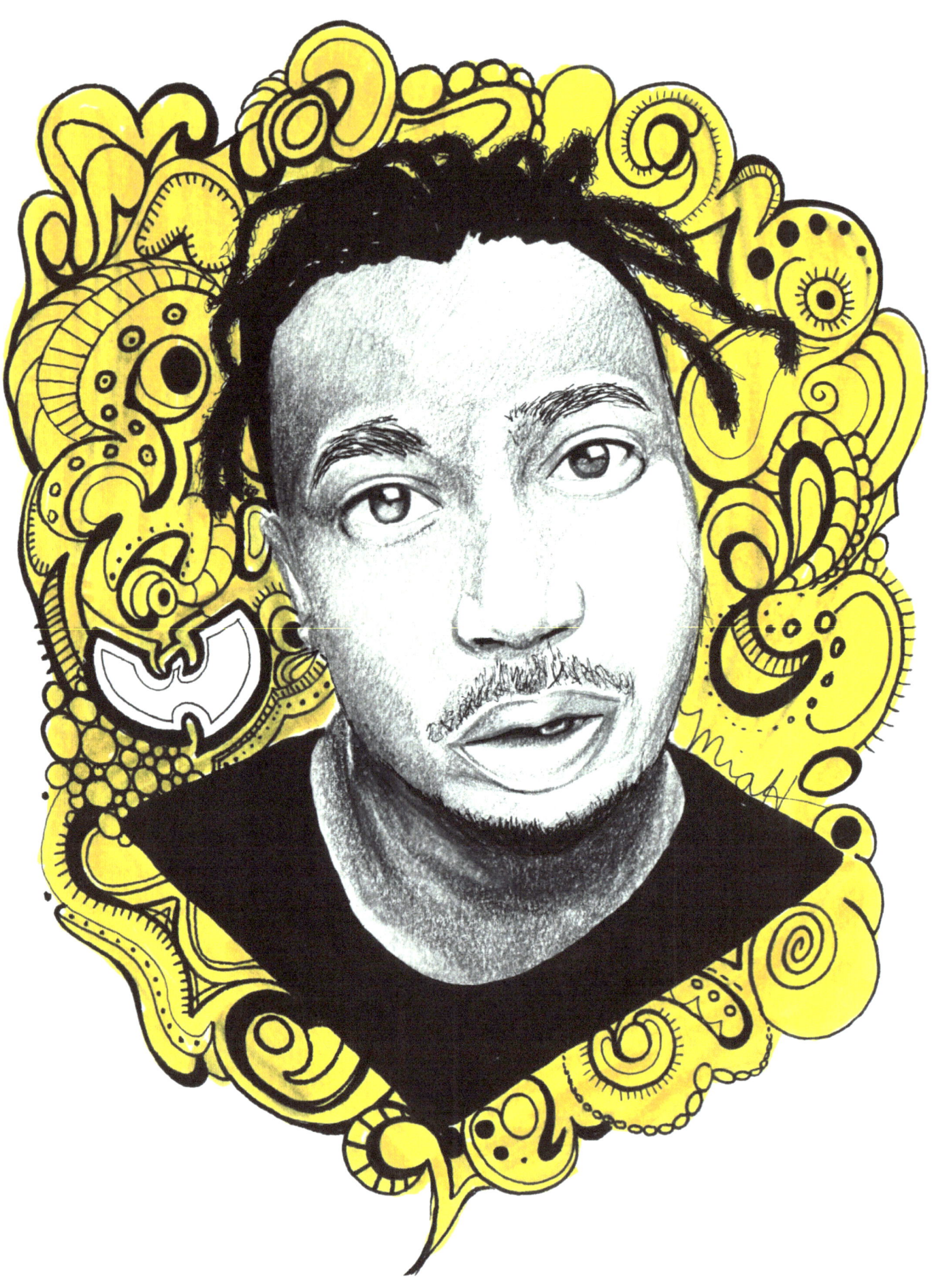

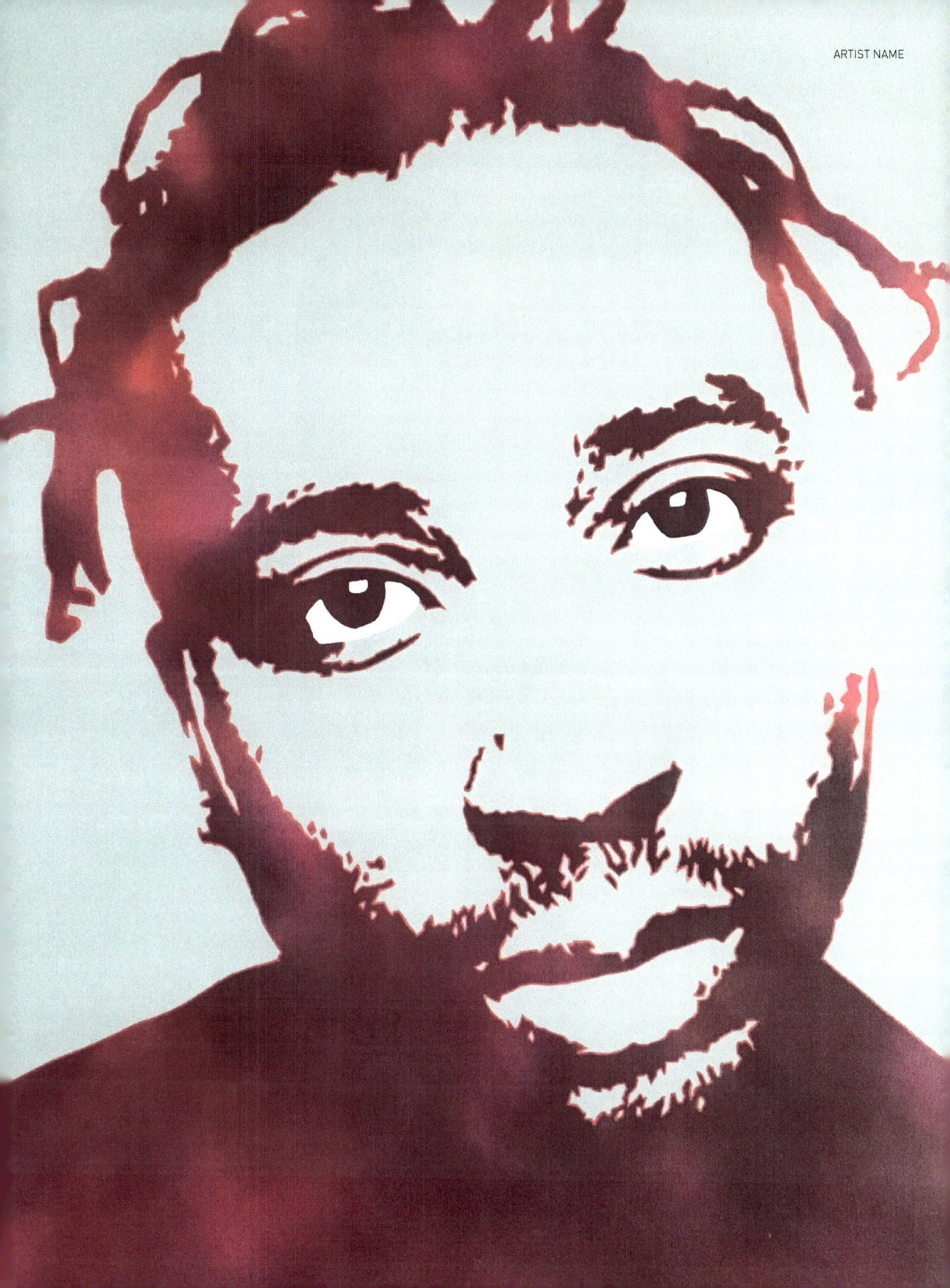
ARTIST NAME

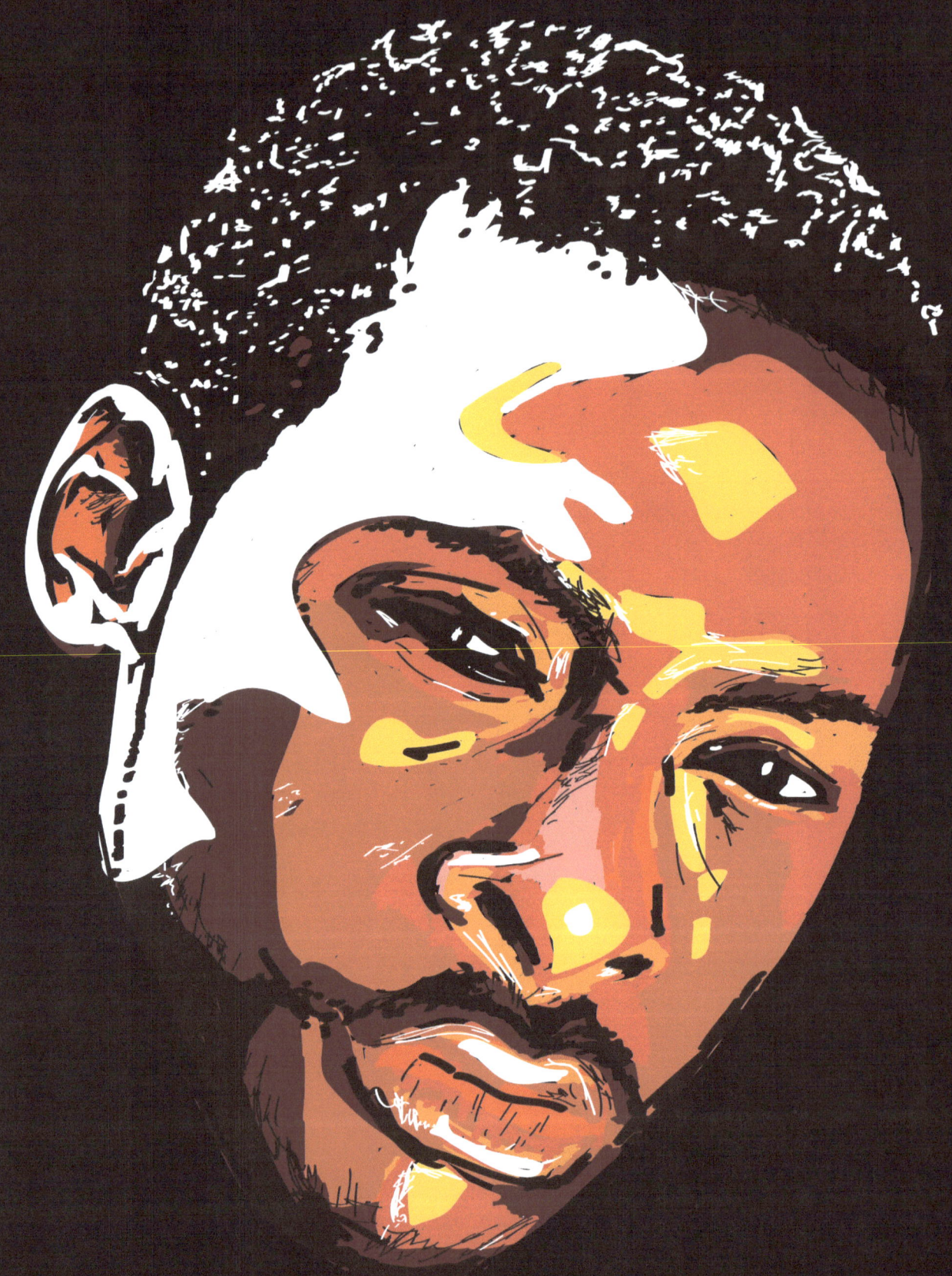

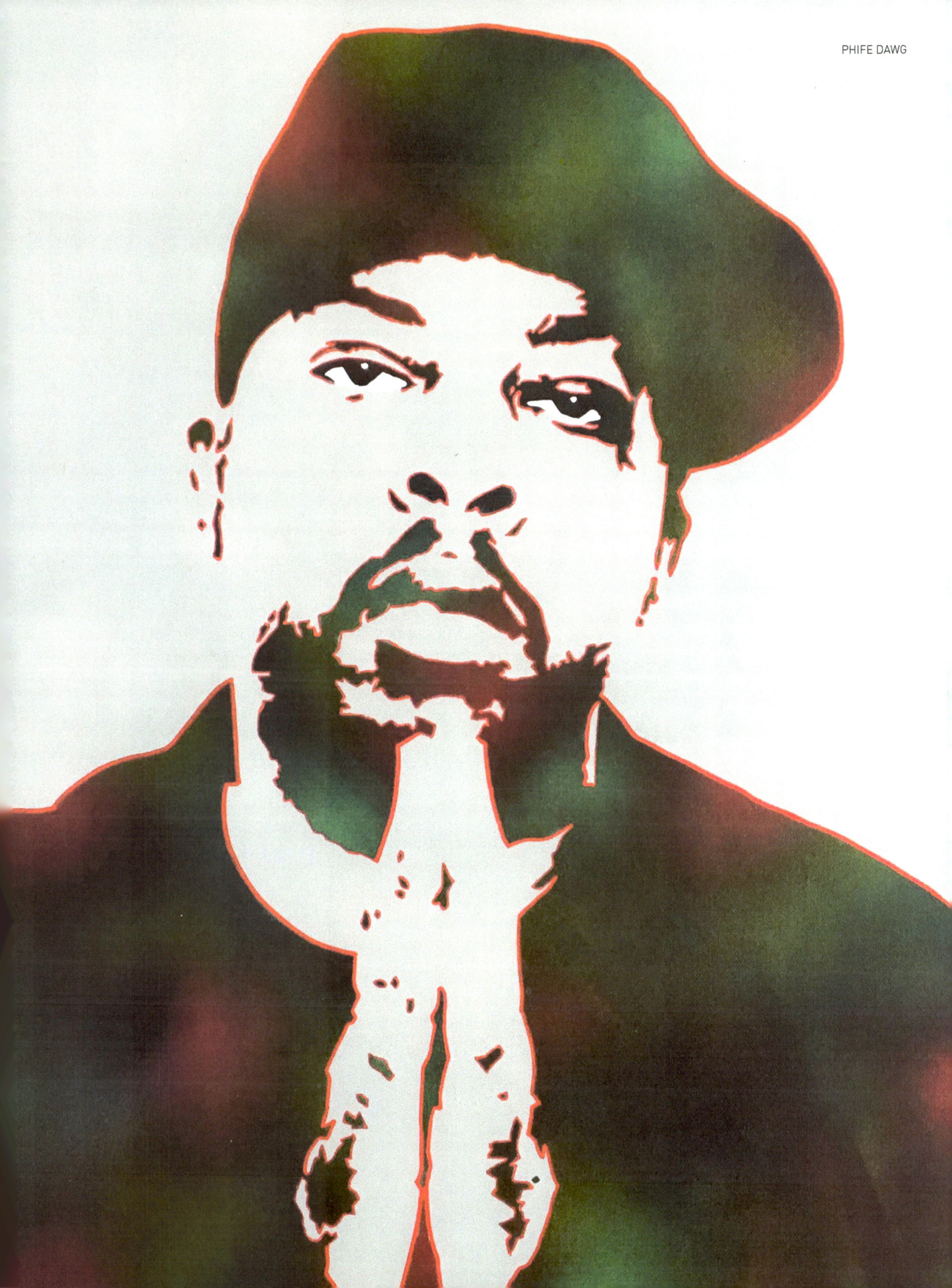
PHIFE DAWG

PUBLIC ENEMY CHUCK D

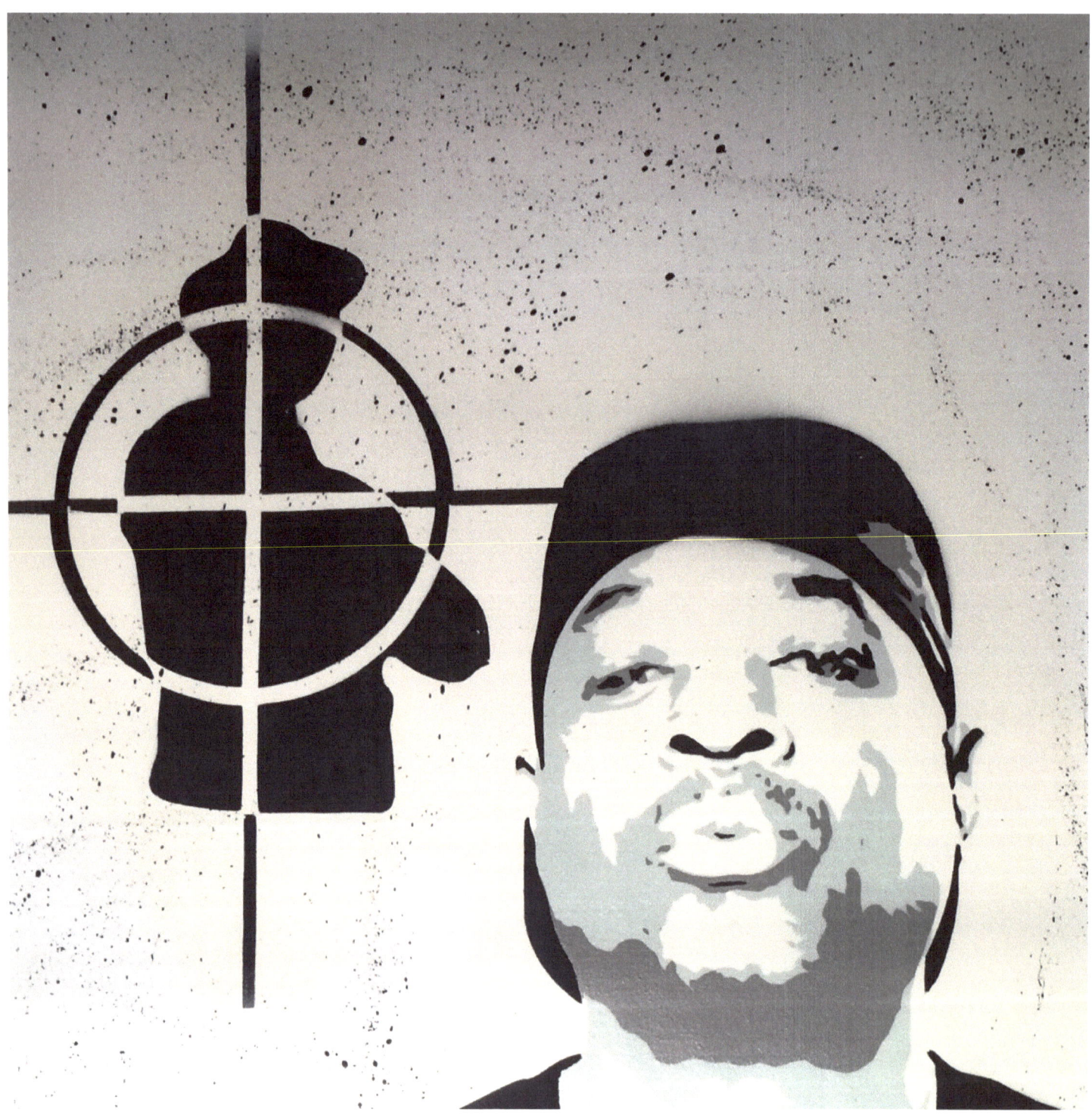

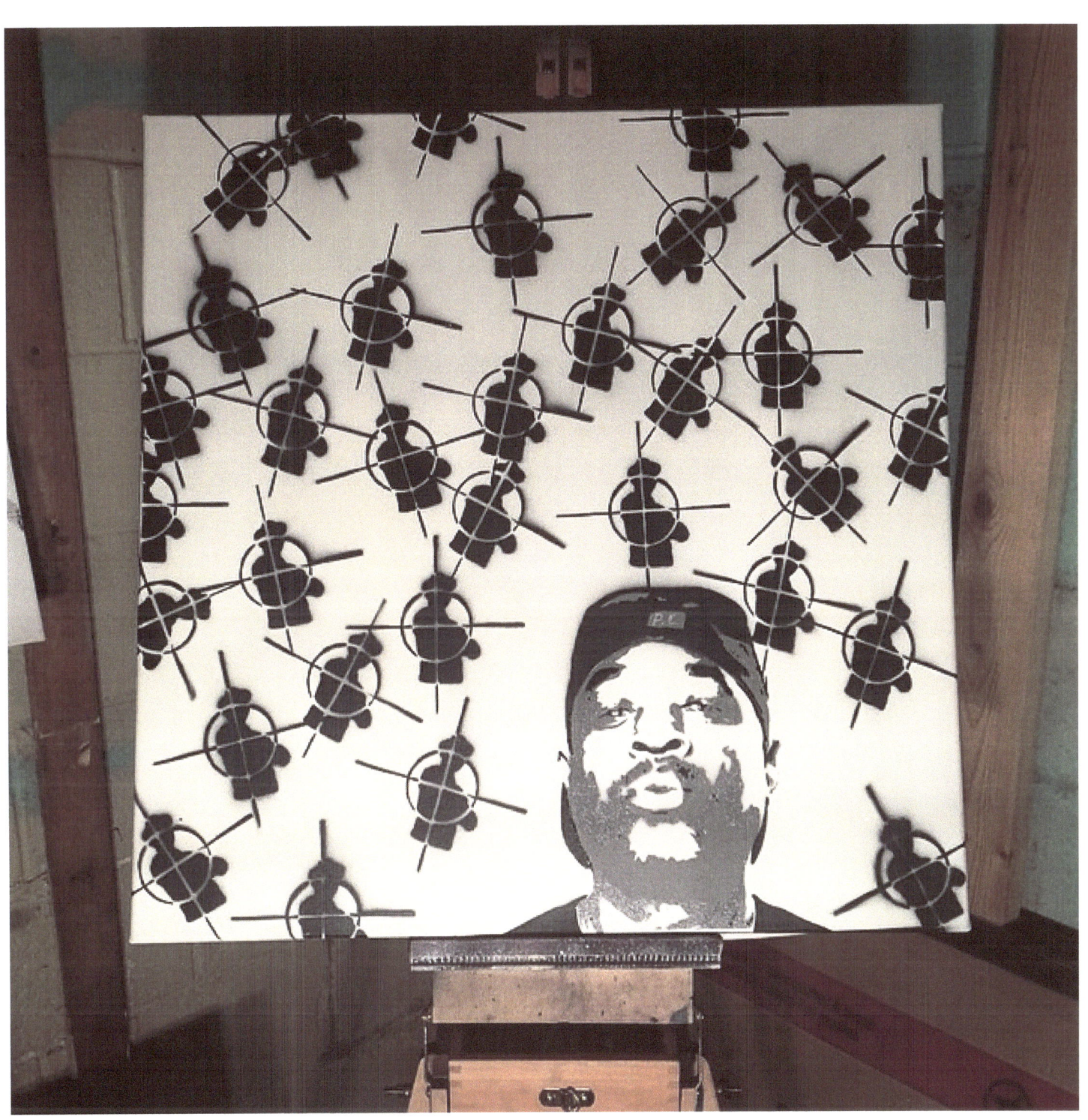

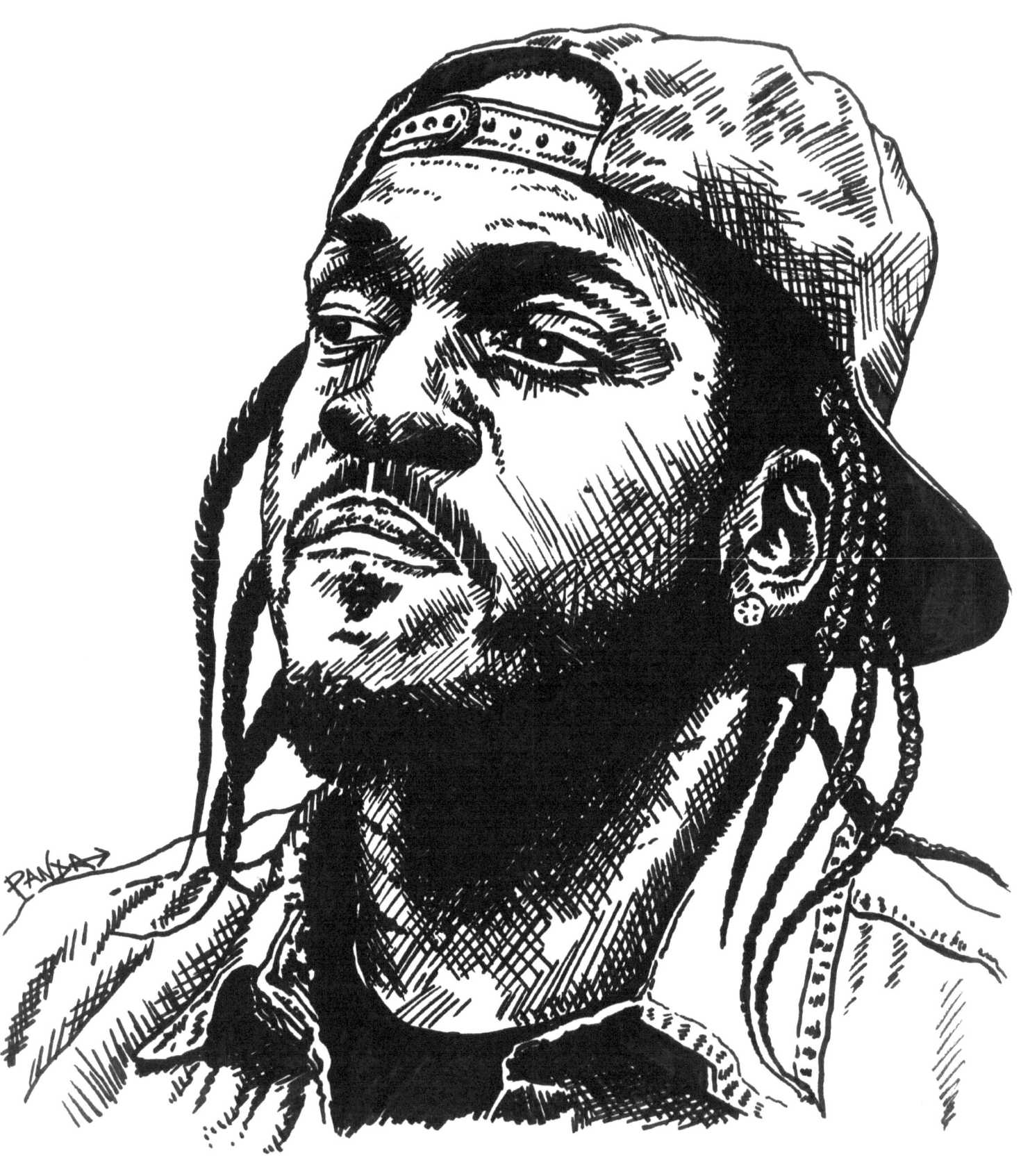

Q TIP

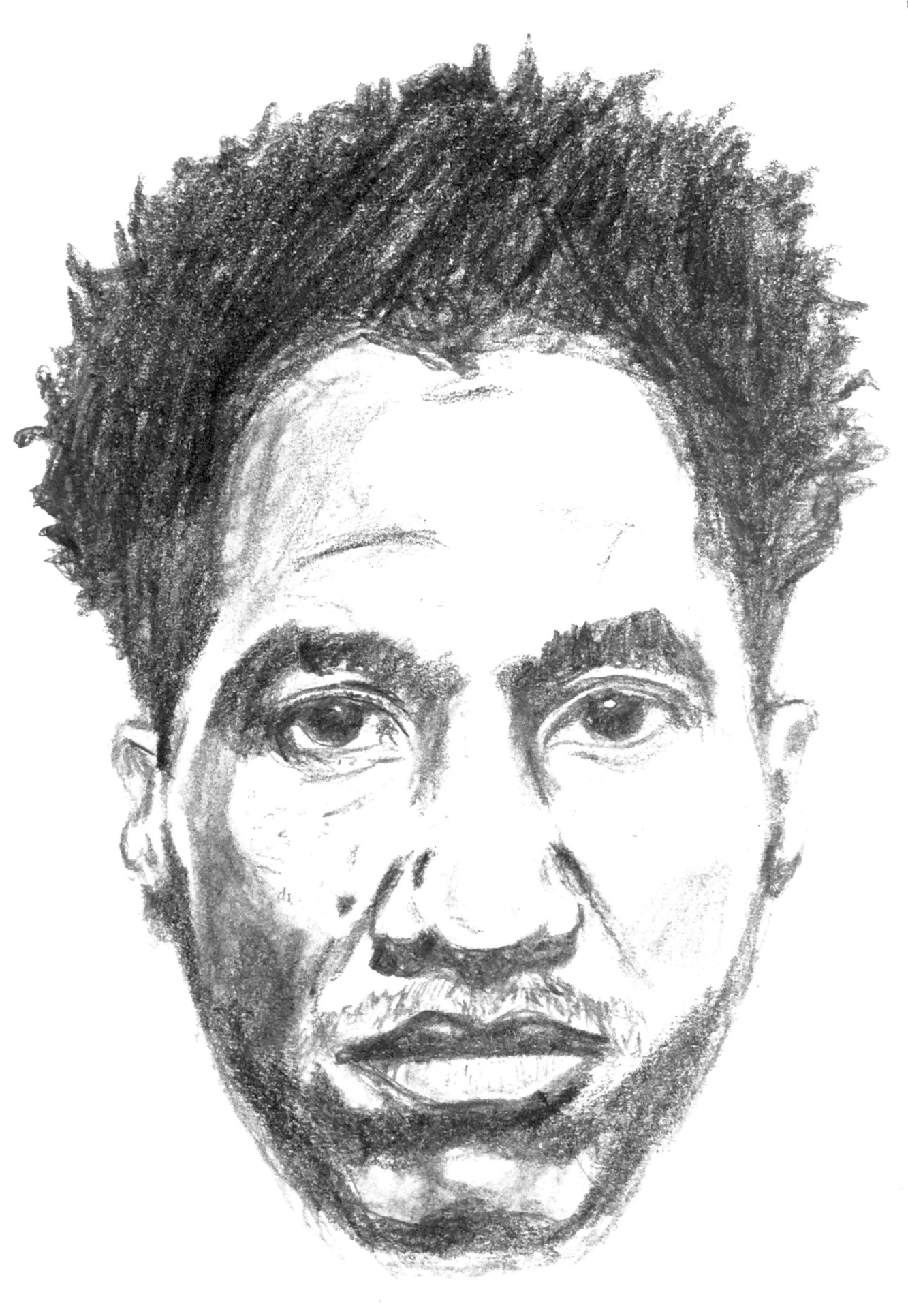

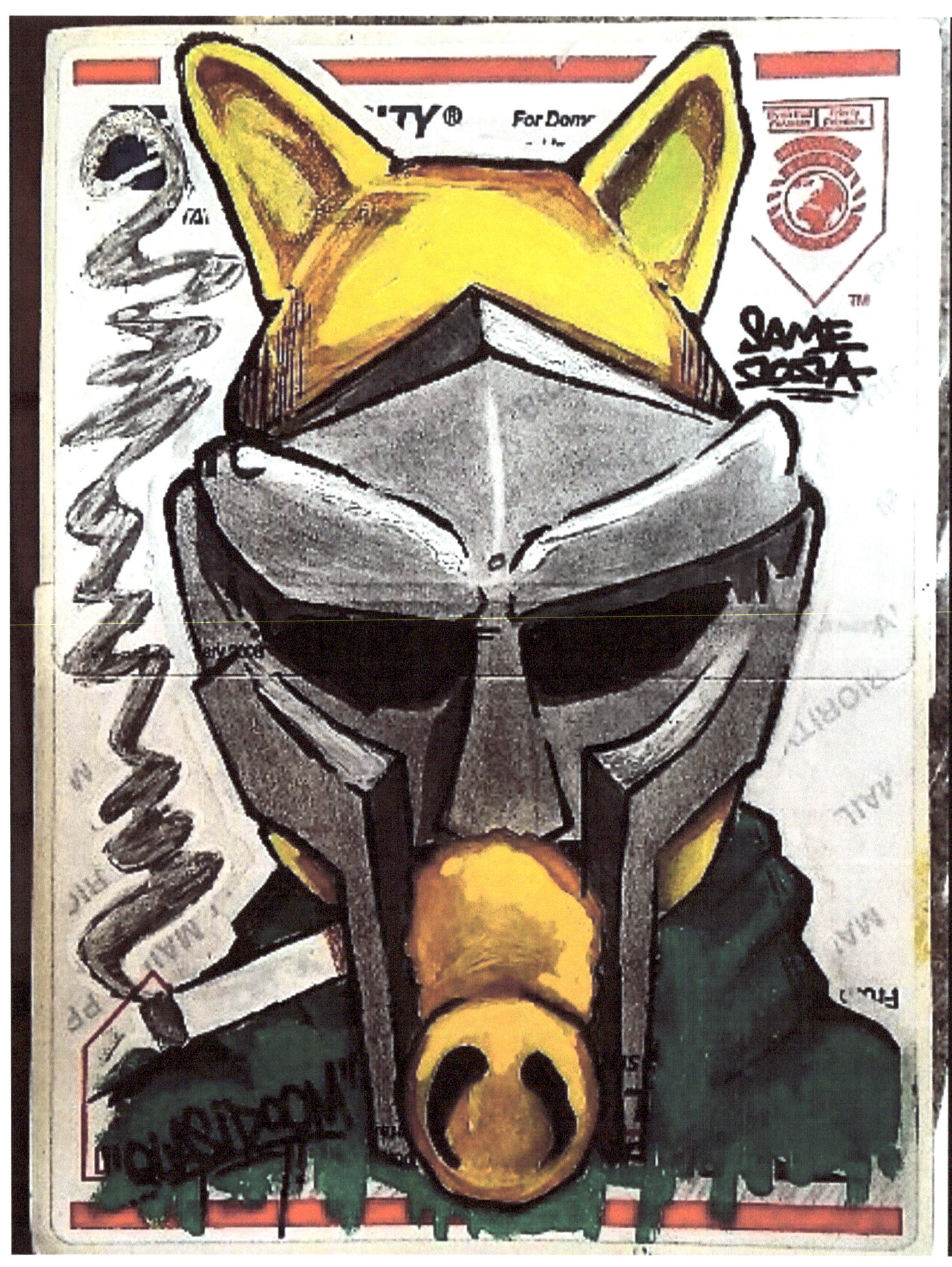

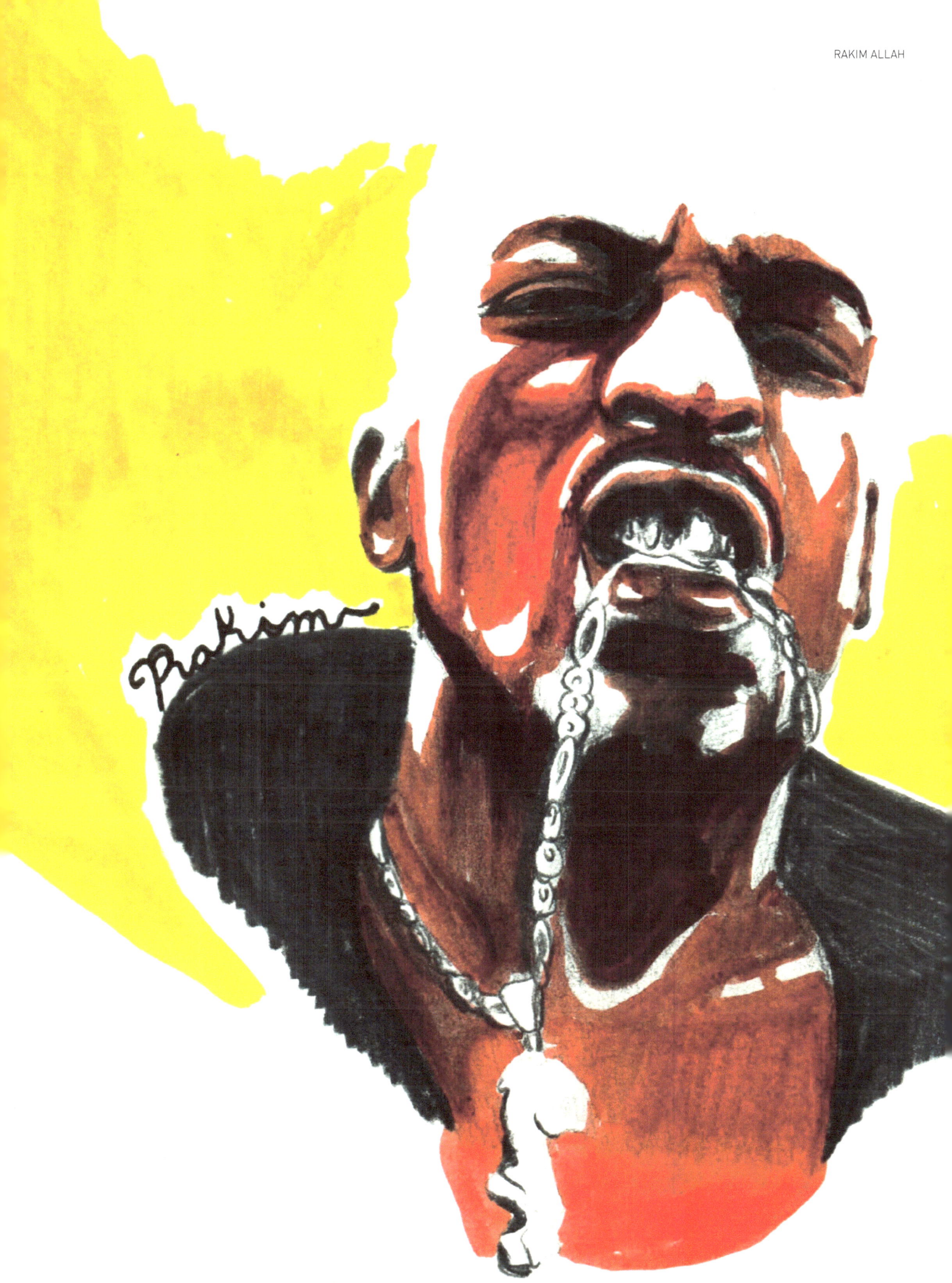

RAKIM ALLAH

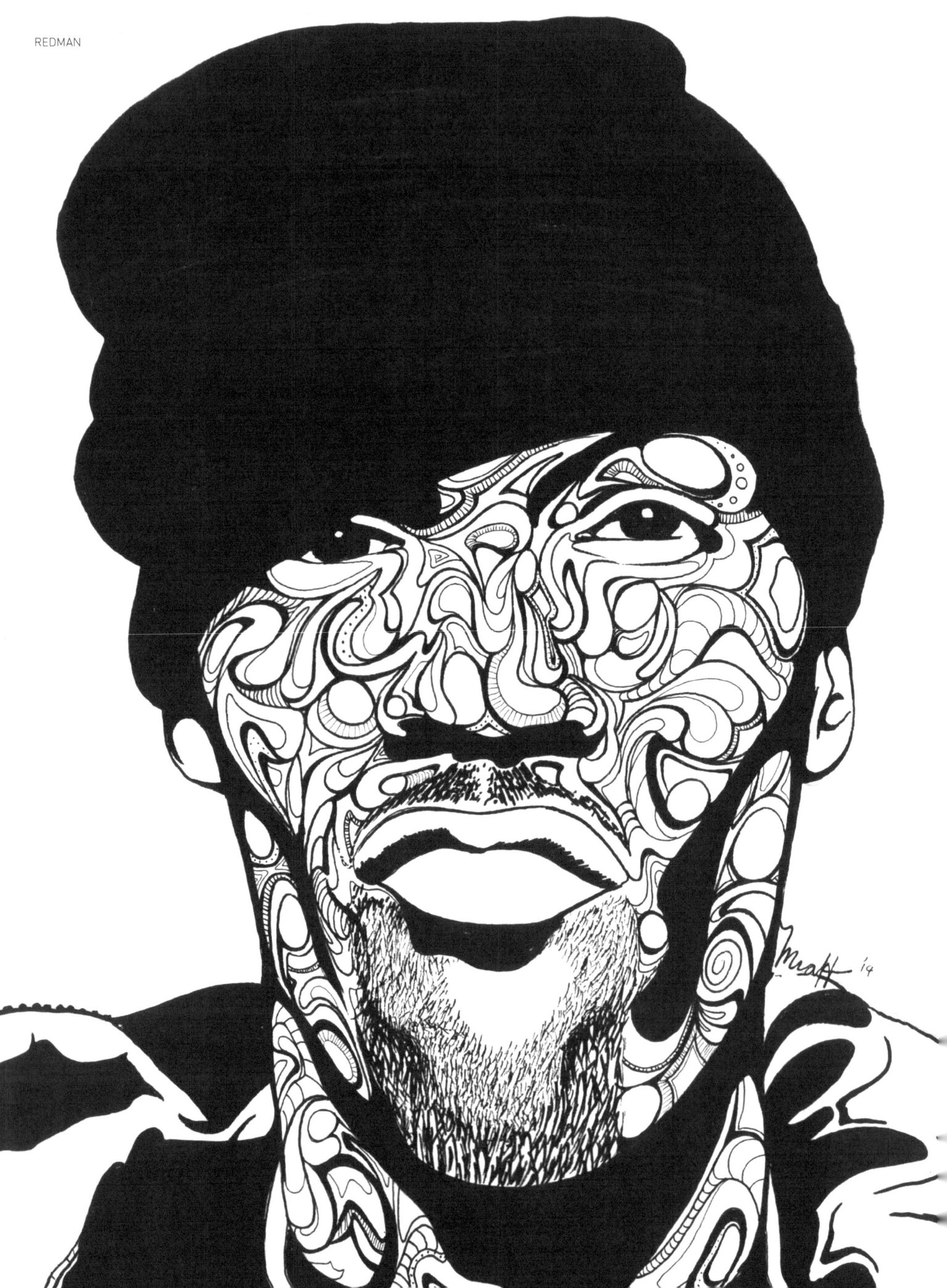

REVERAND RUN

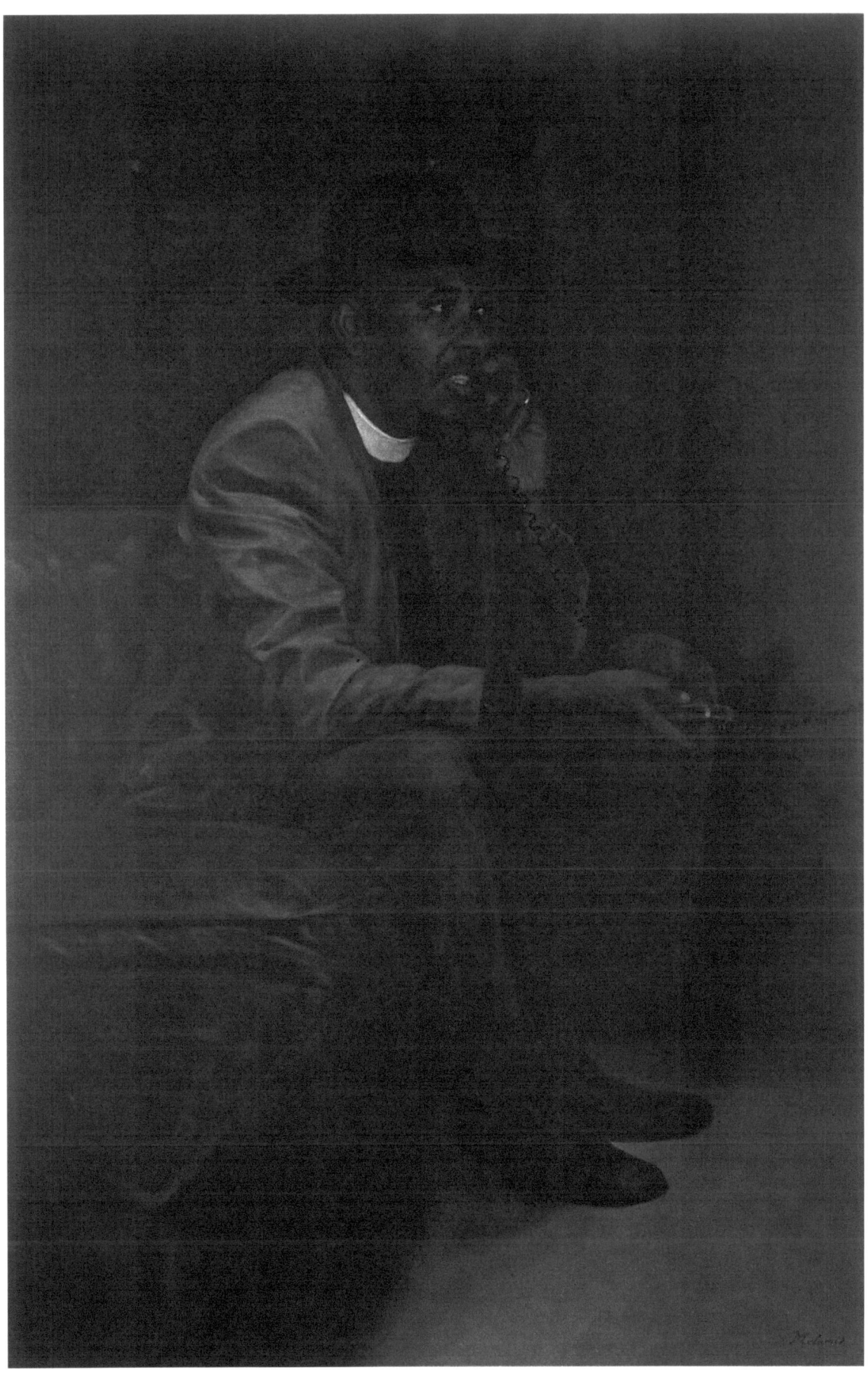

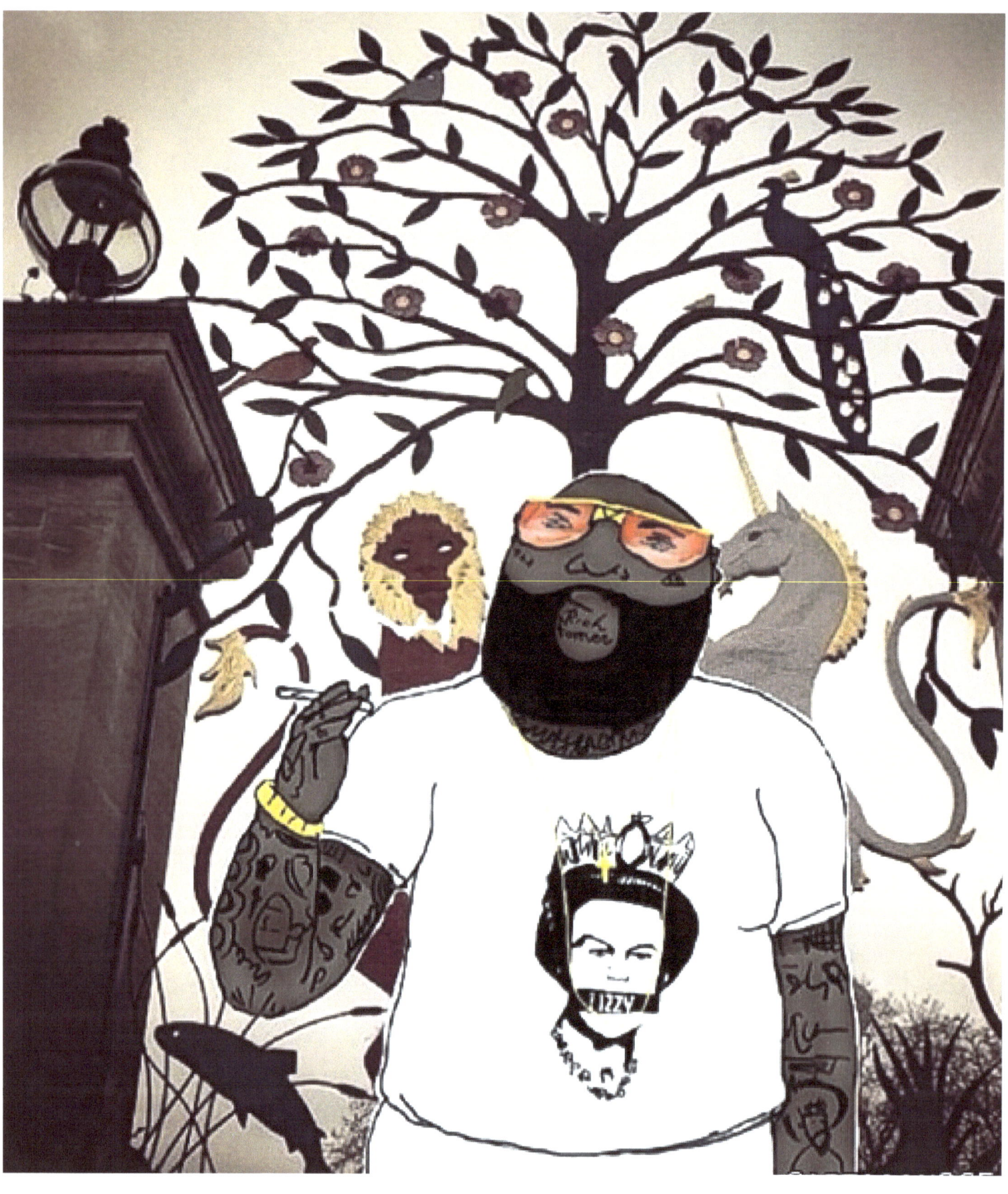

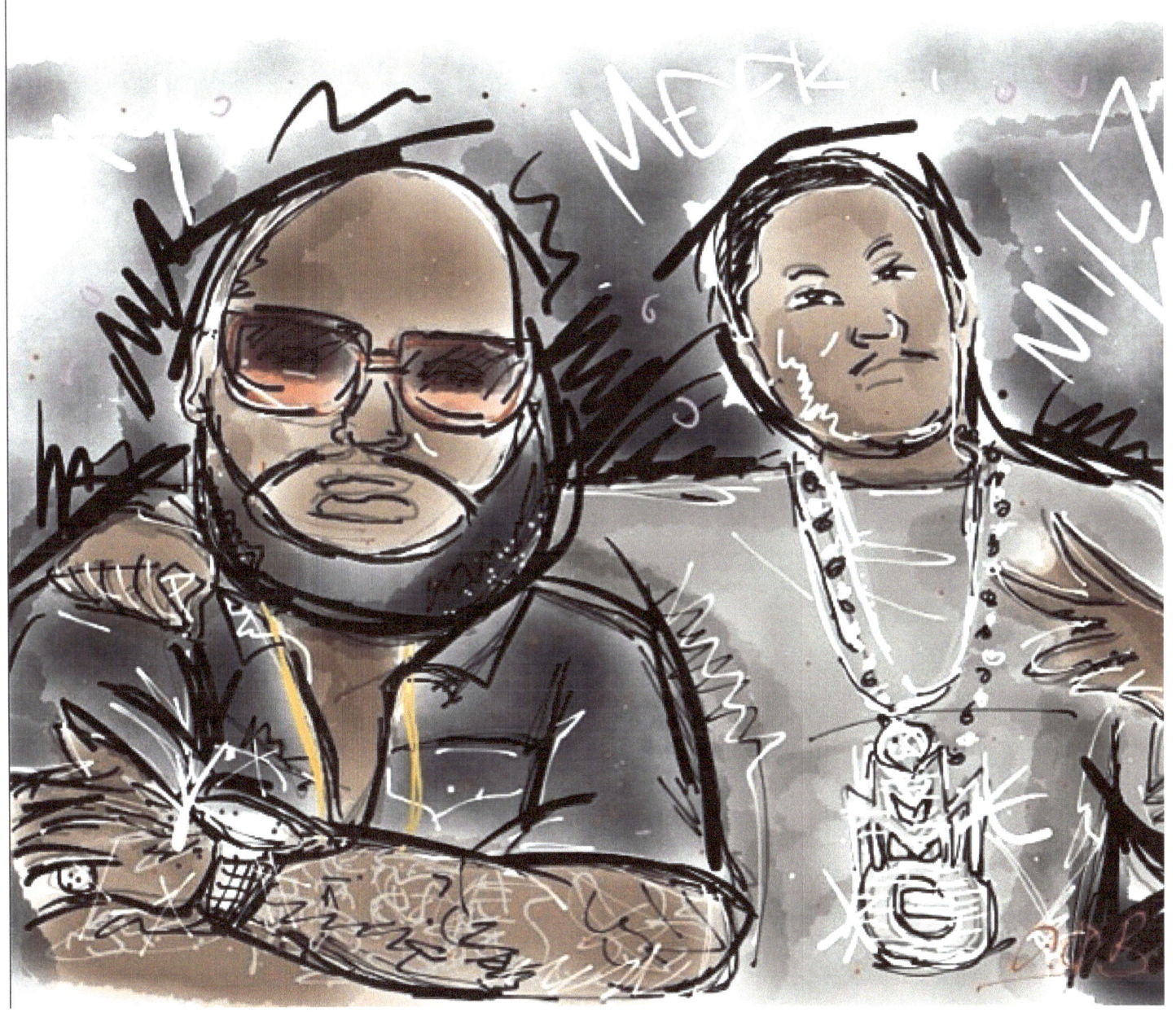

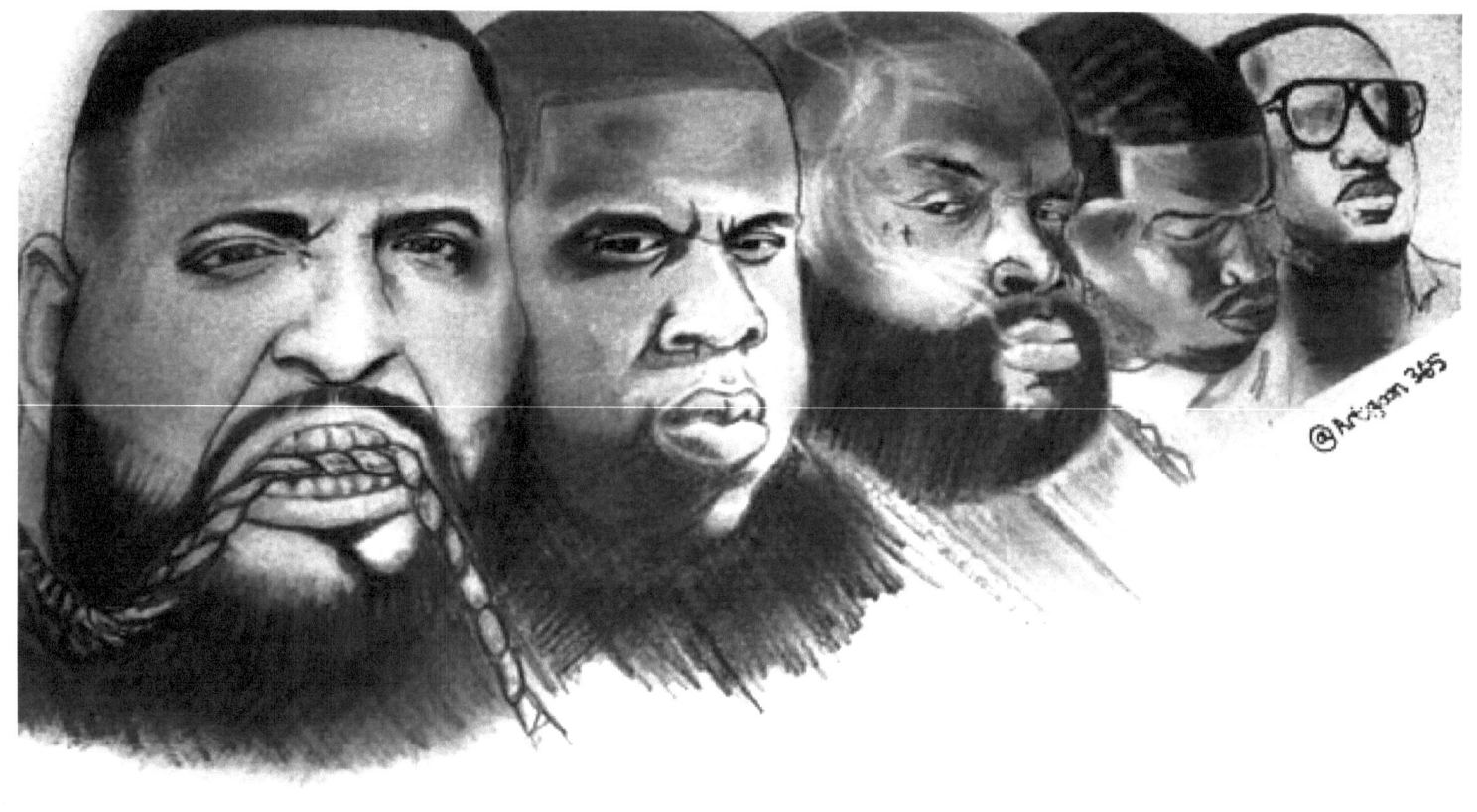

RICK ROSS & FRIENDS (DJ KHALID, JAY Z, MEEK MIL & FRENCH MONTANA)

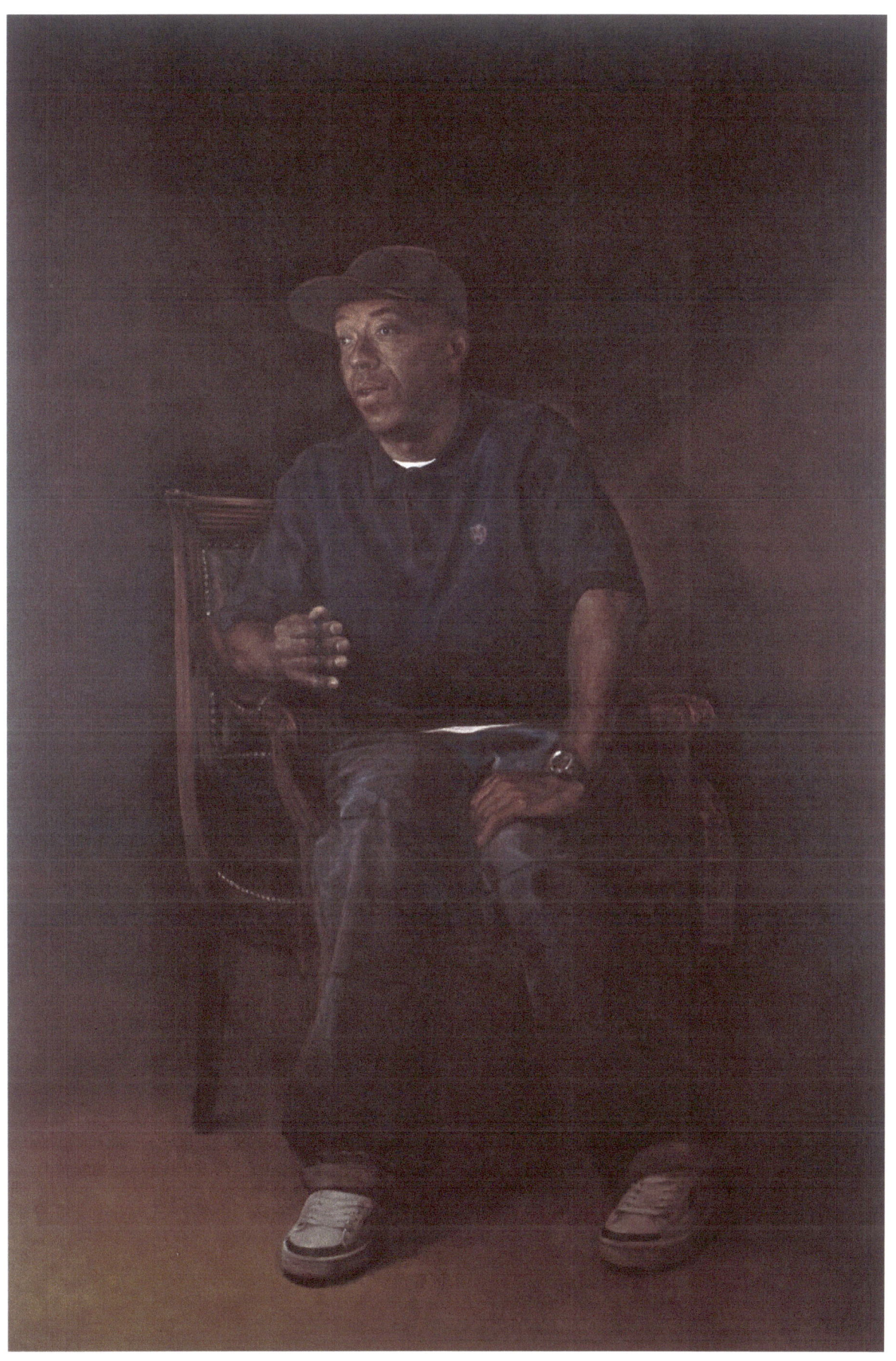

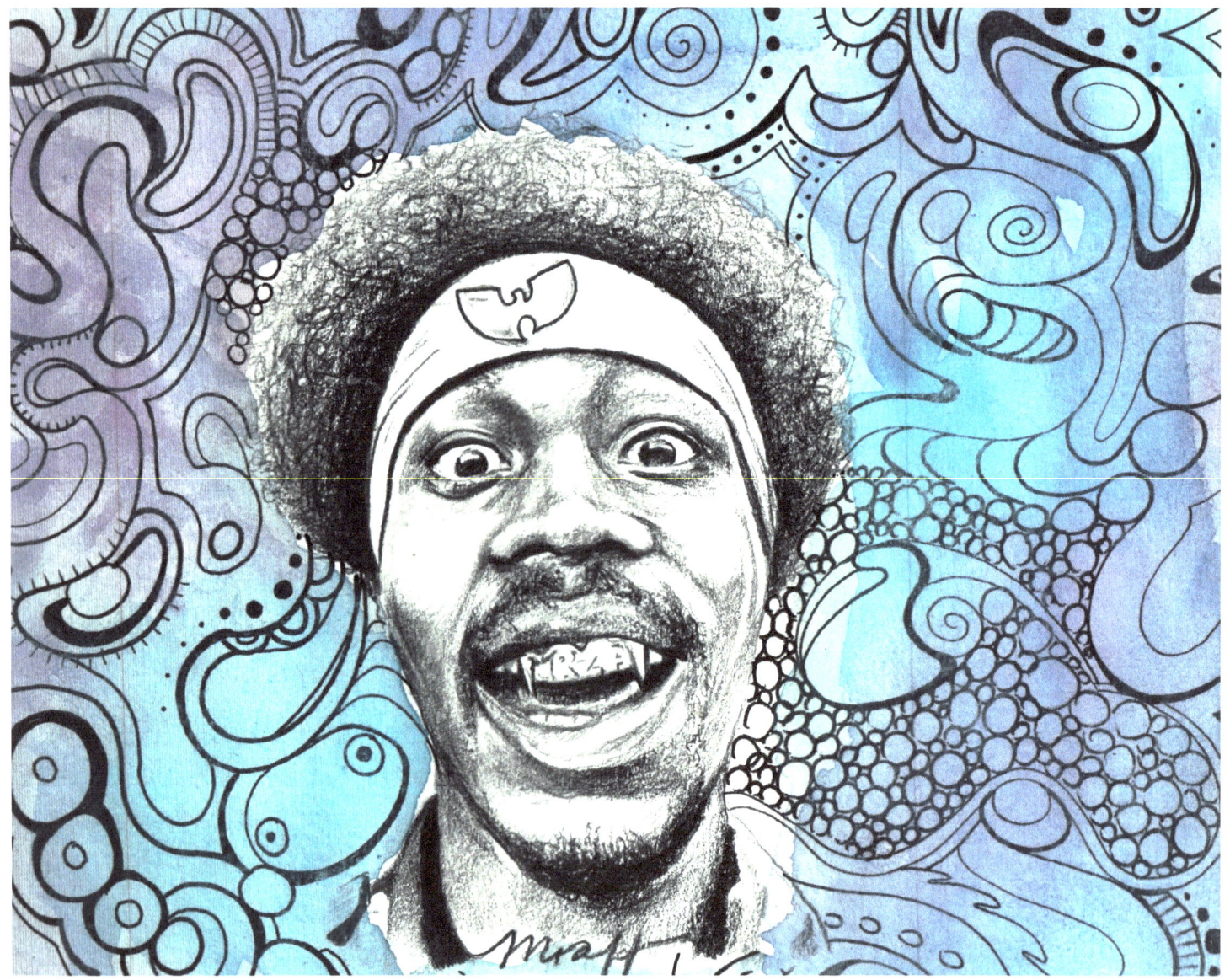

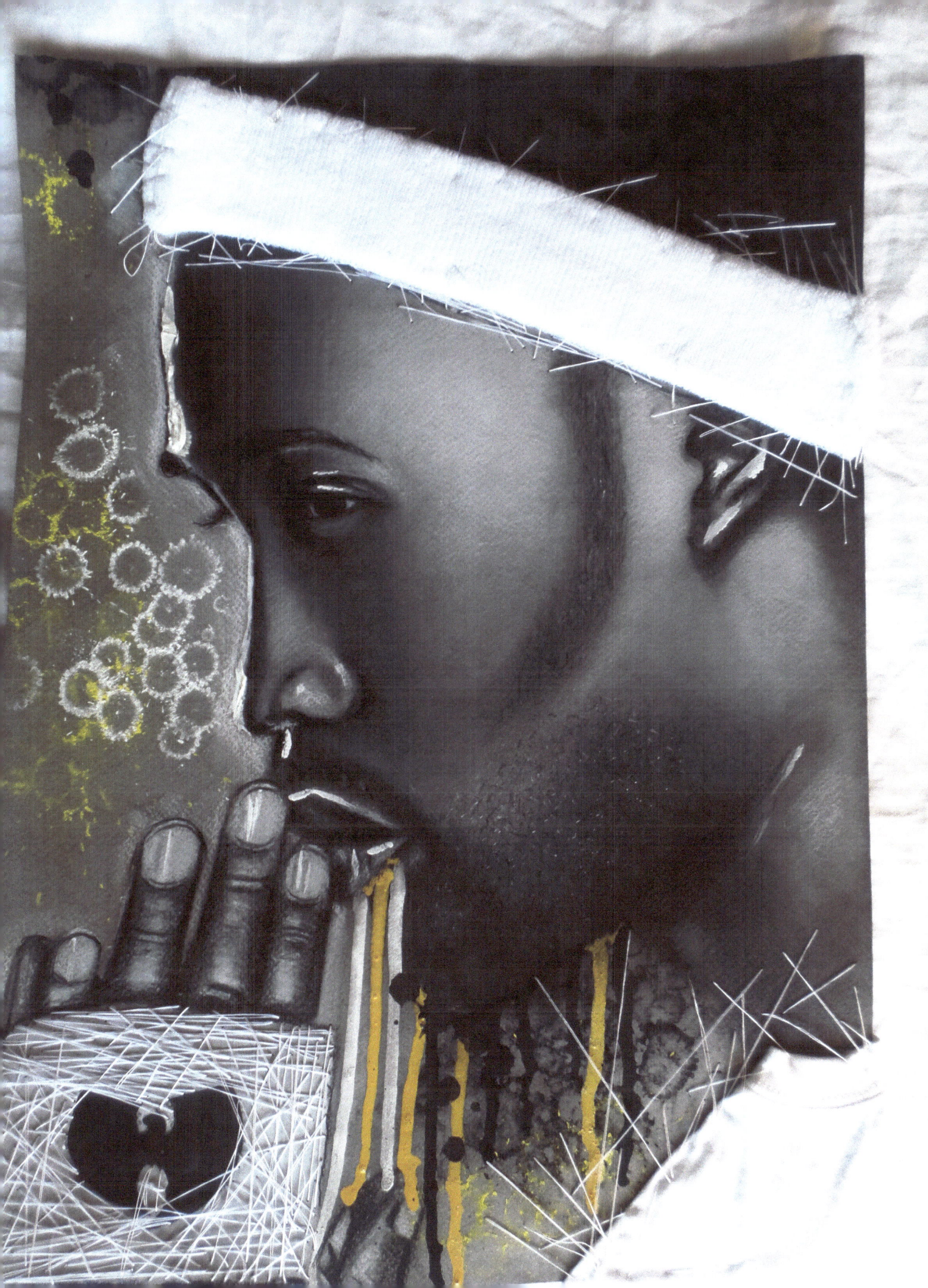

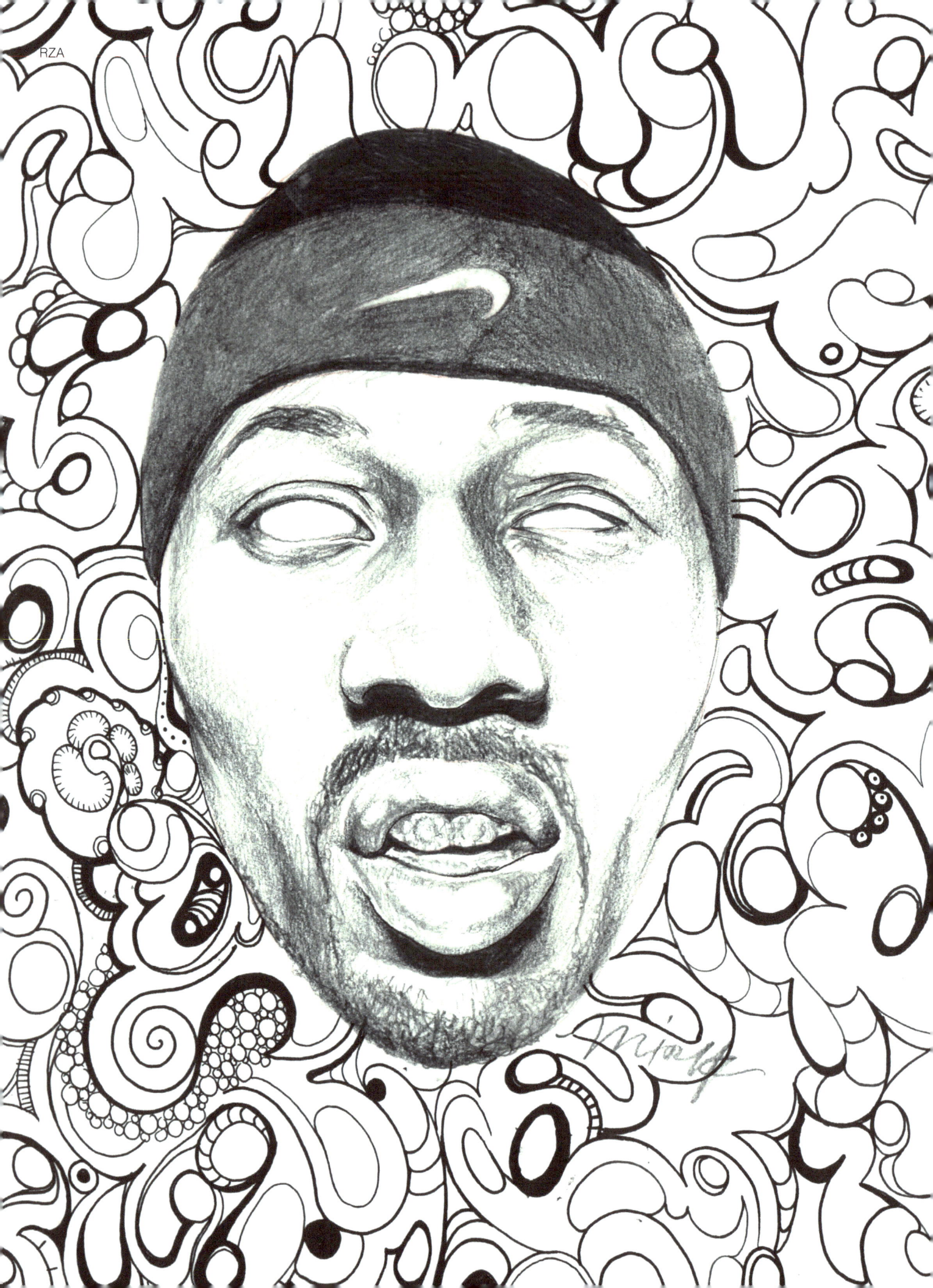

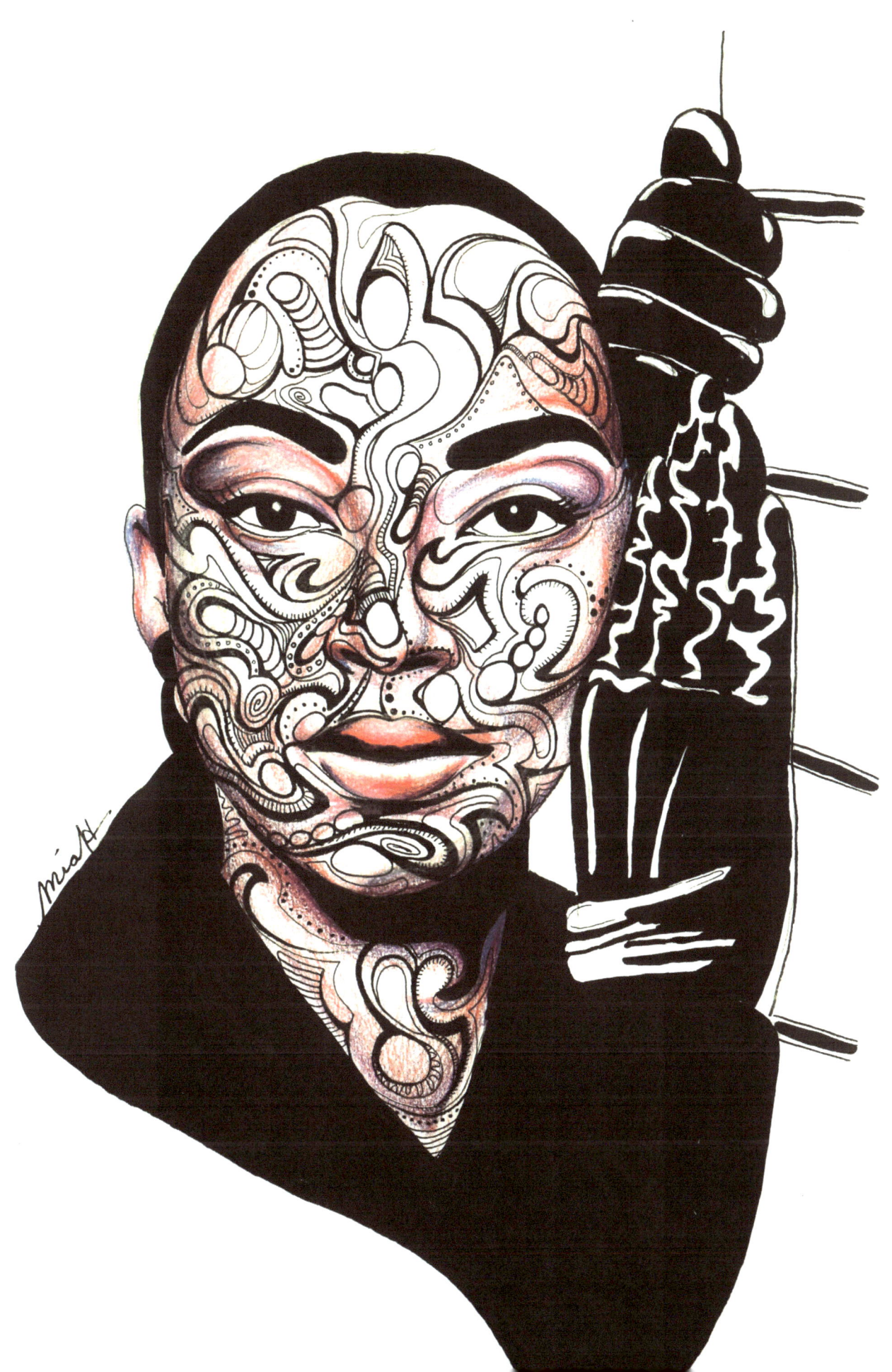

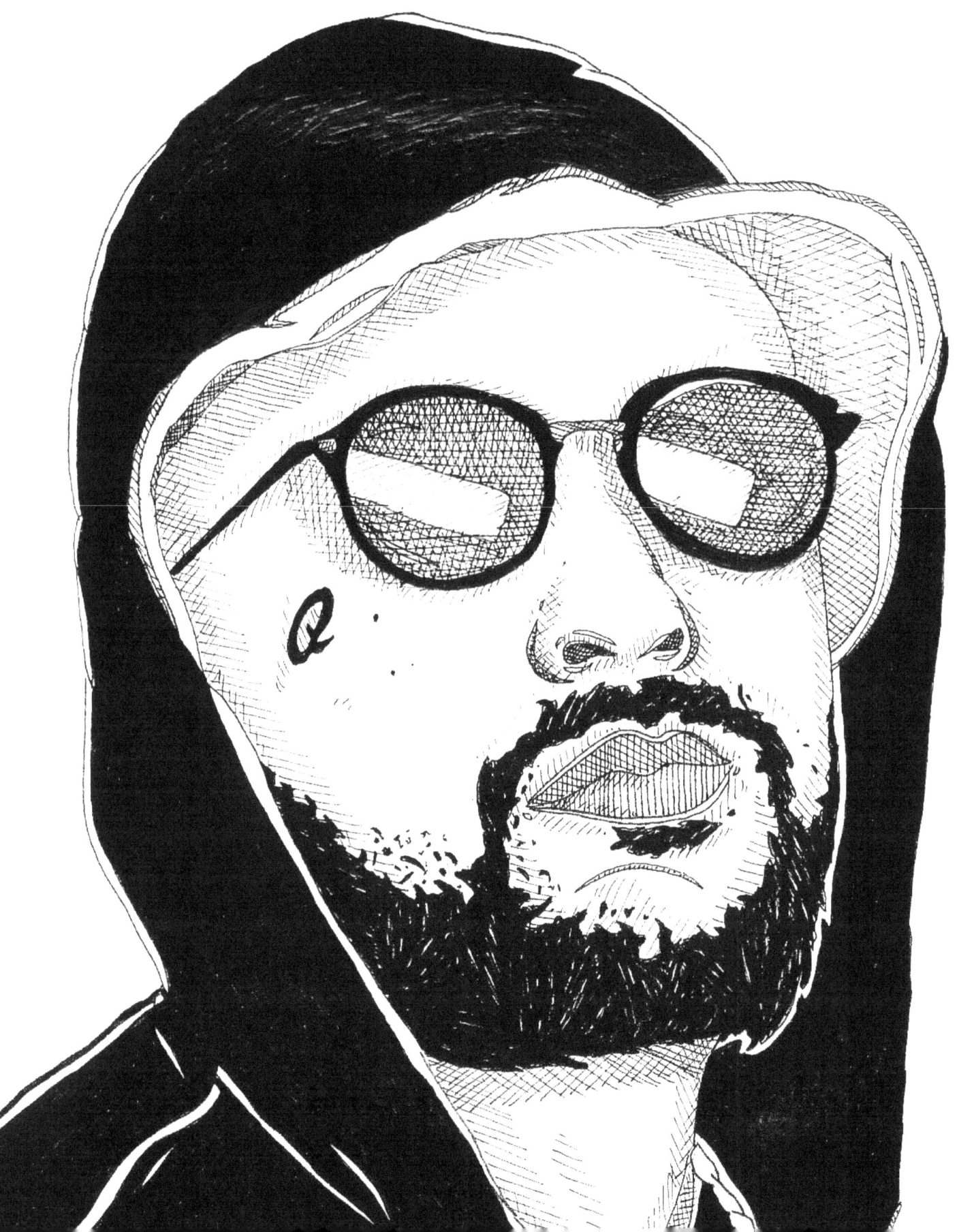

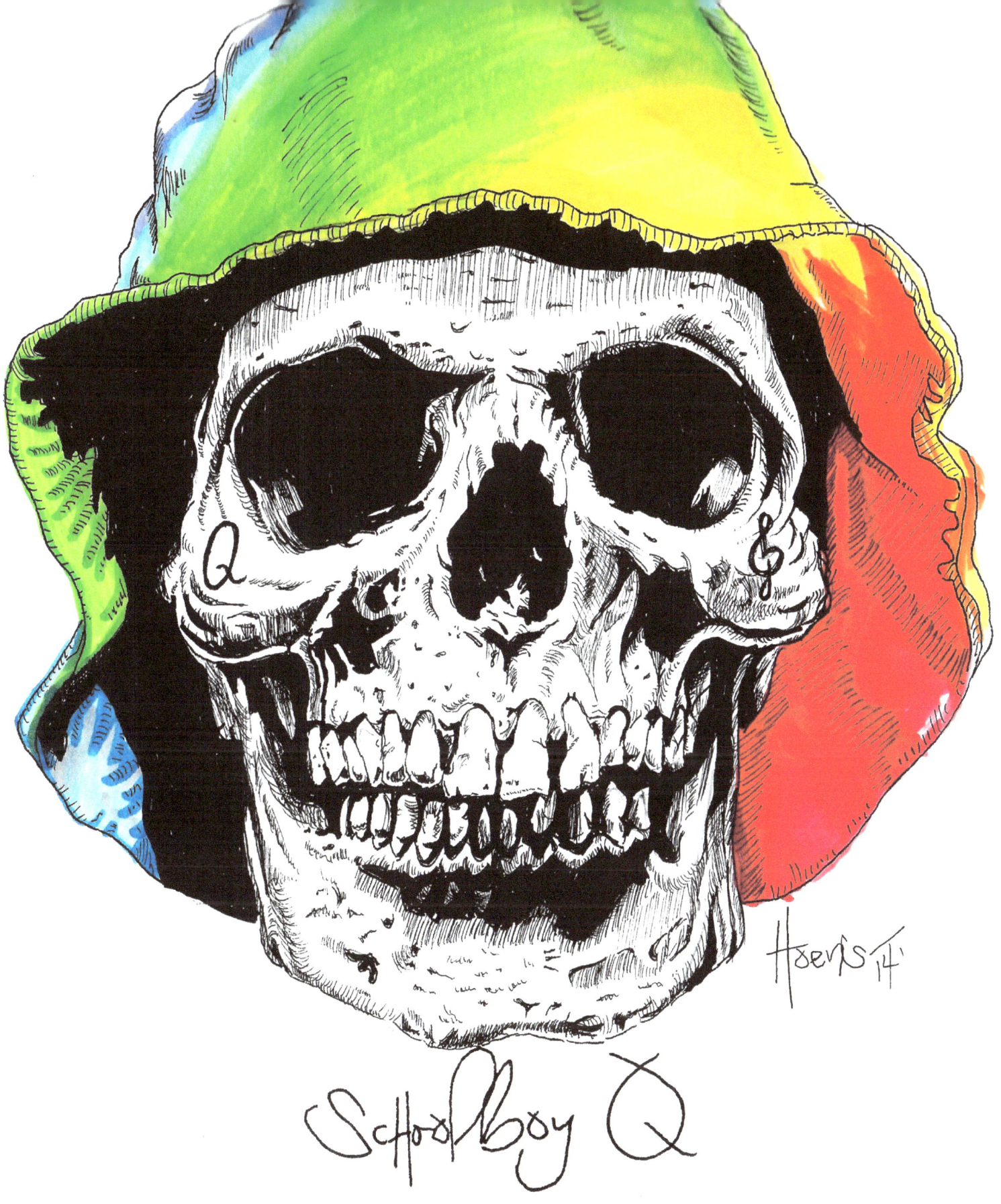

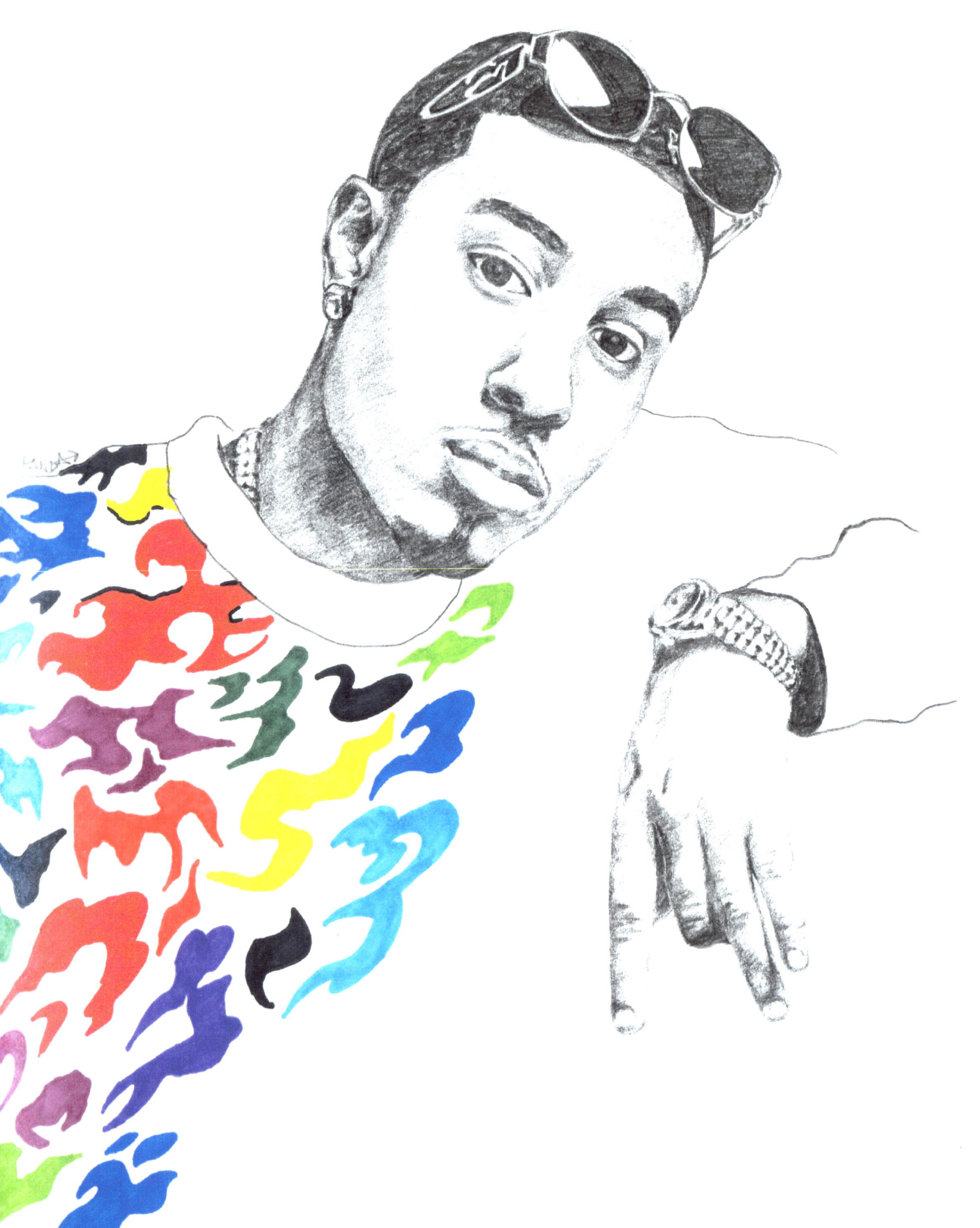

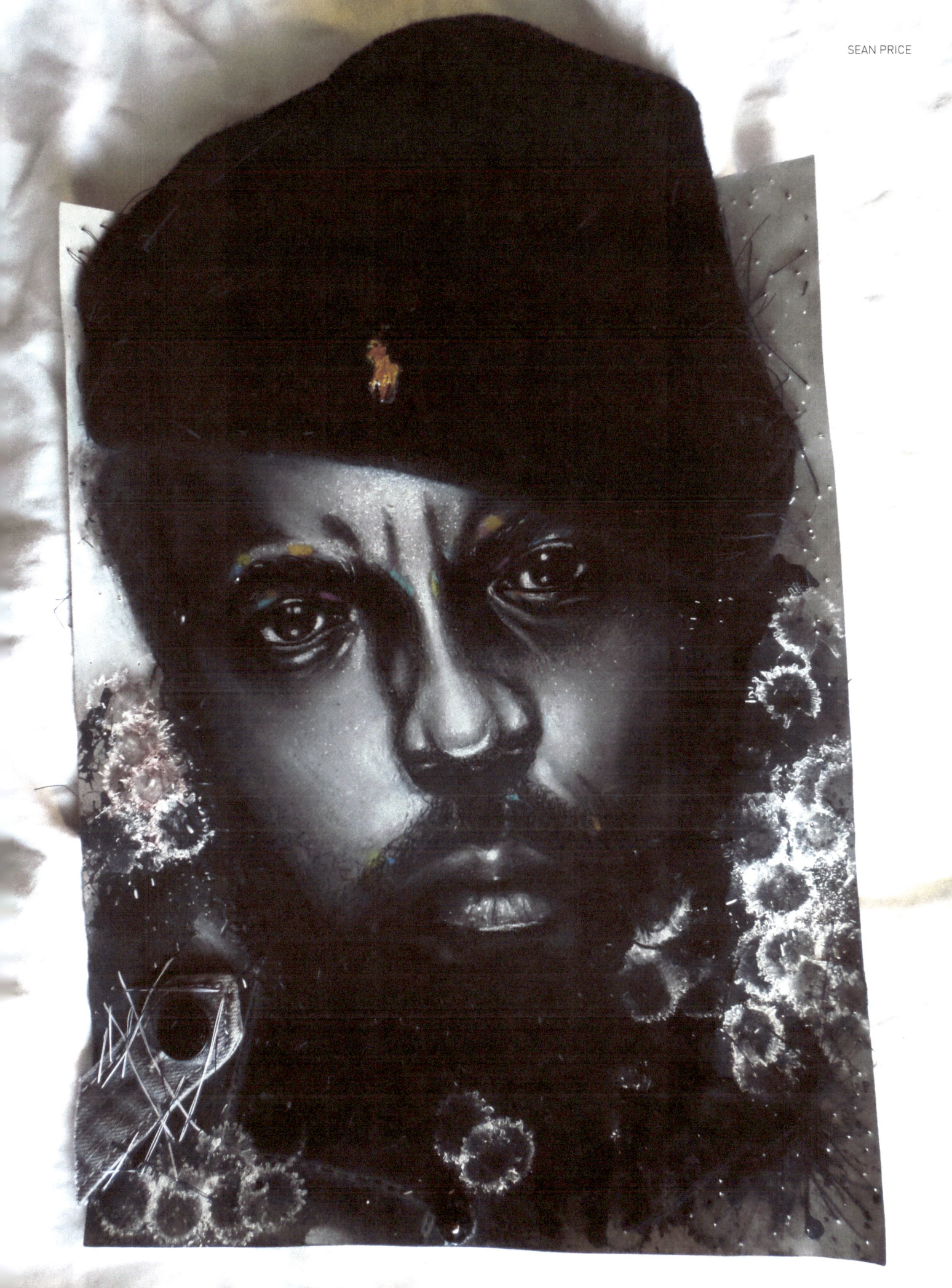

SEAN PRICE

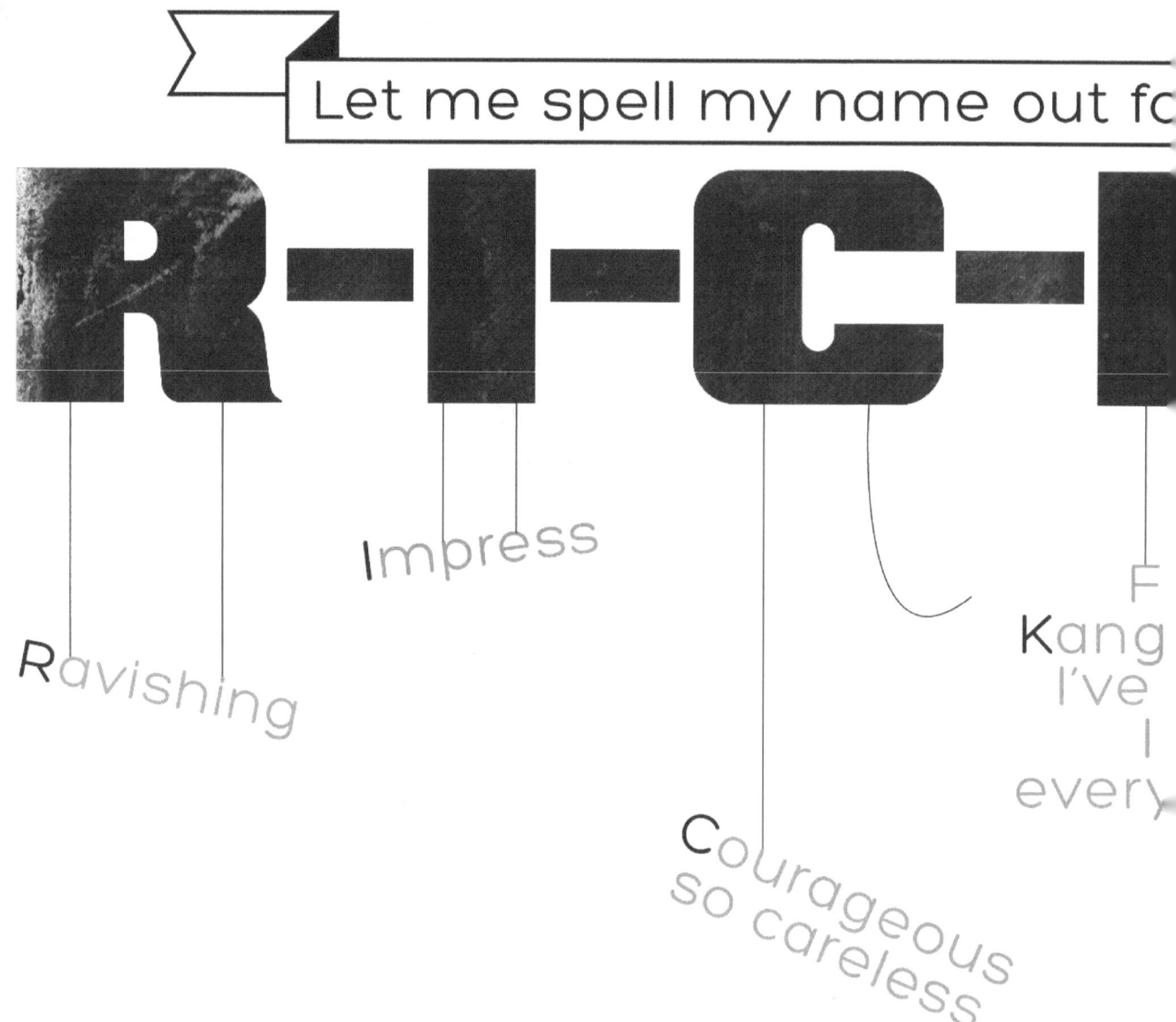

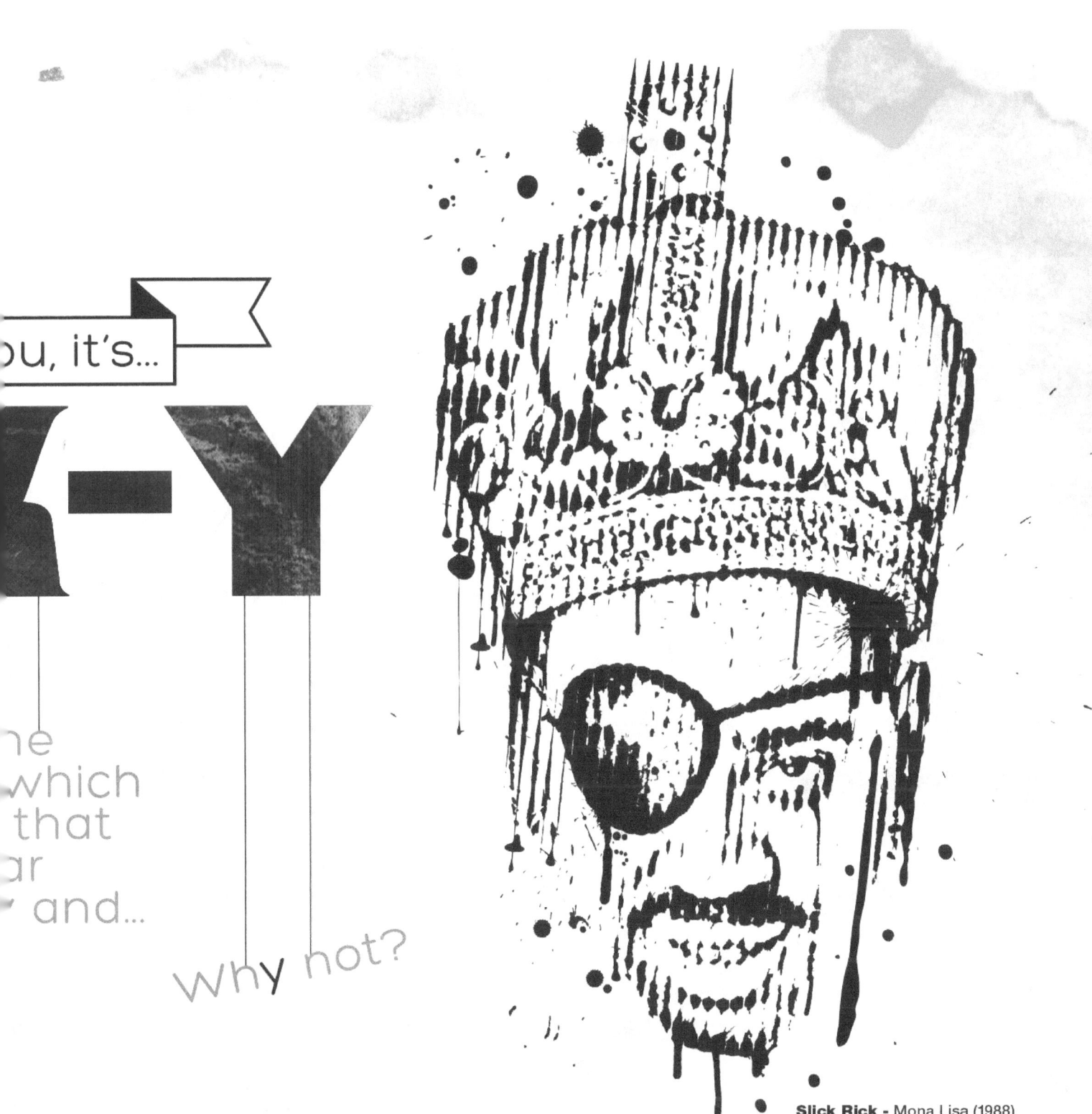

Slick Rick - Mona Lisa (1988)

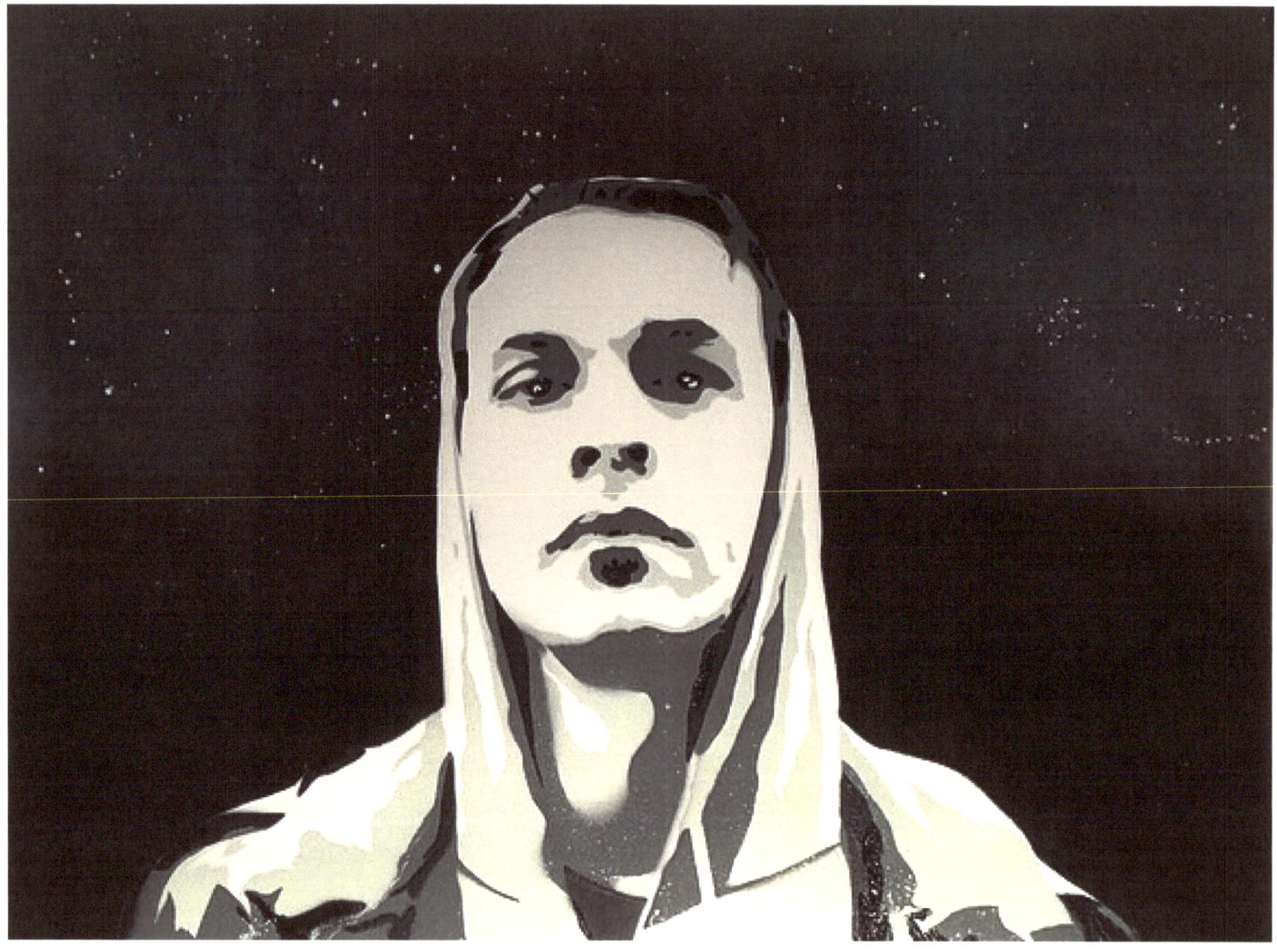

SMOKE DZA

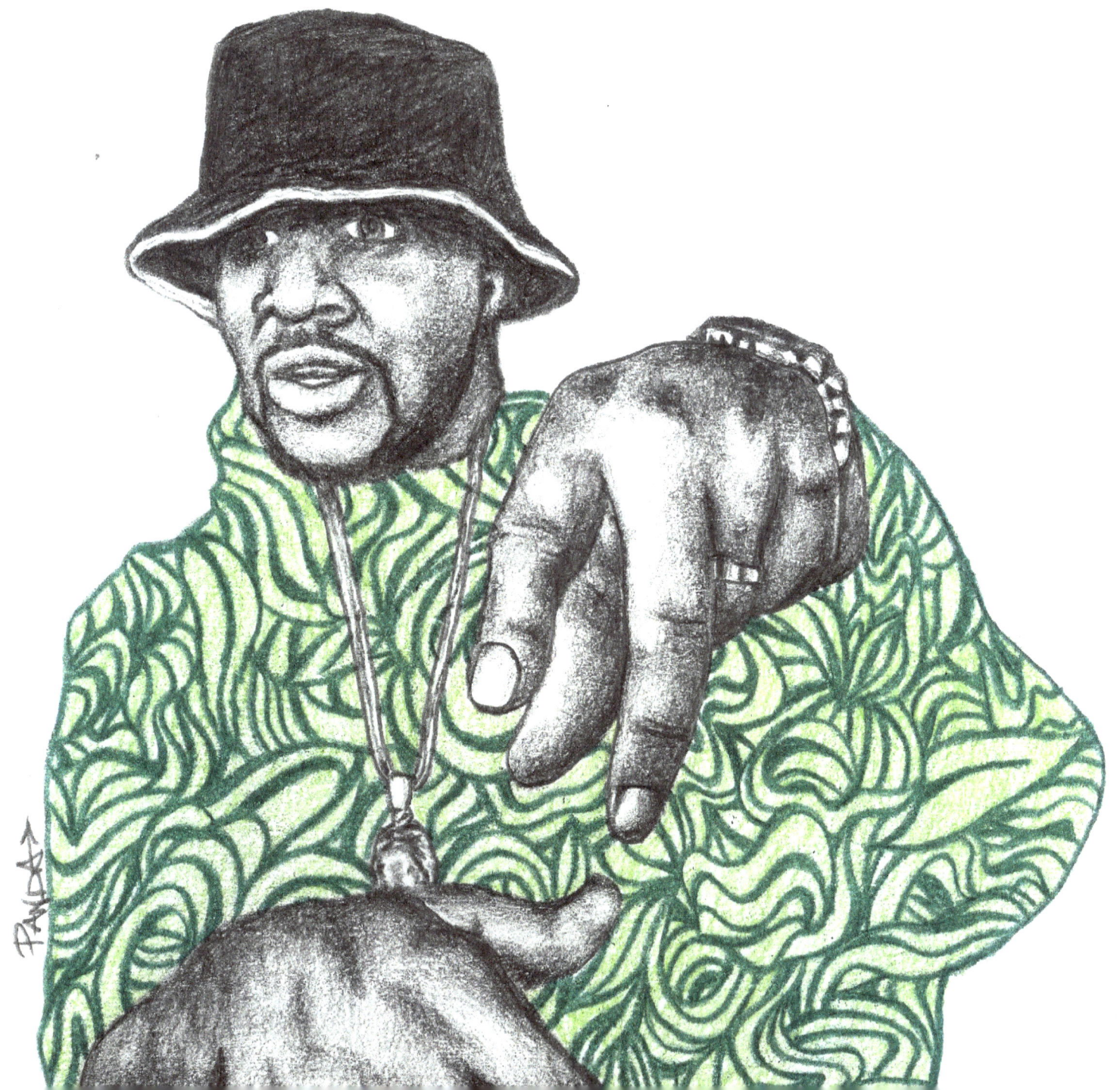

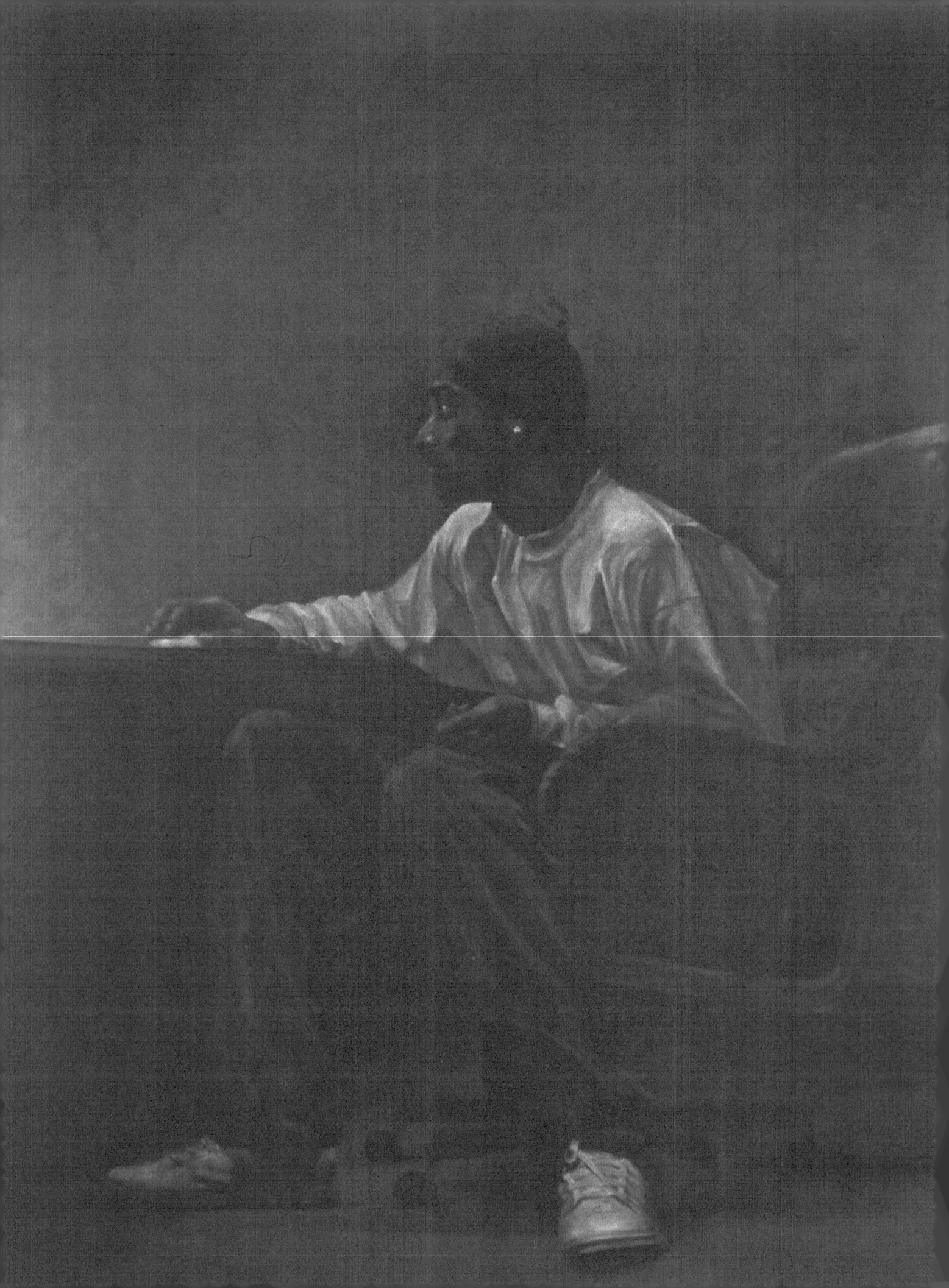

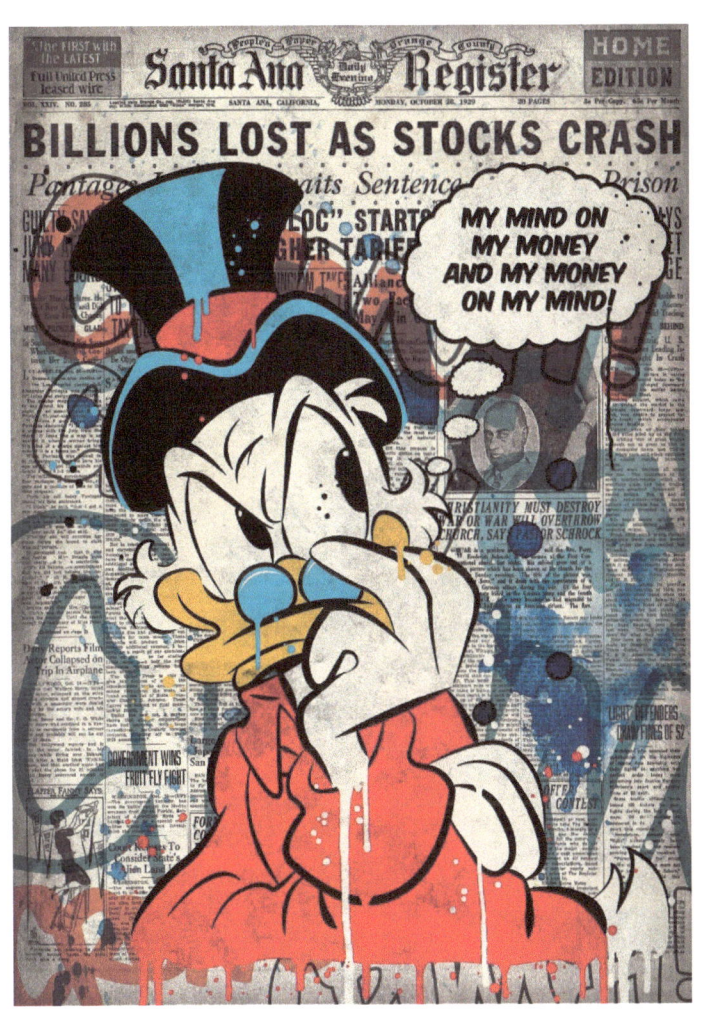
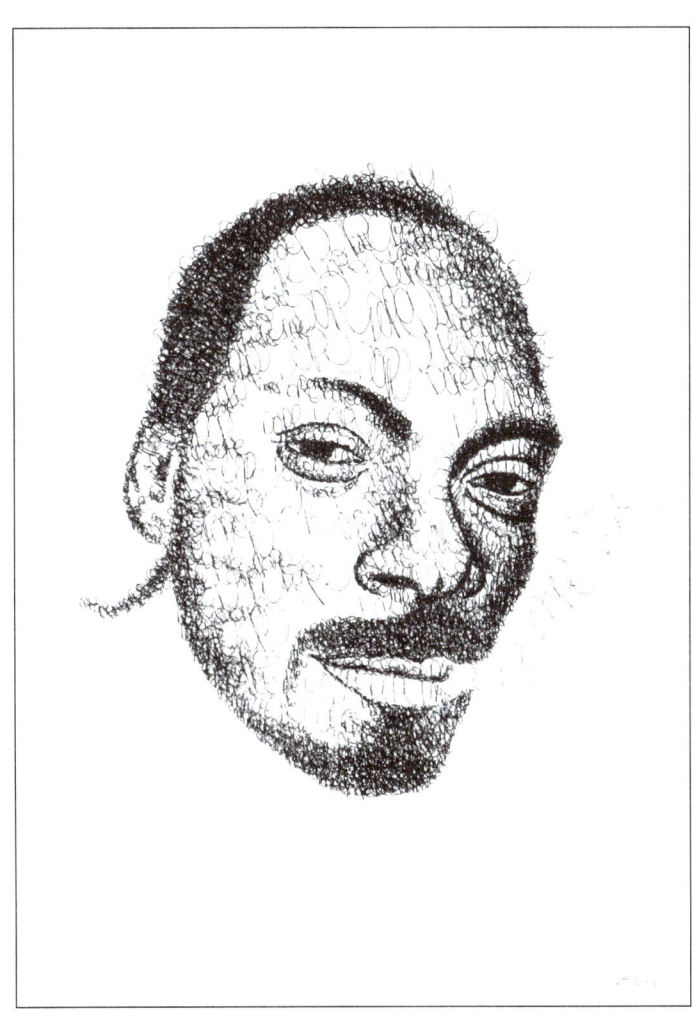

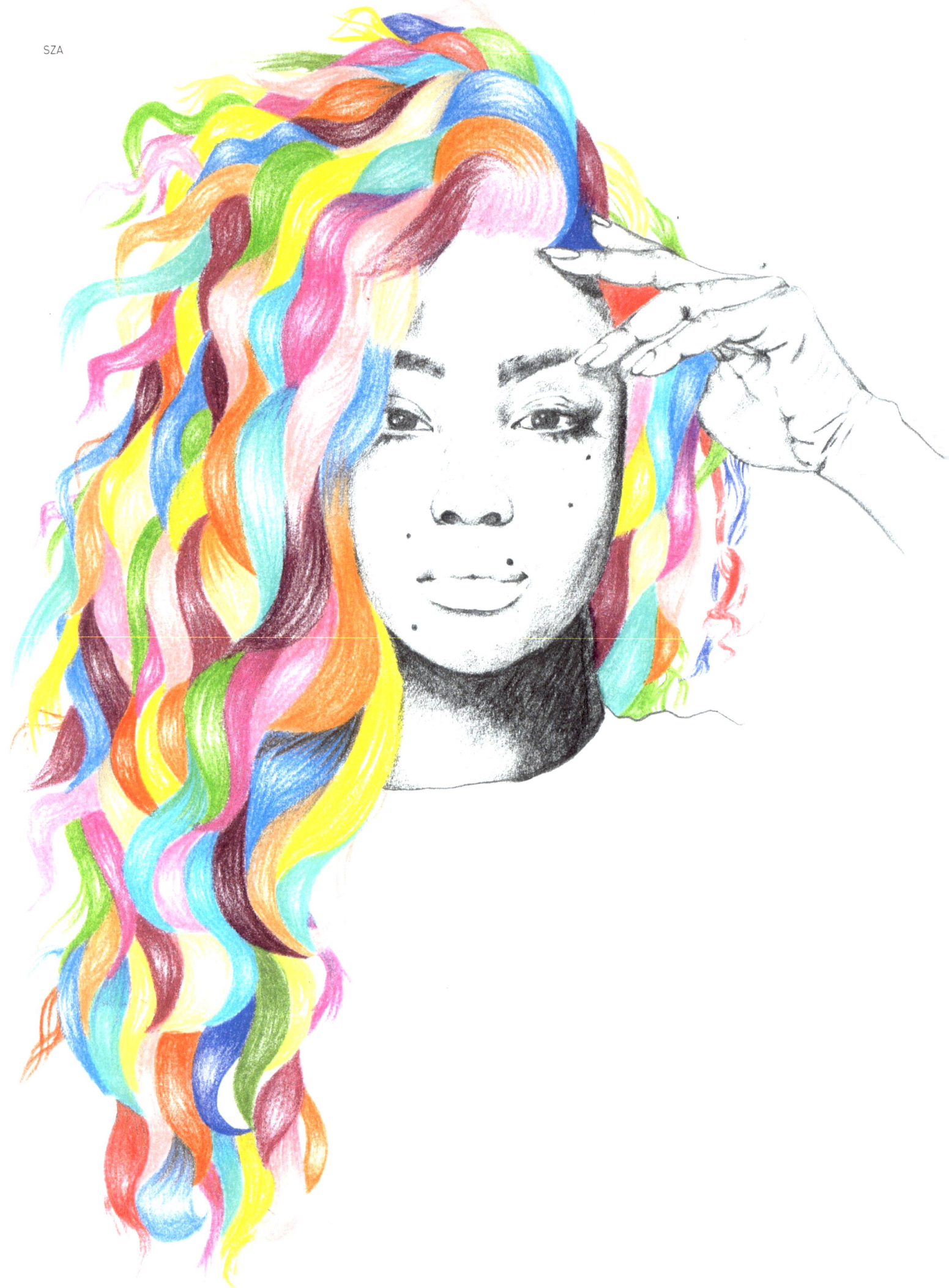

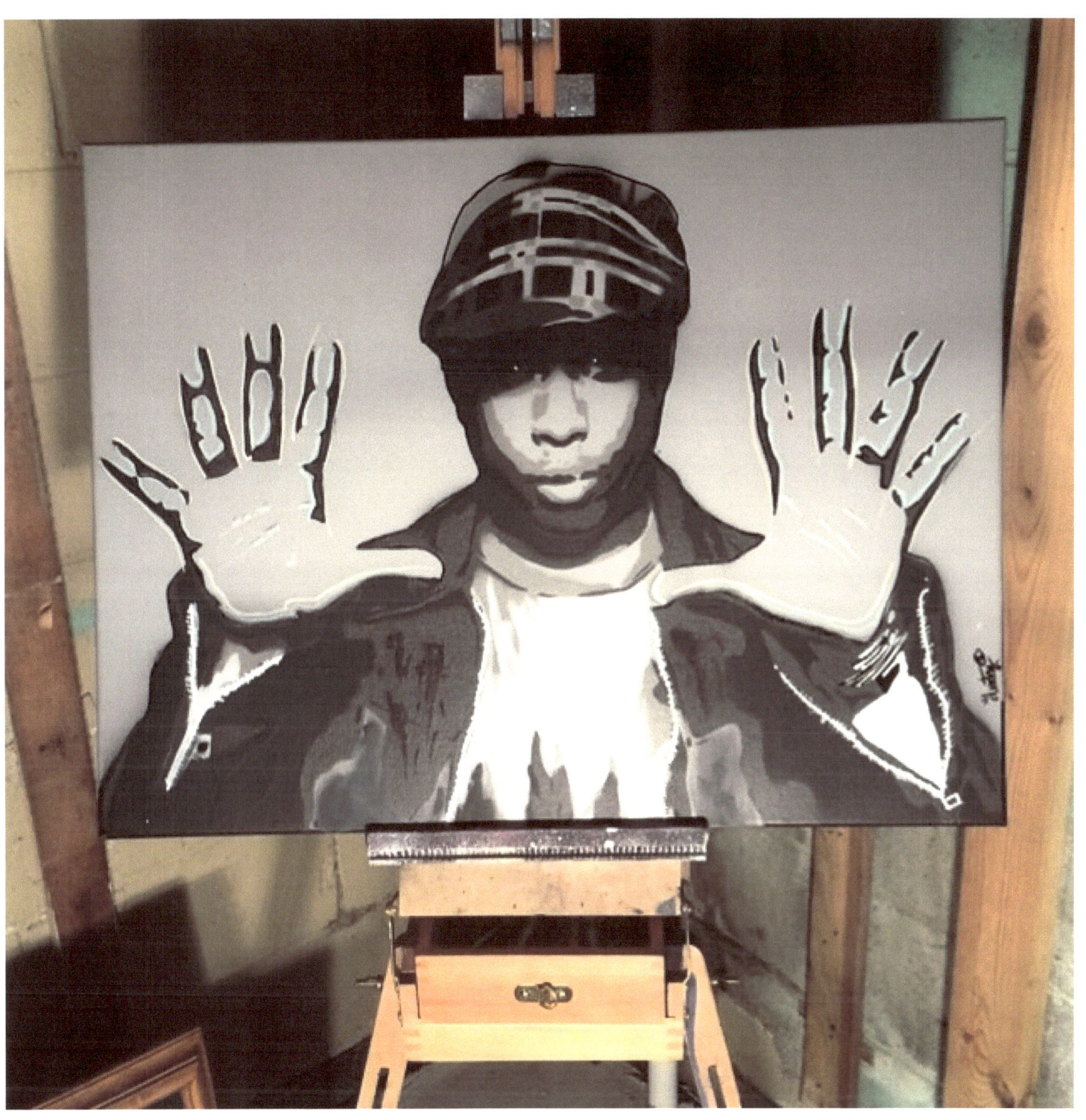

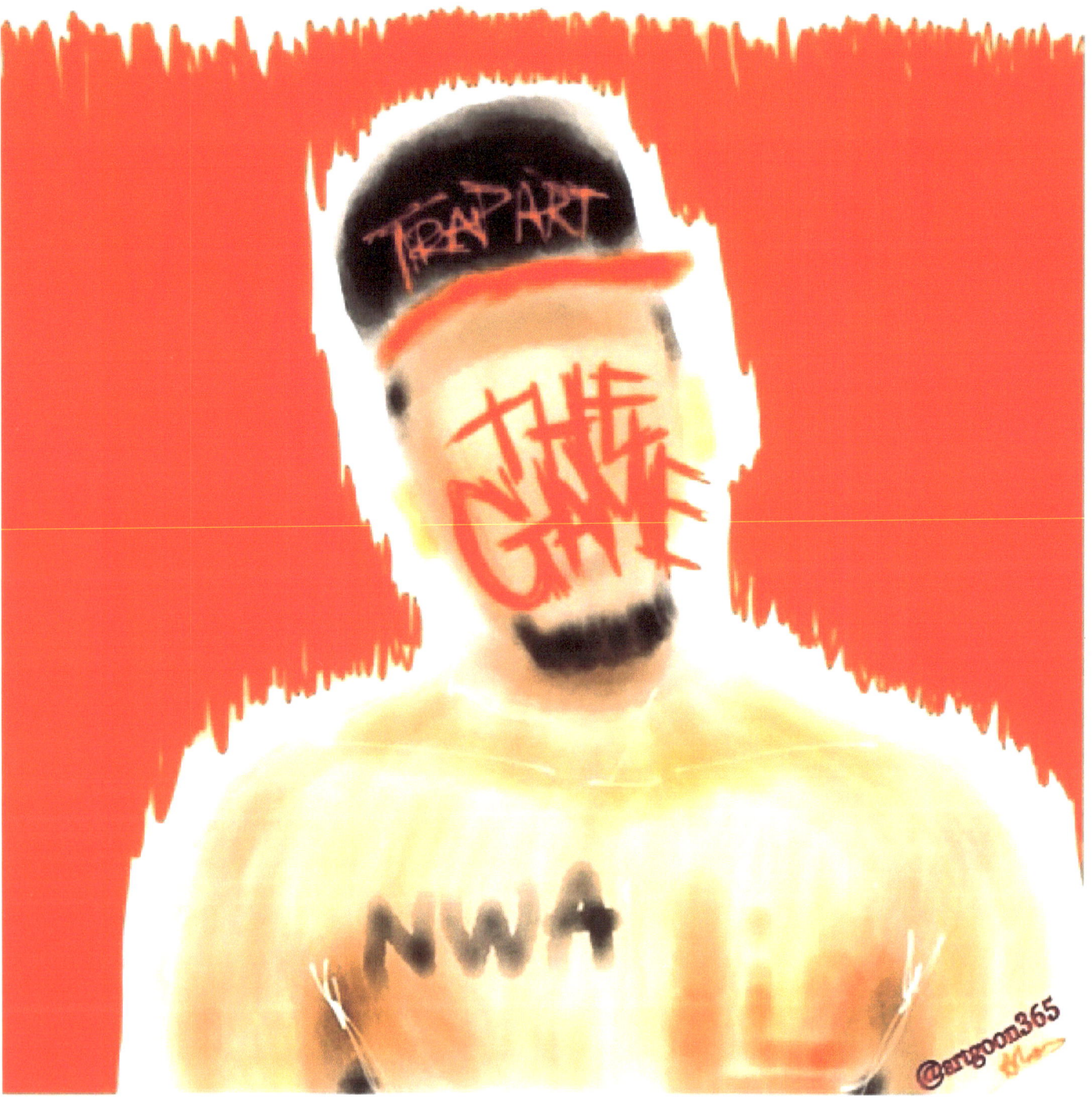

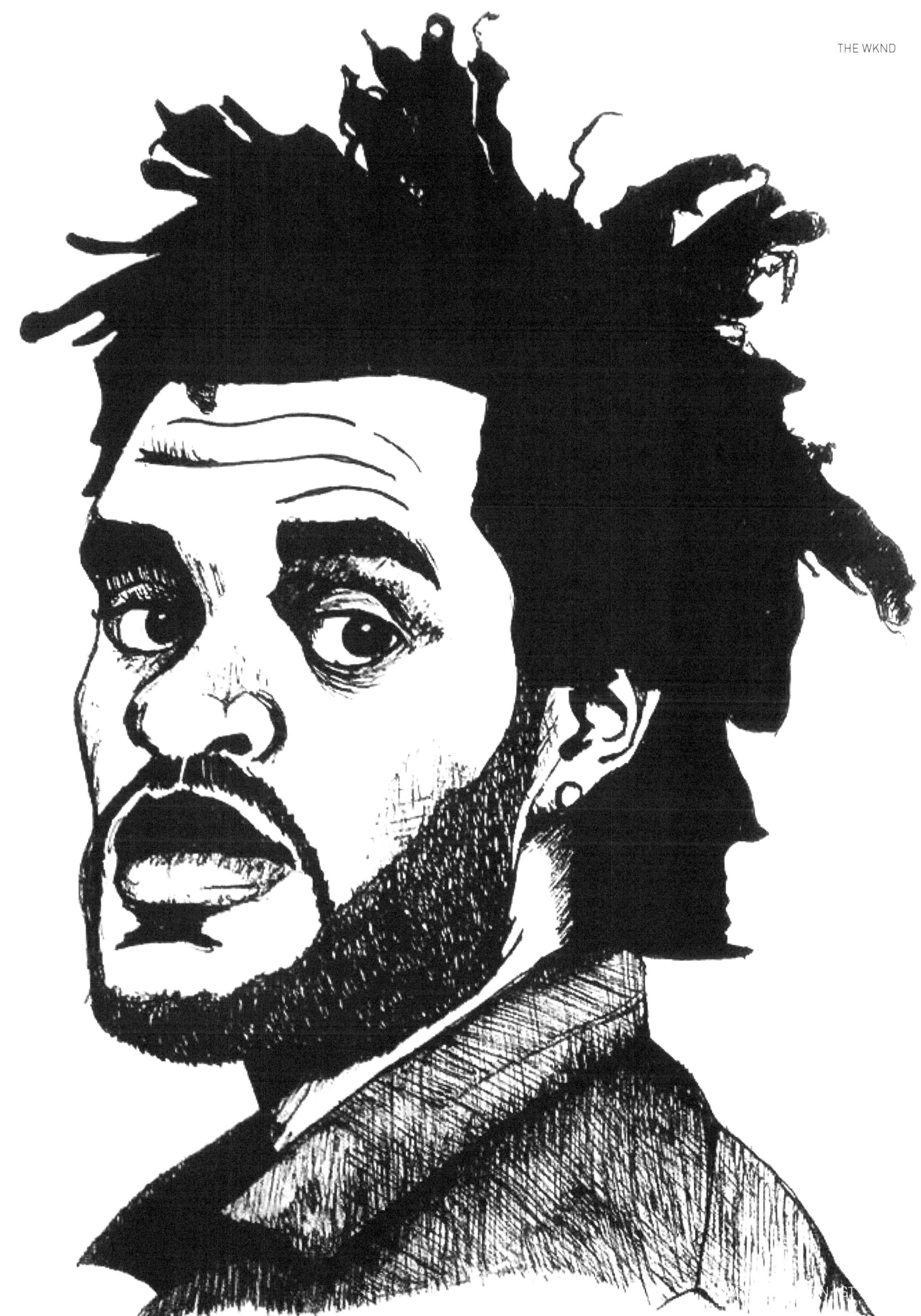

THE WKND

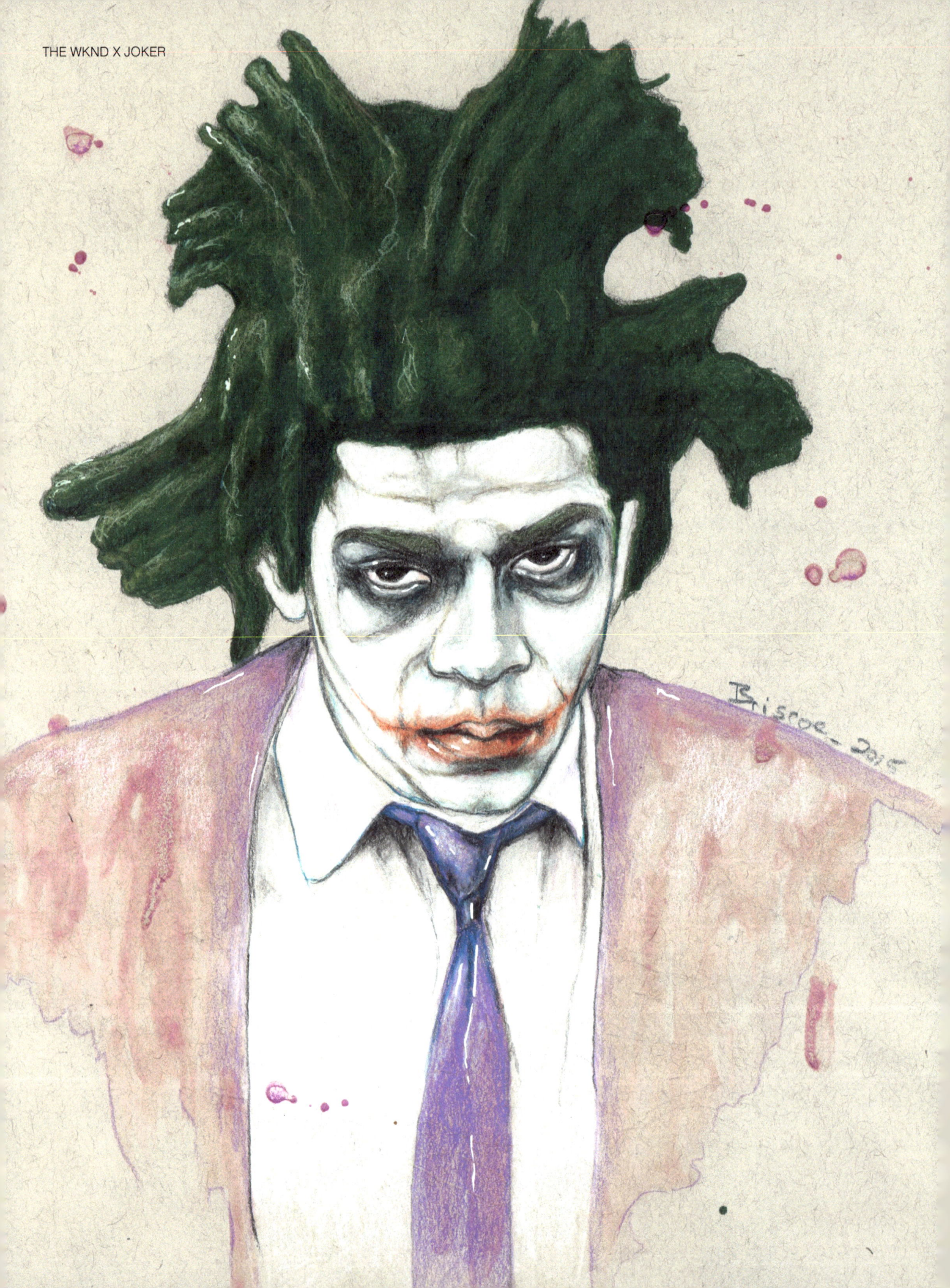

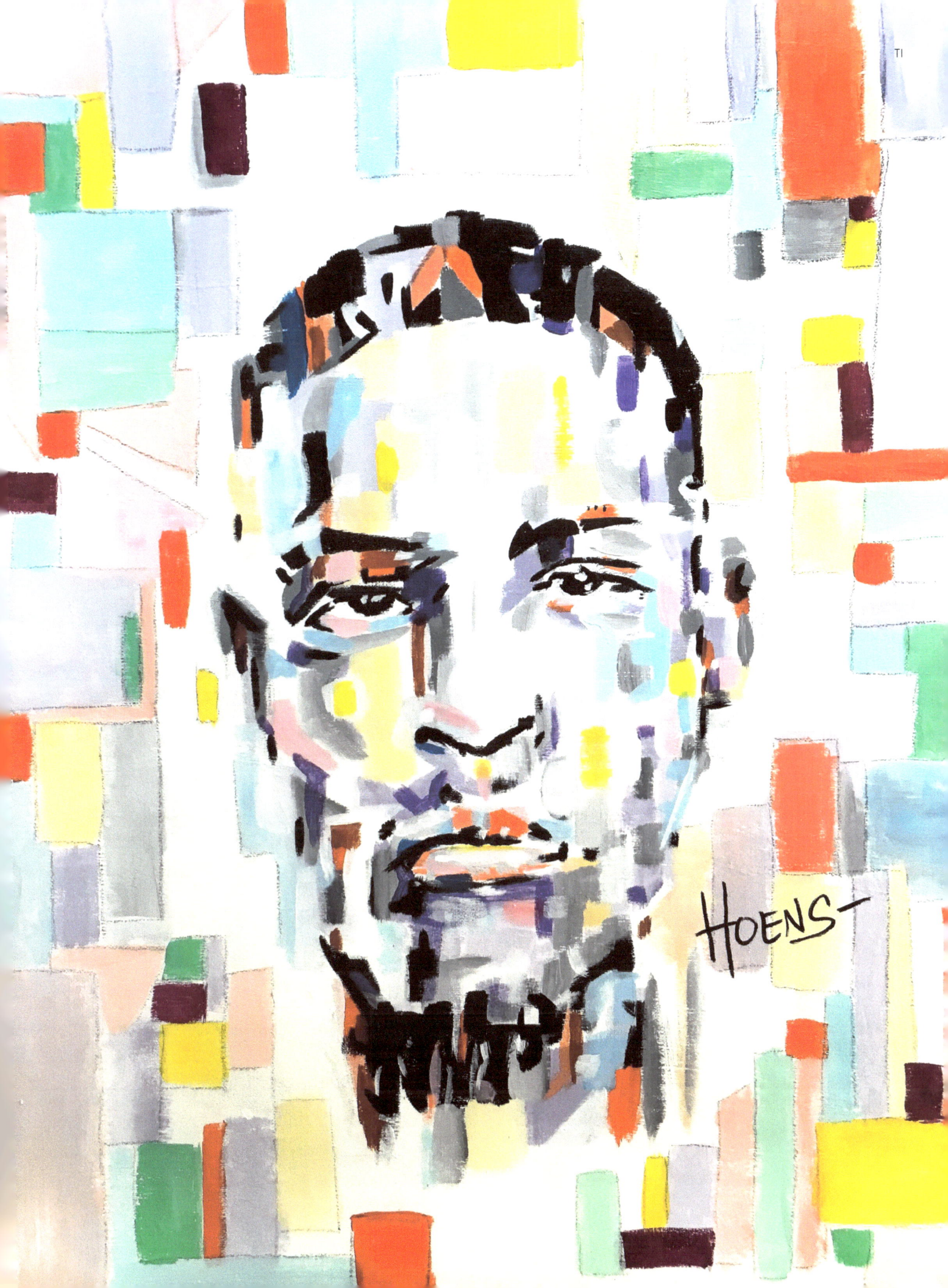

TRAVIS SCOTT

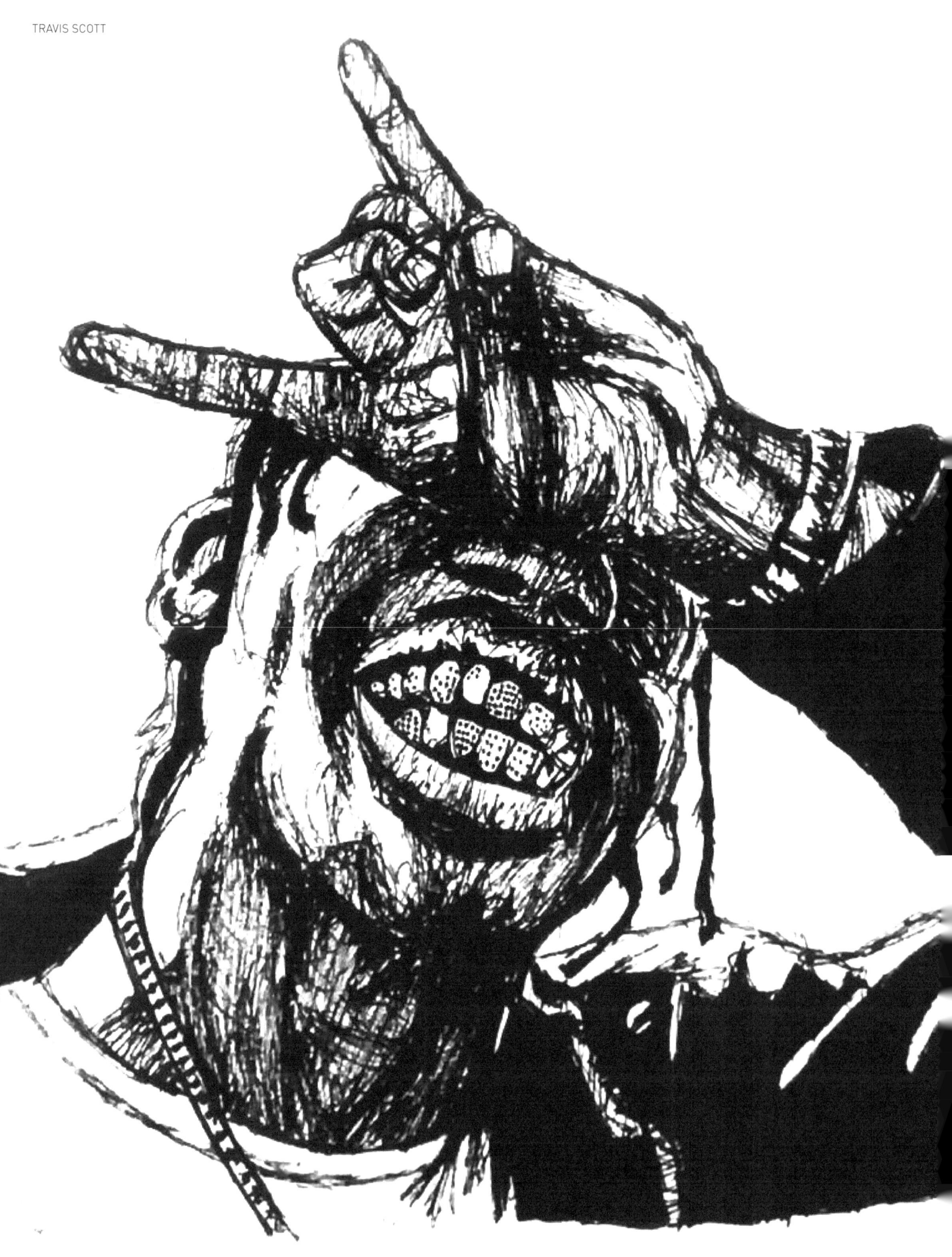

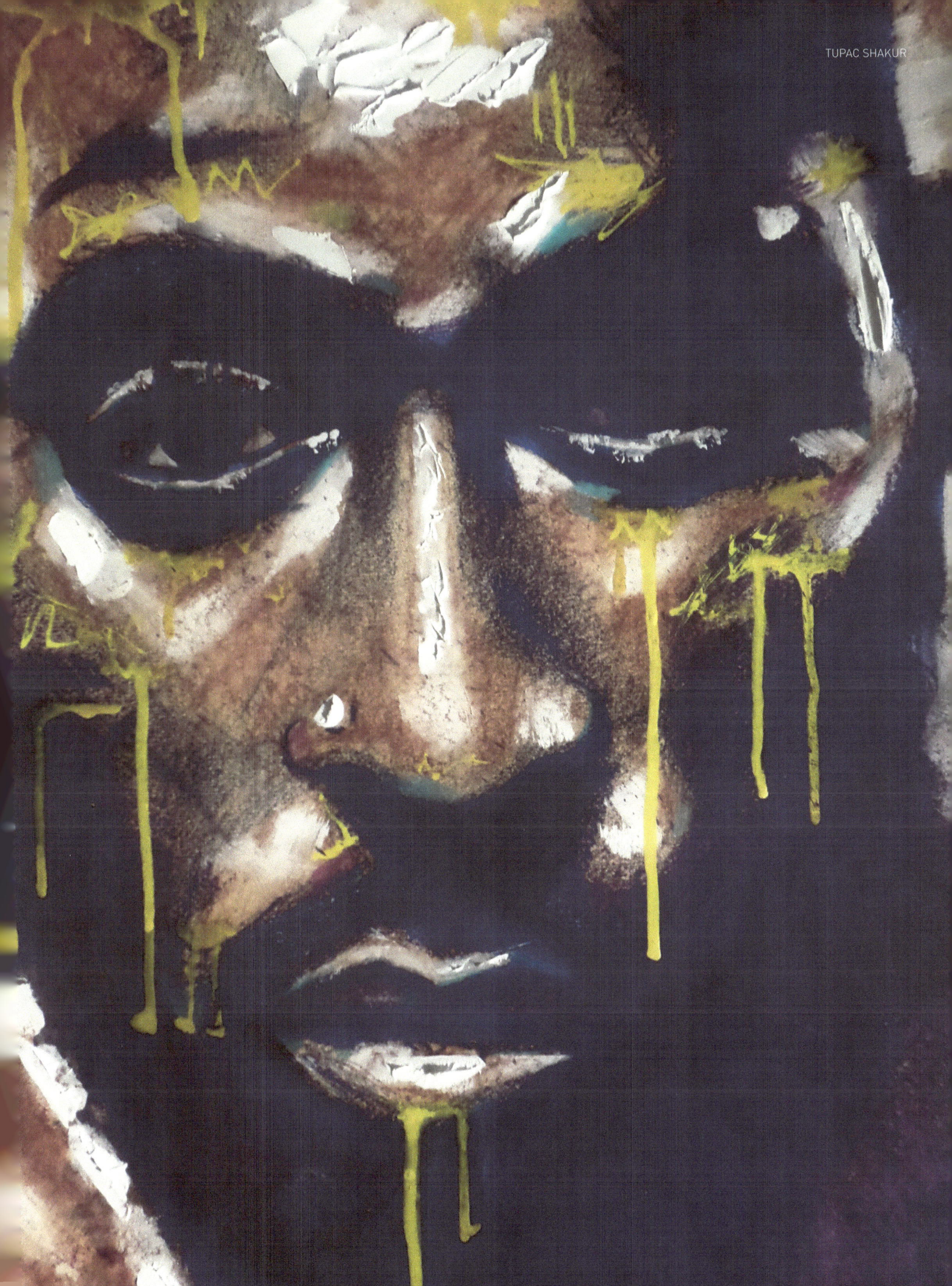
TUPAC SHAKUR

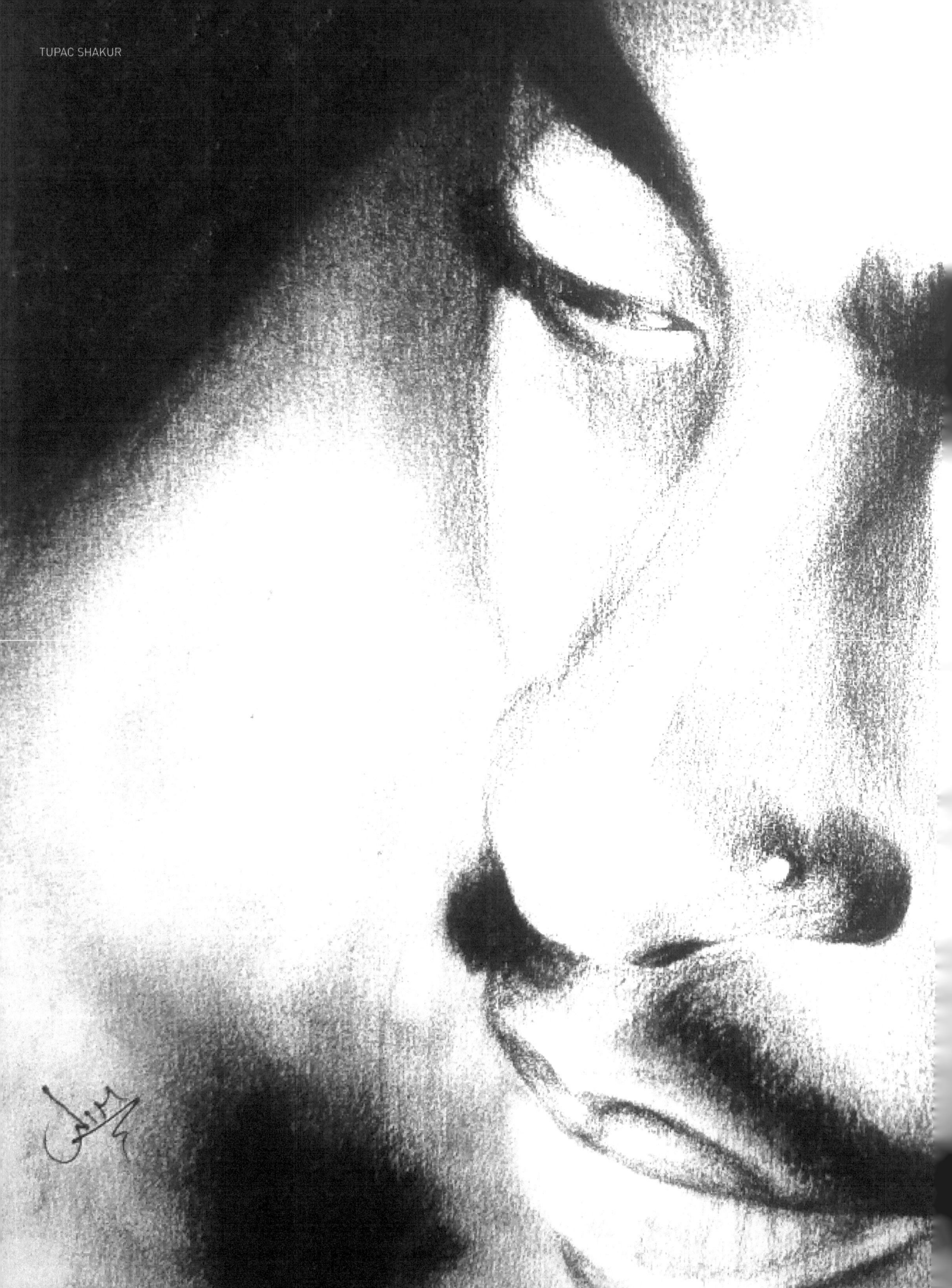

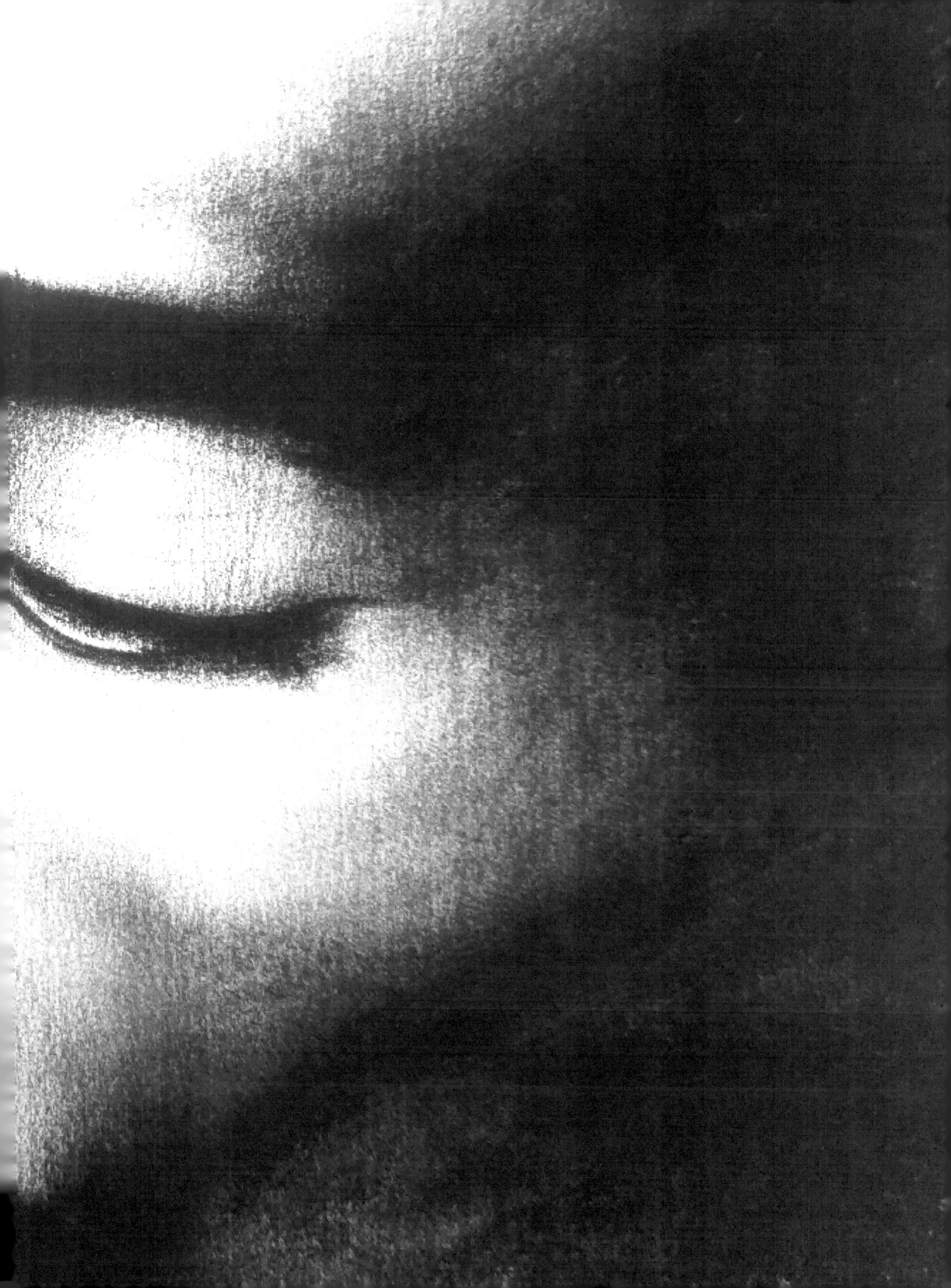

TUPAC SHAKUR

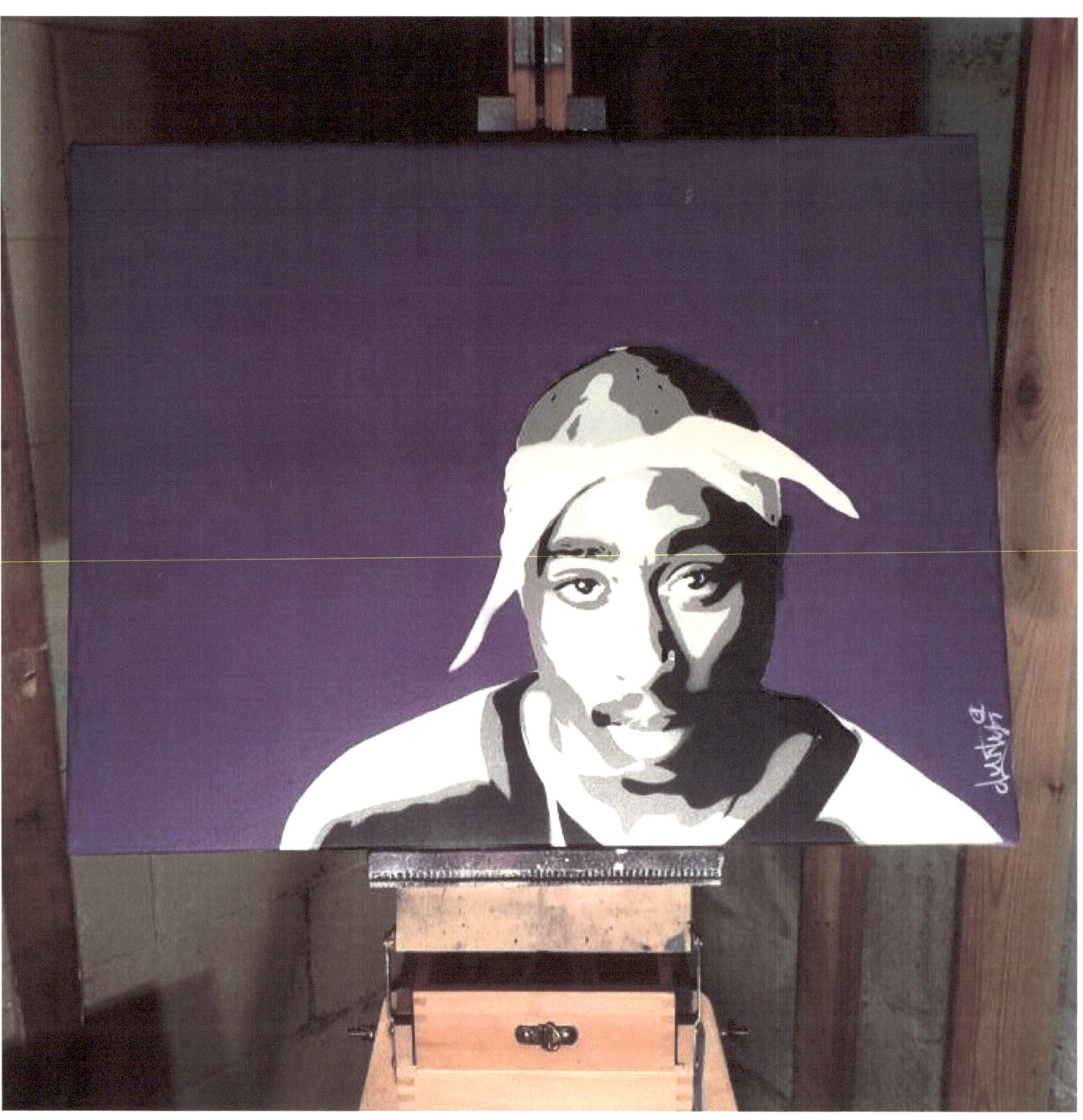

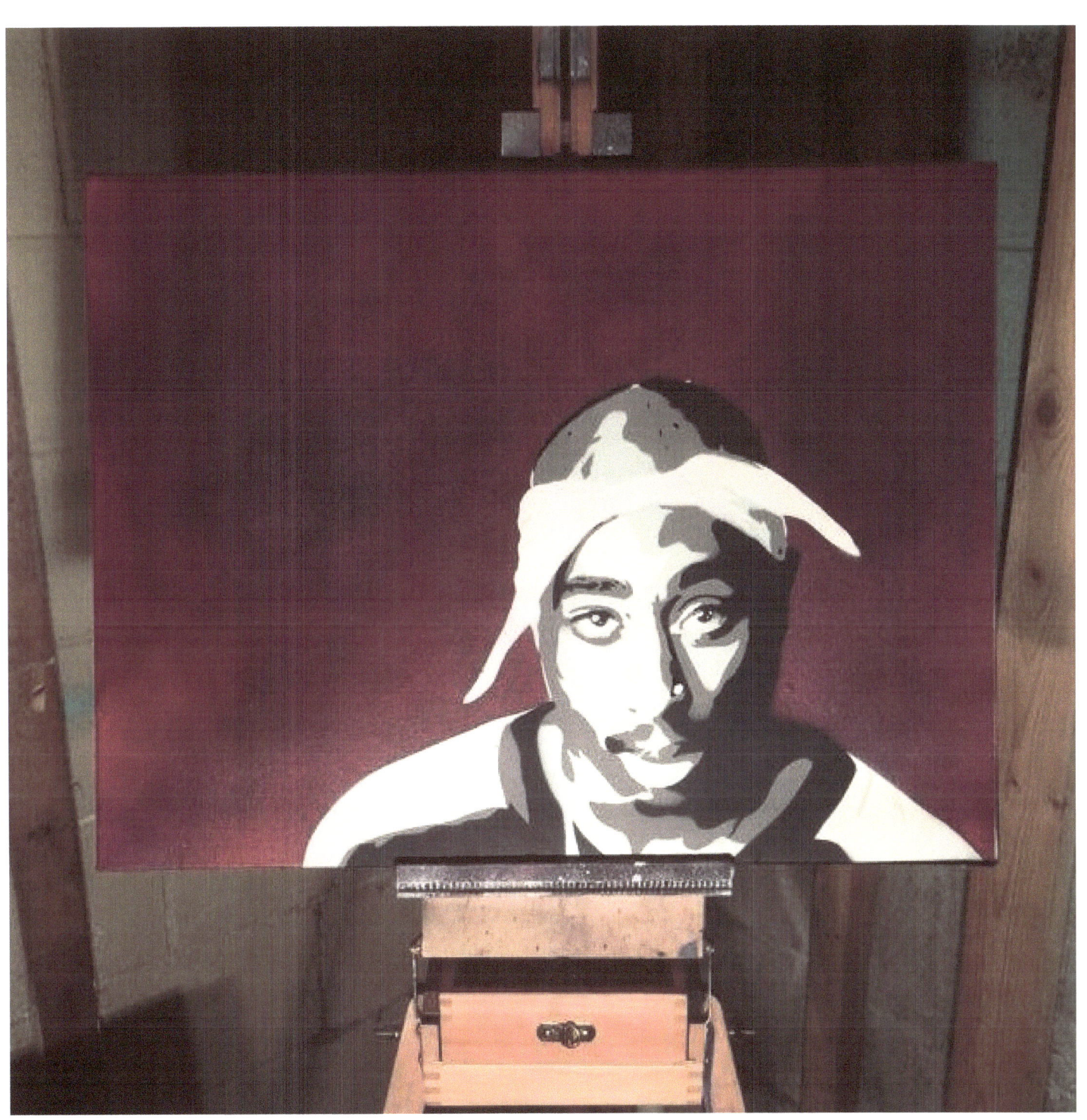

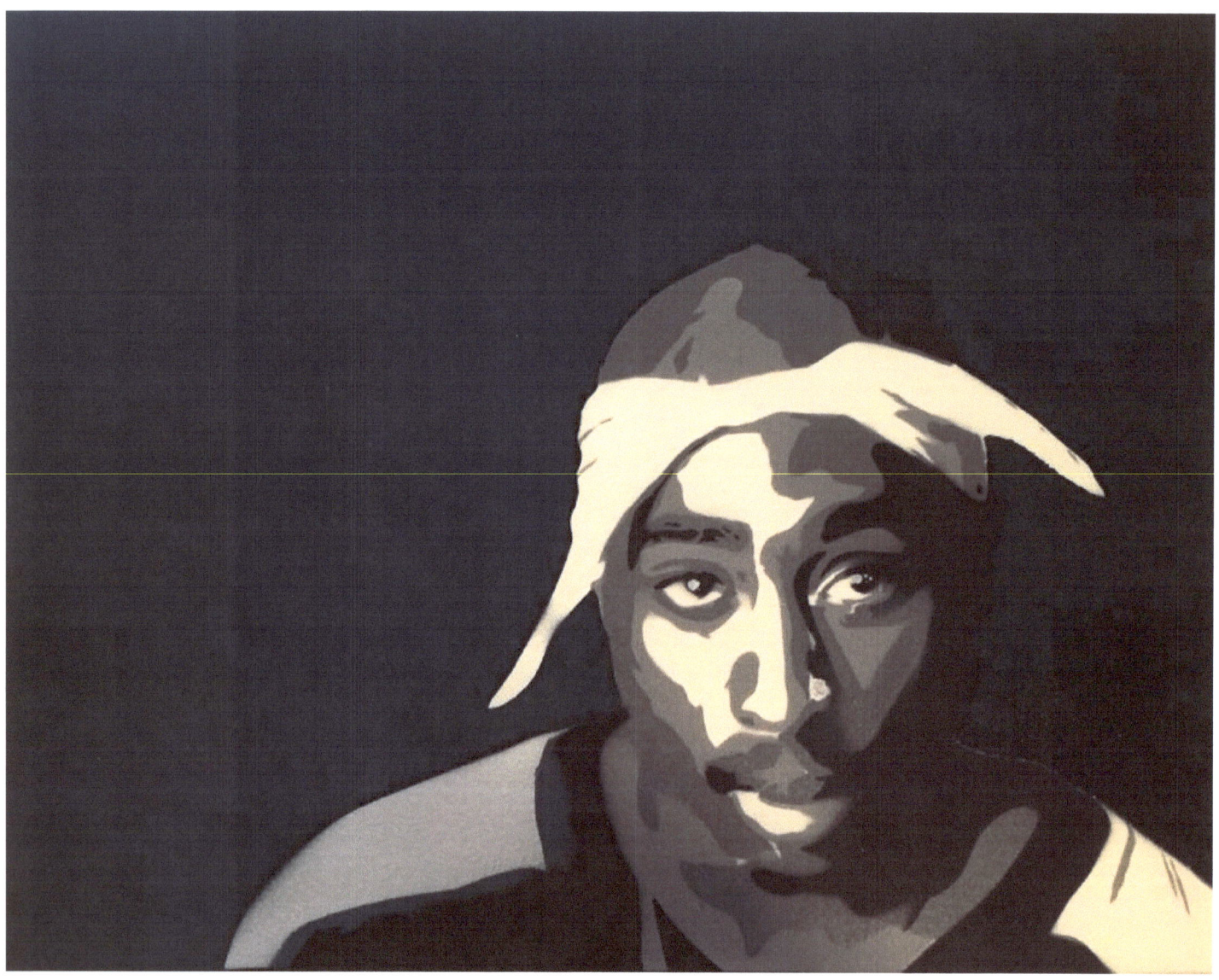

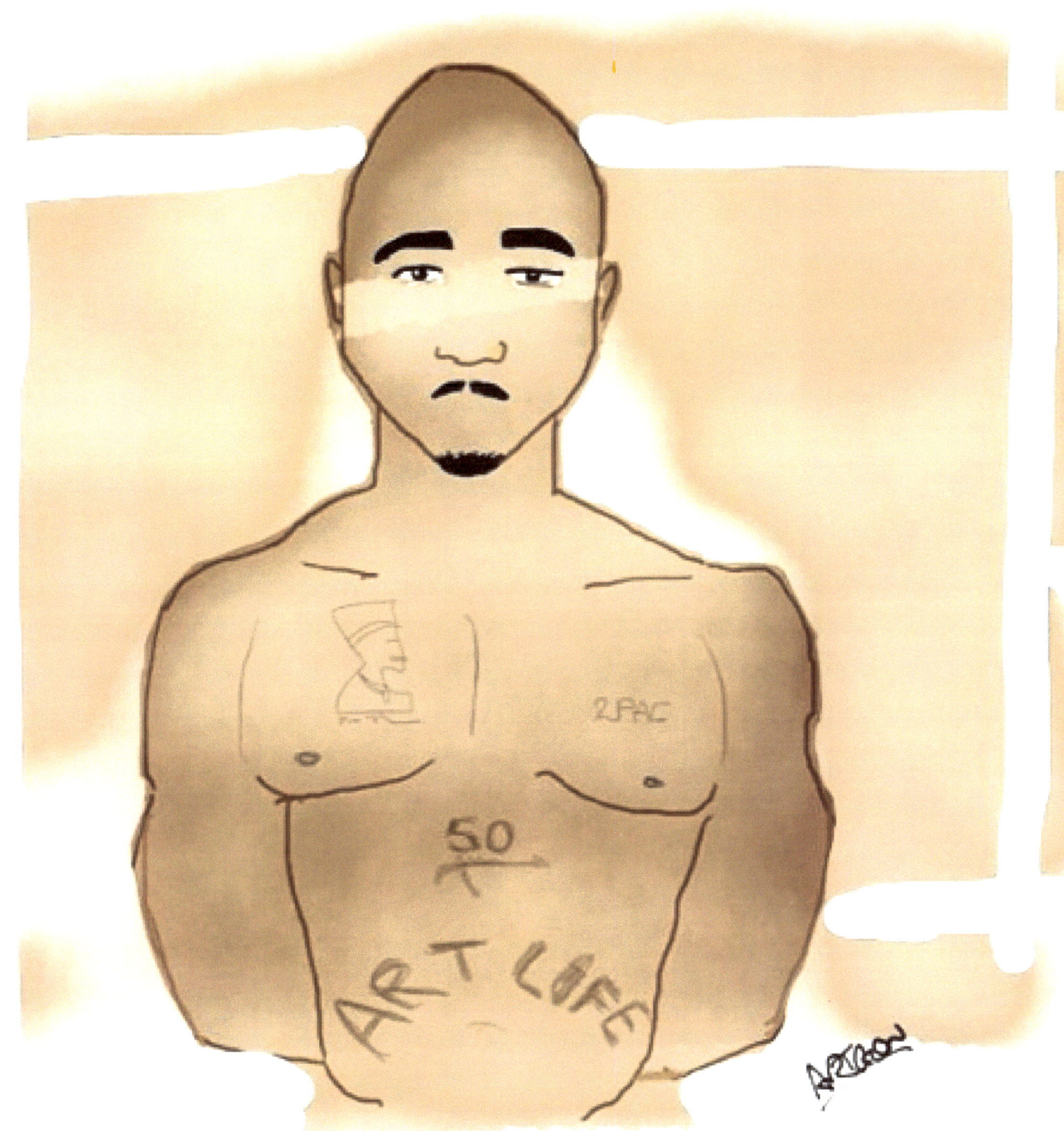

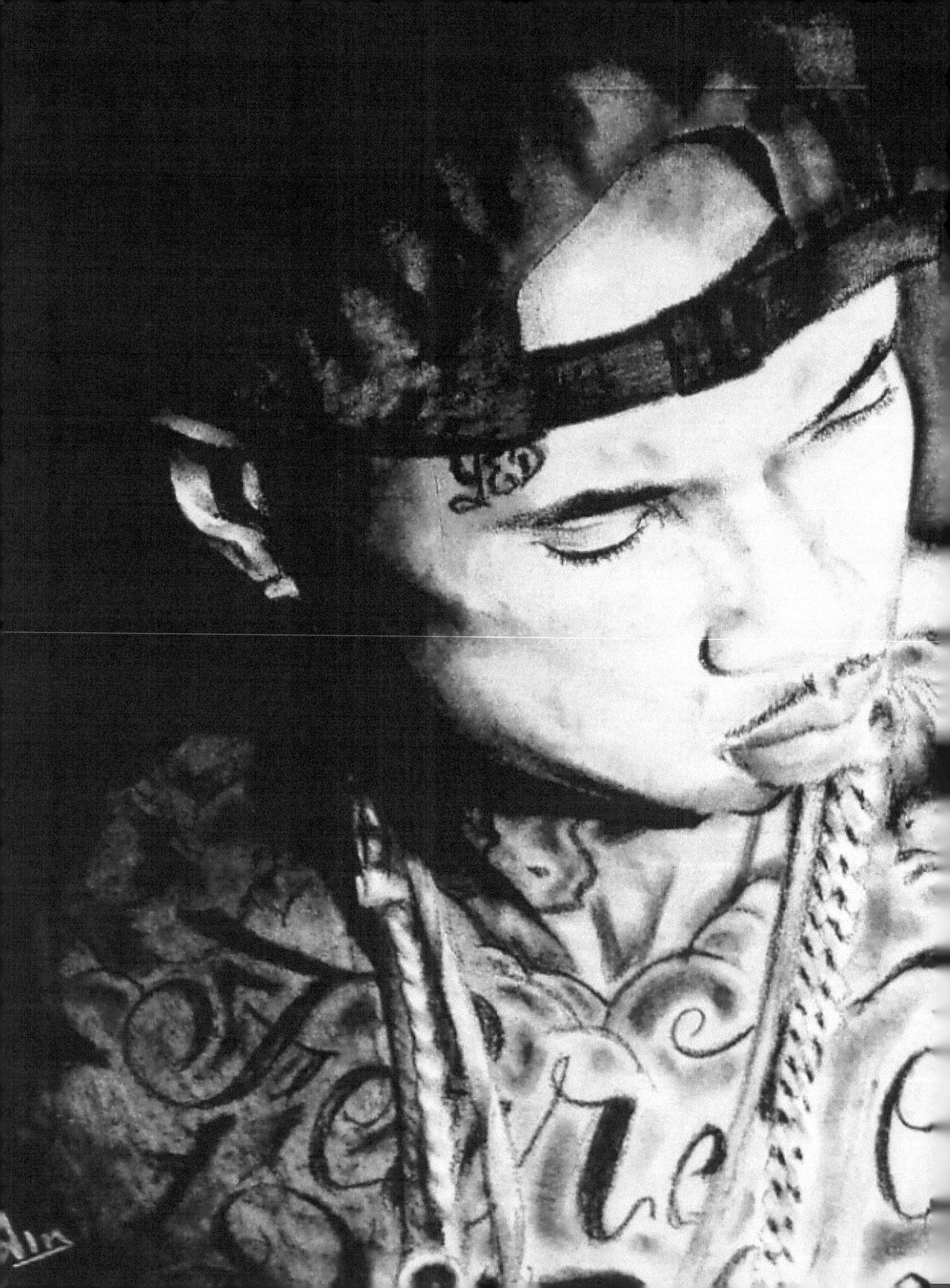

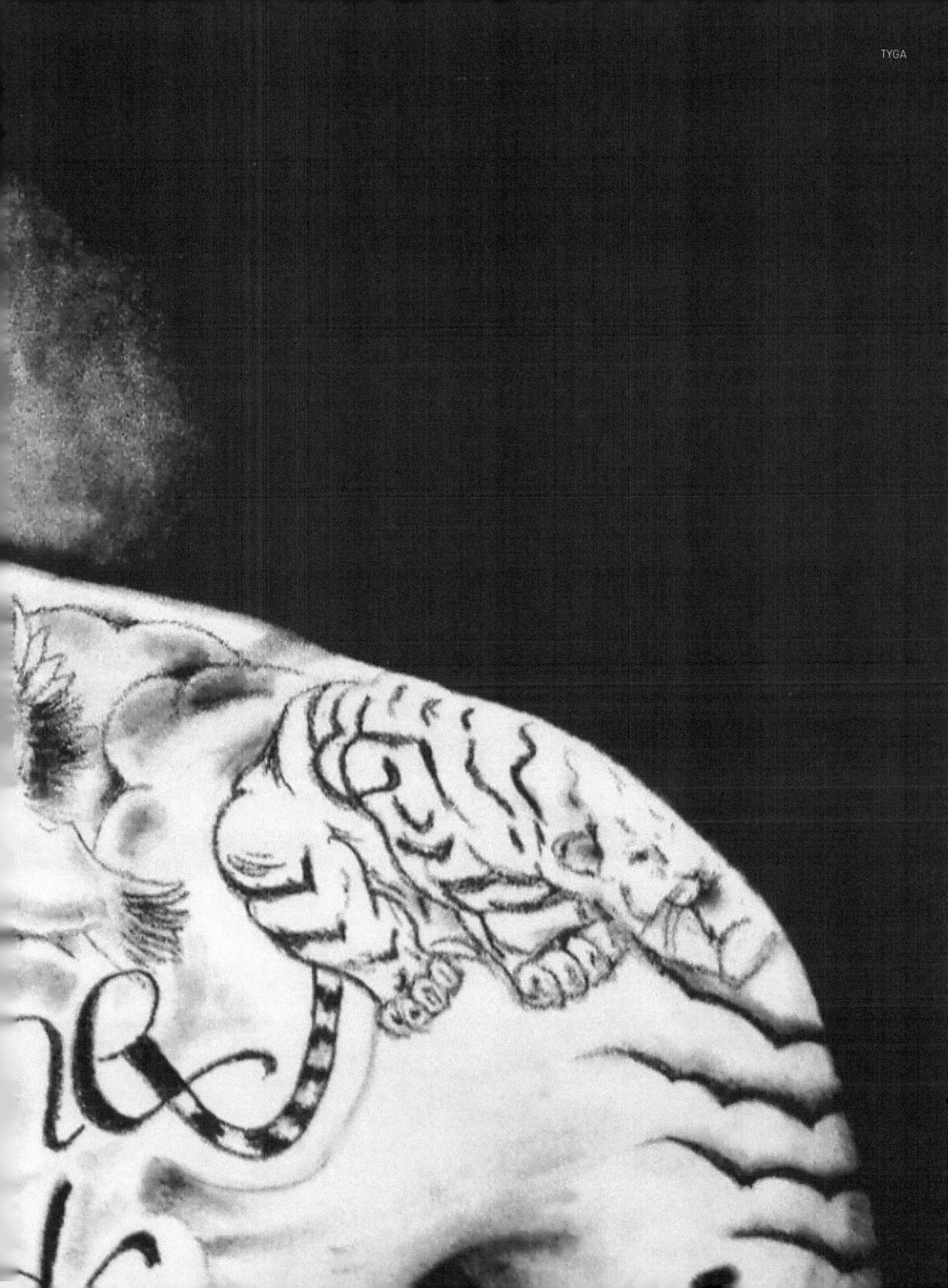

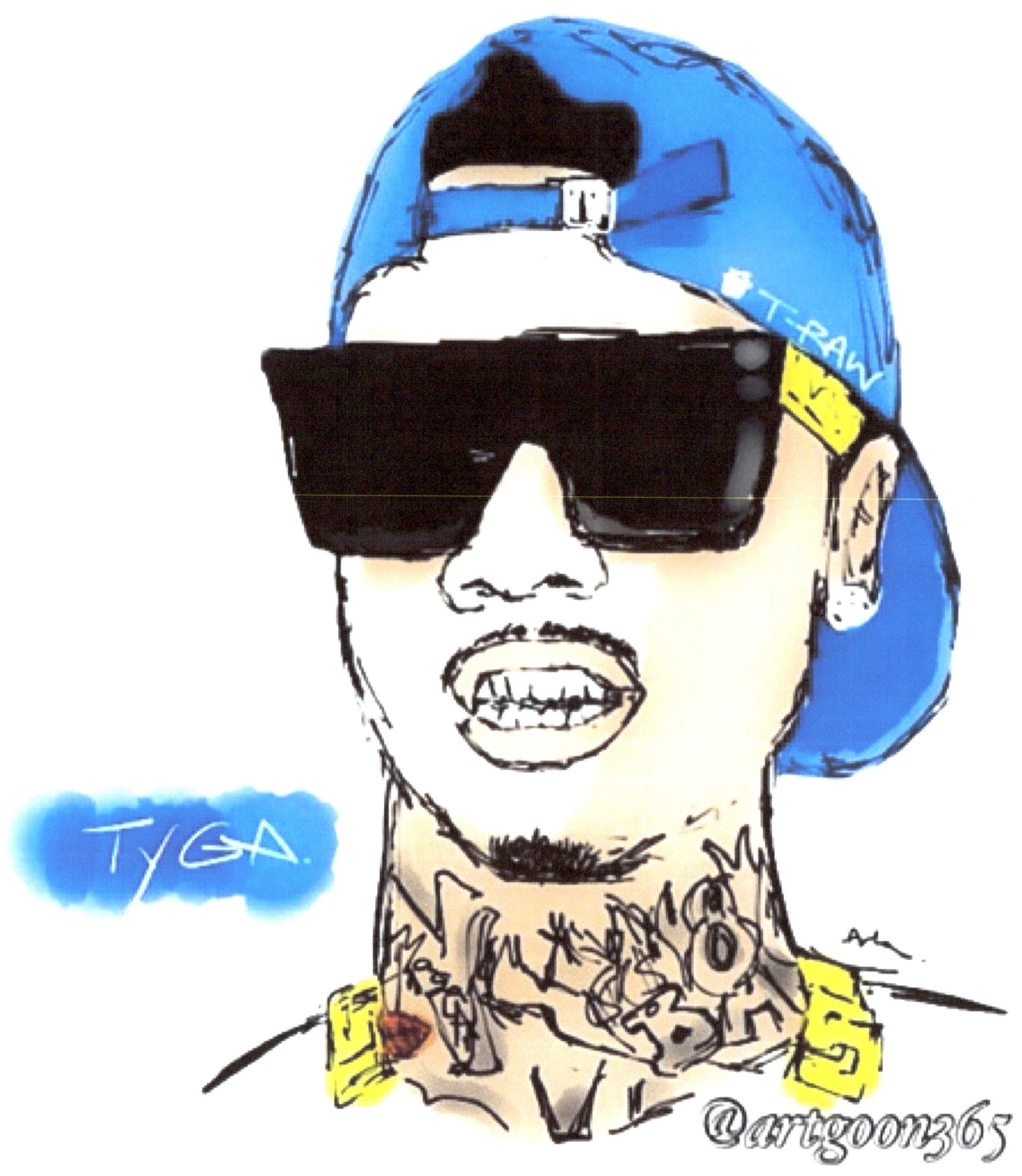

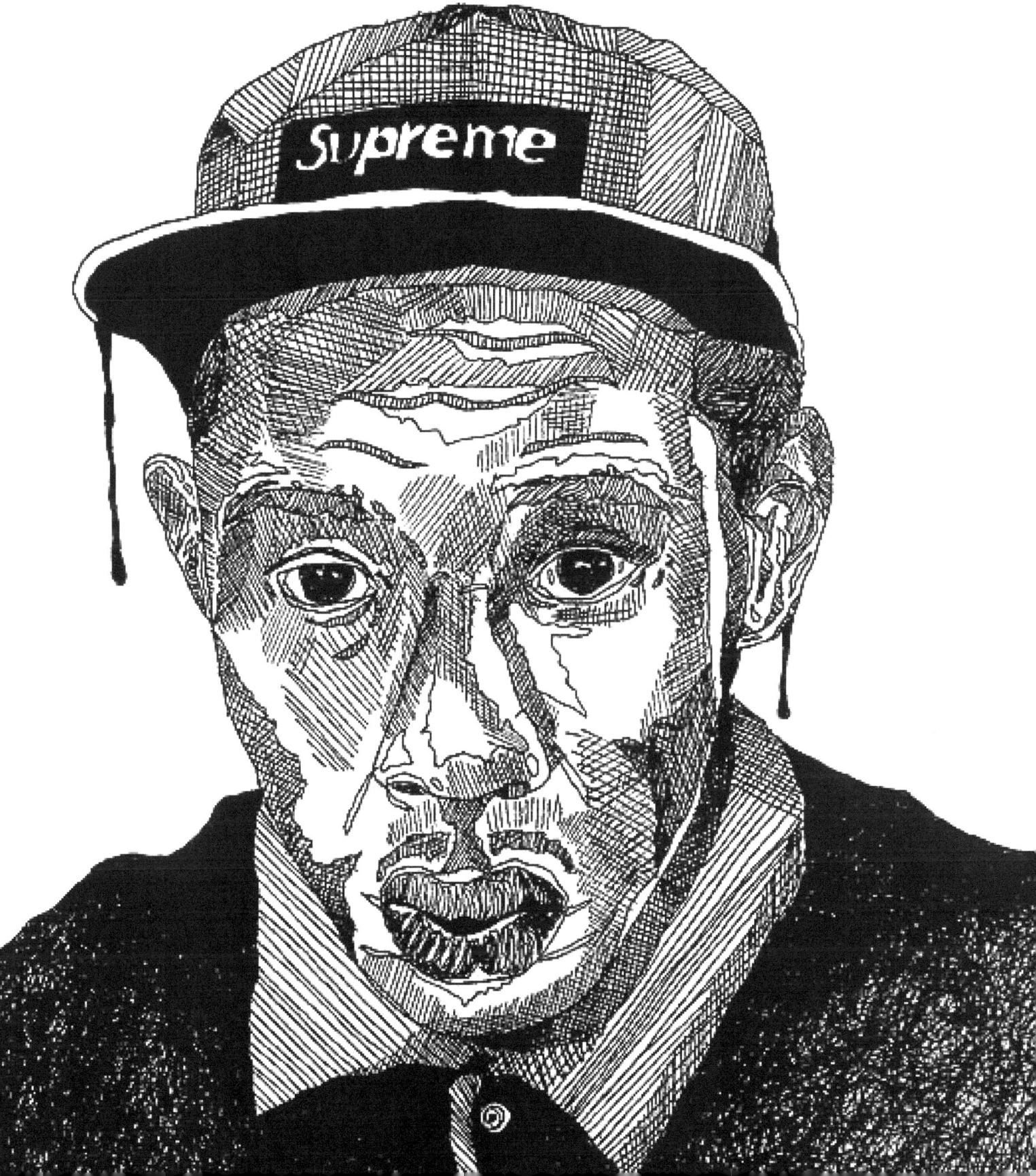

TYLER THE CREATOR

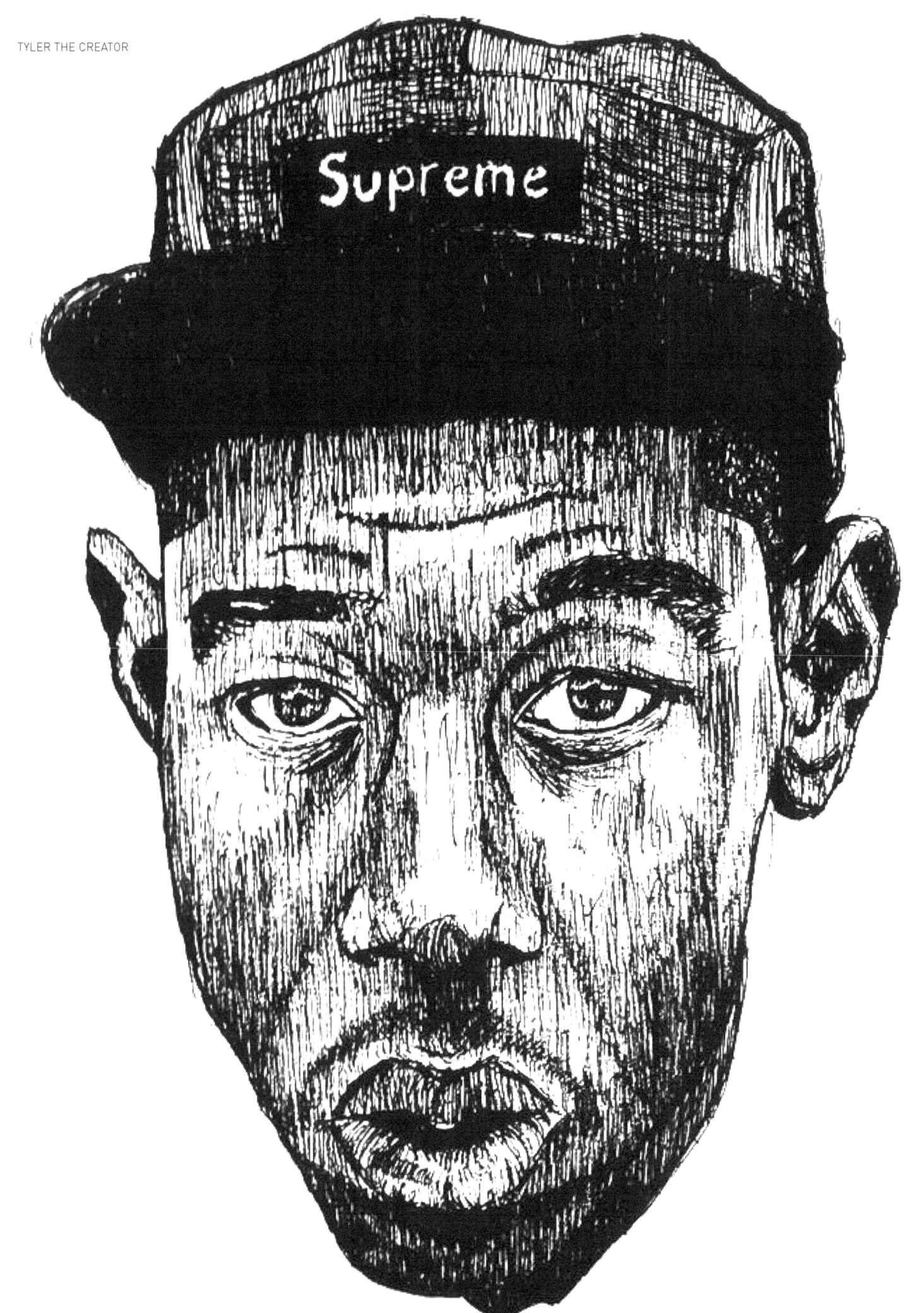

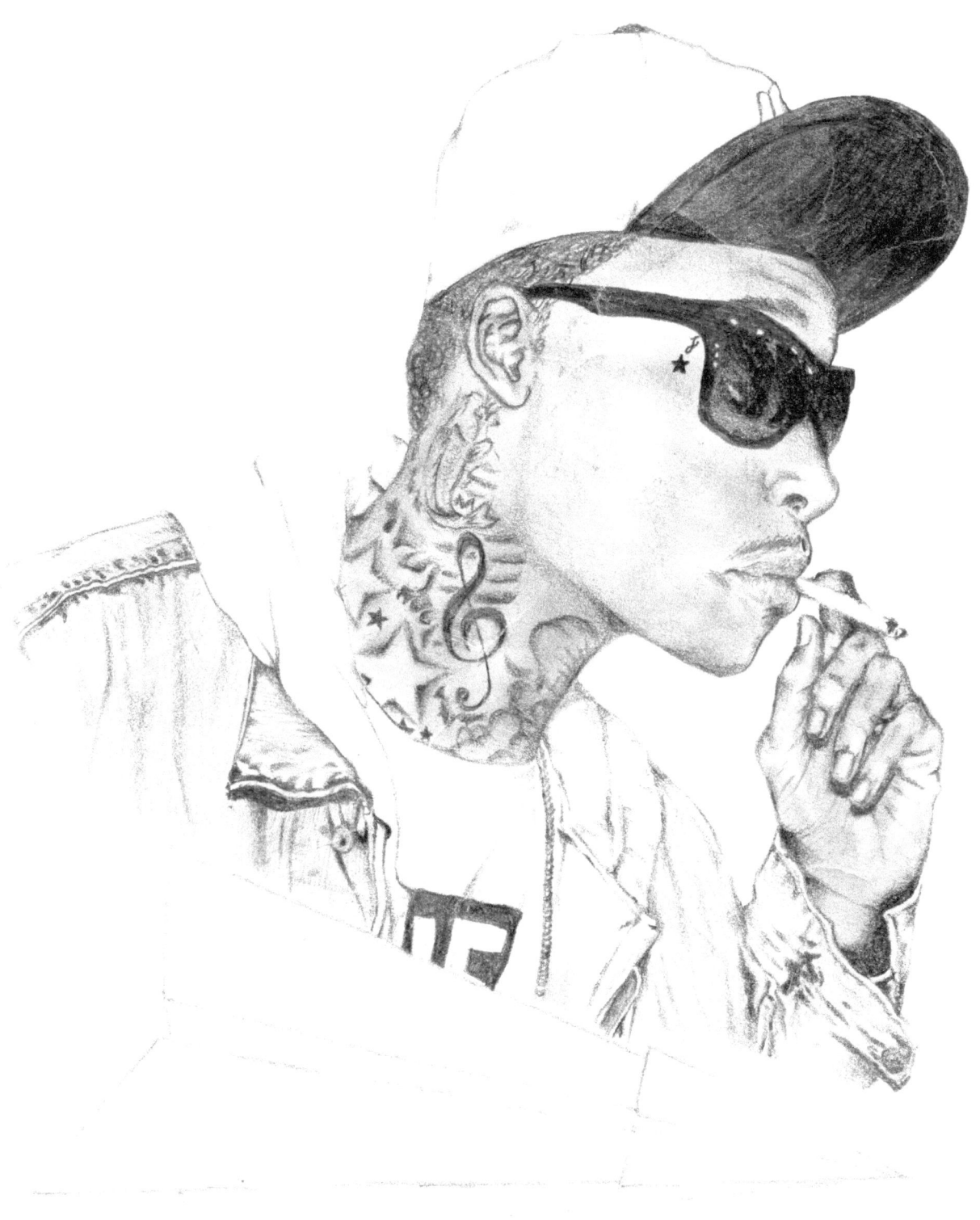

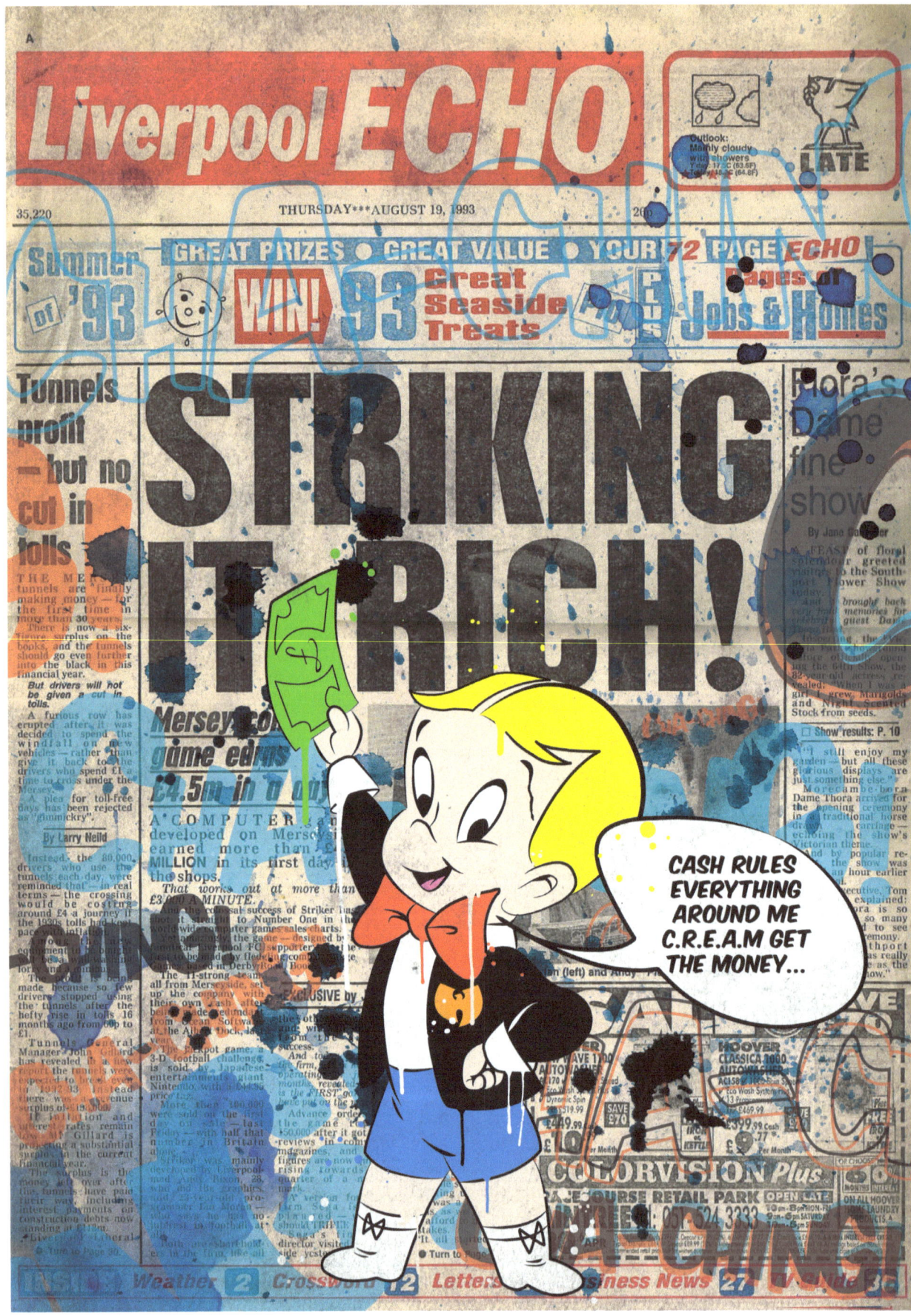

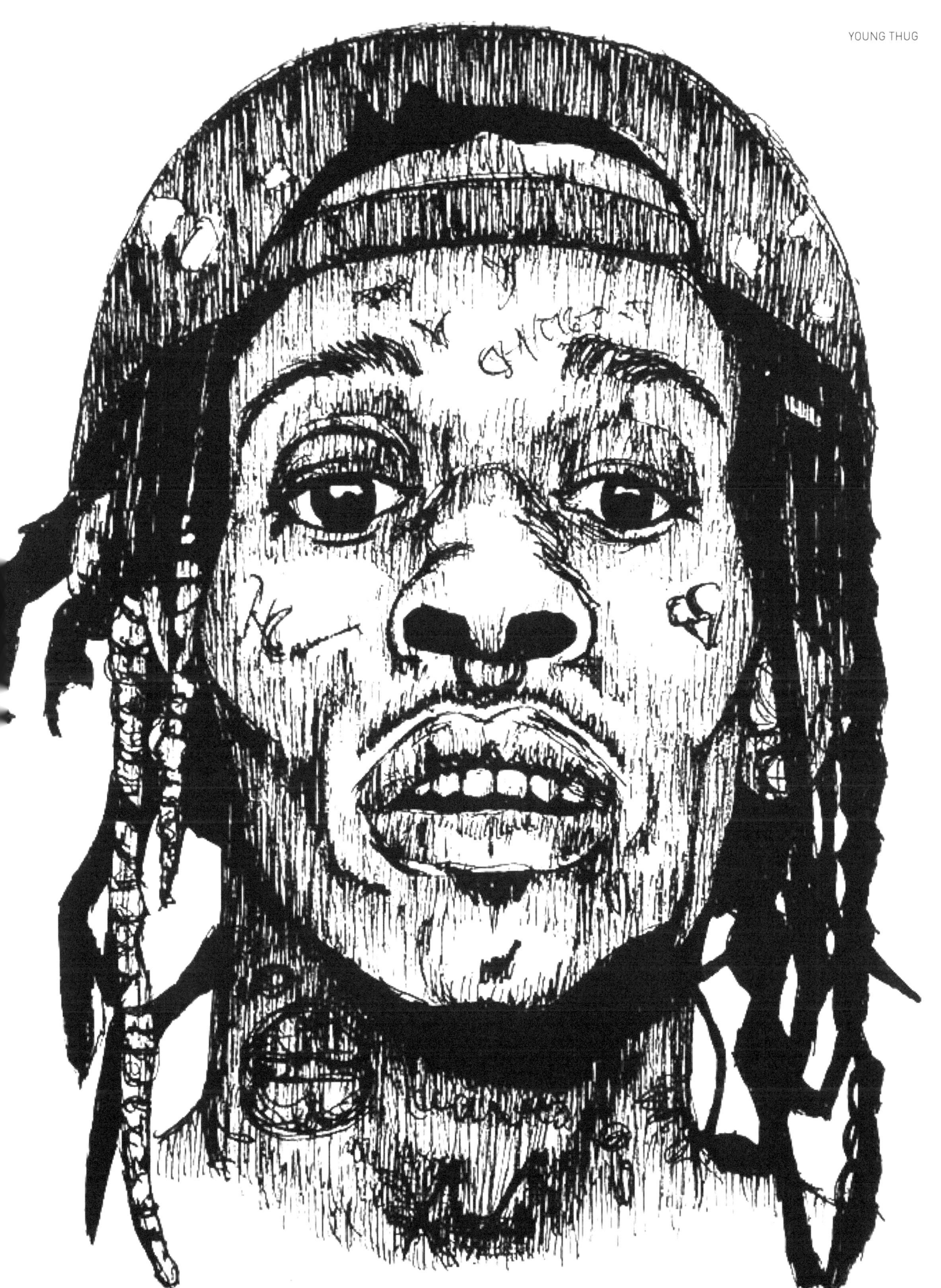

YOUNG THUG

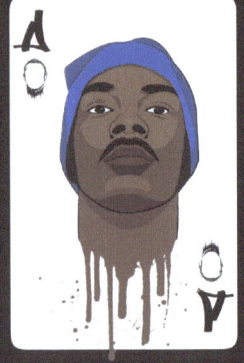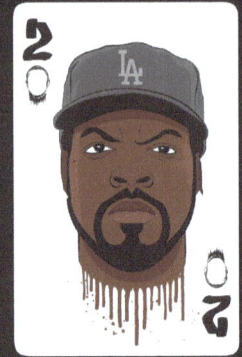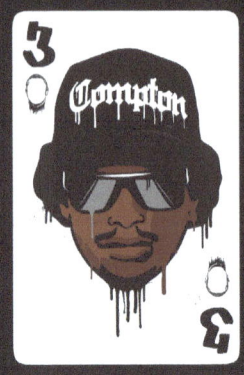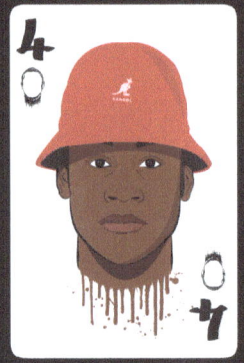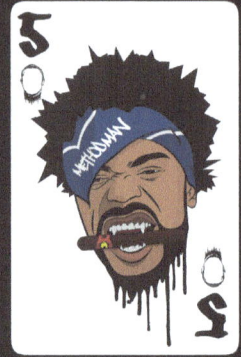
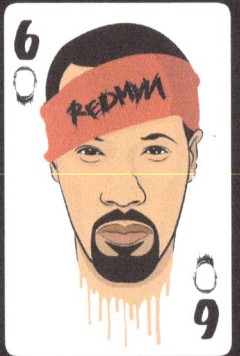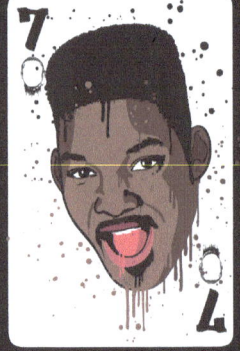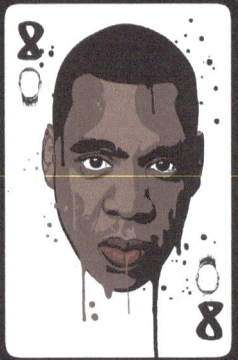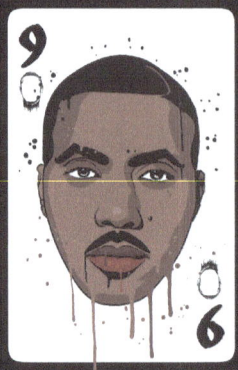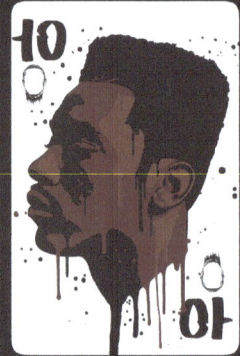
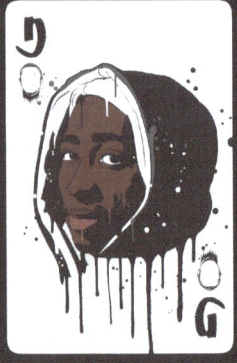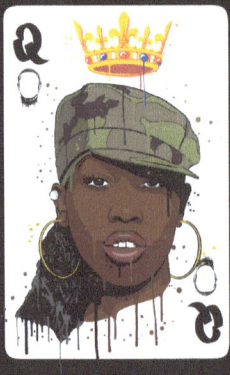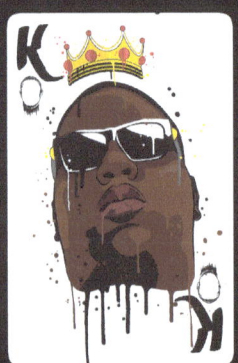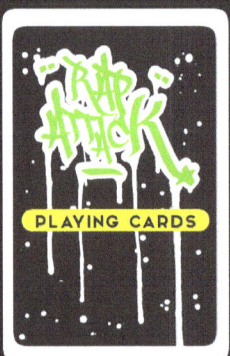

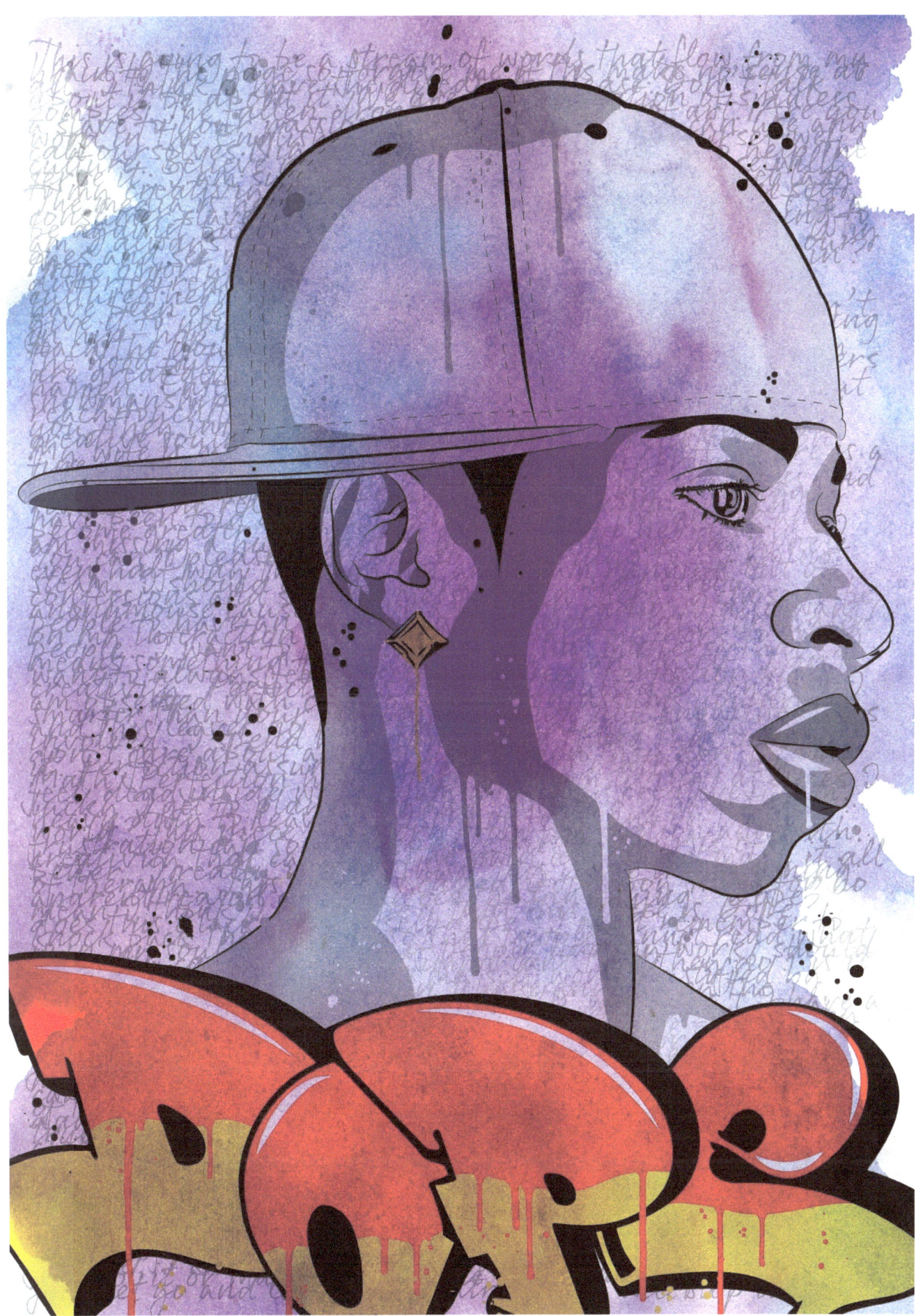

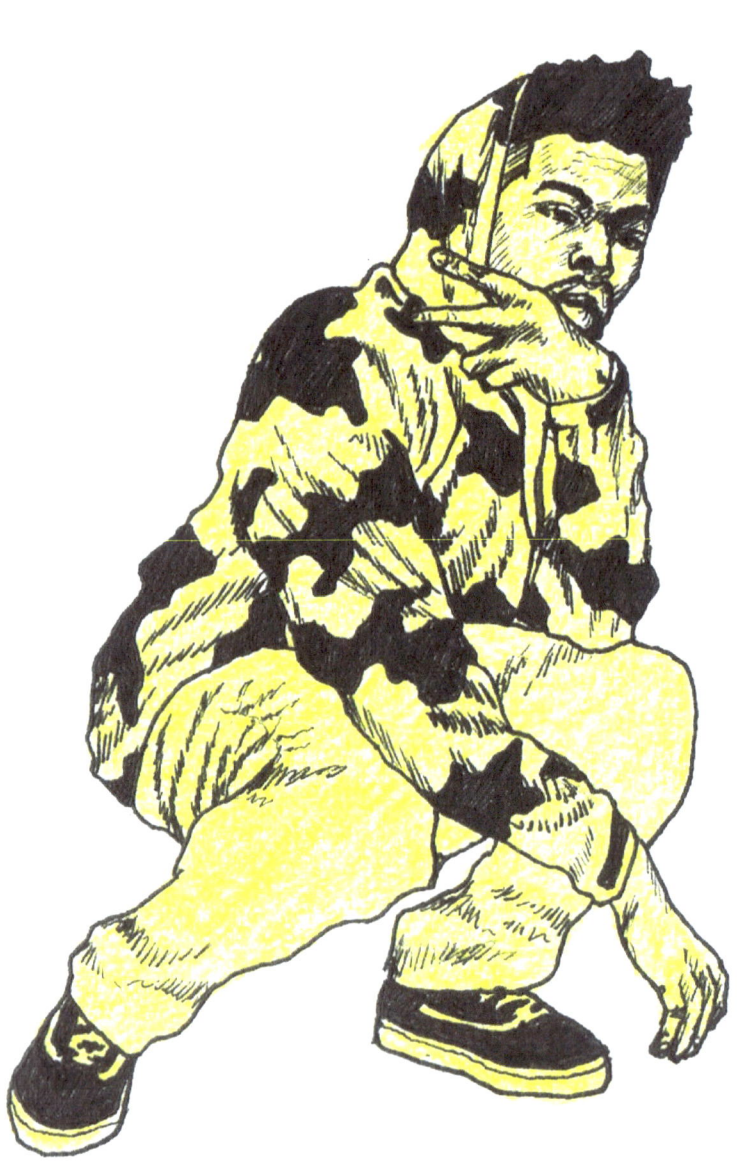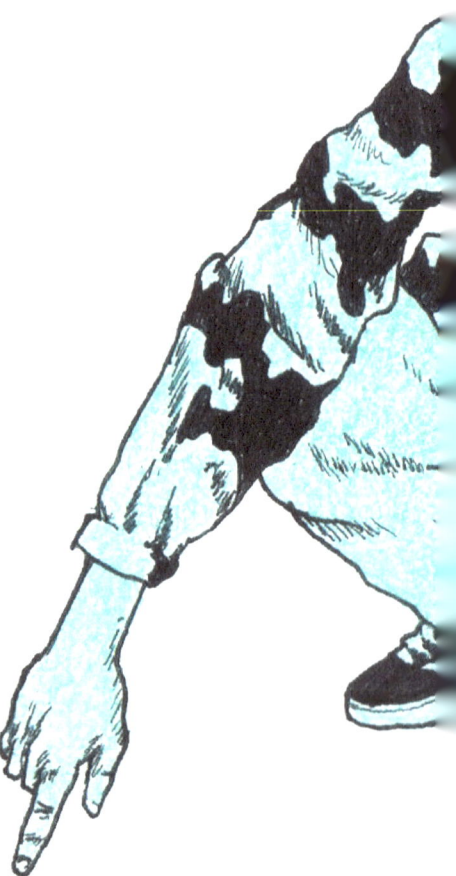

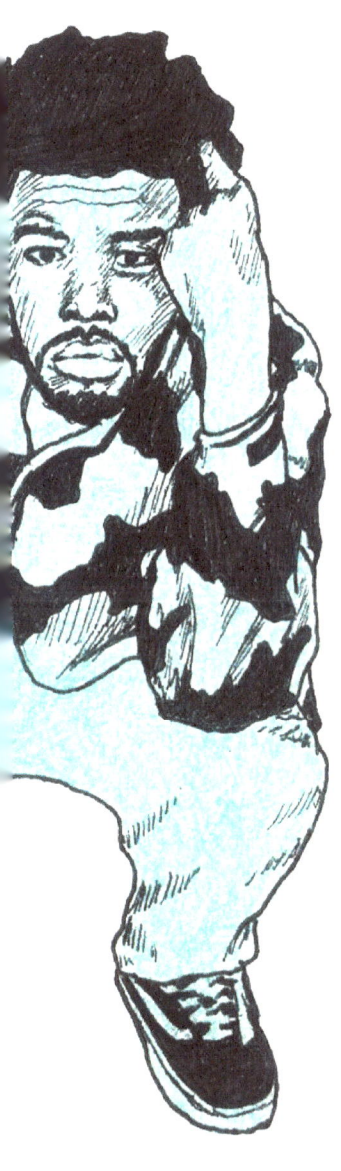
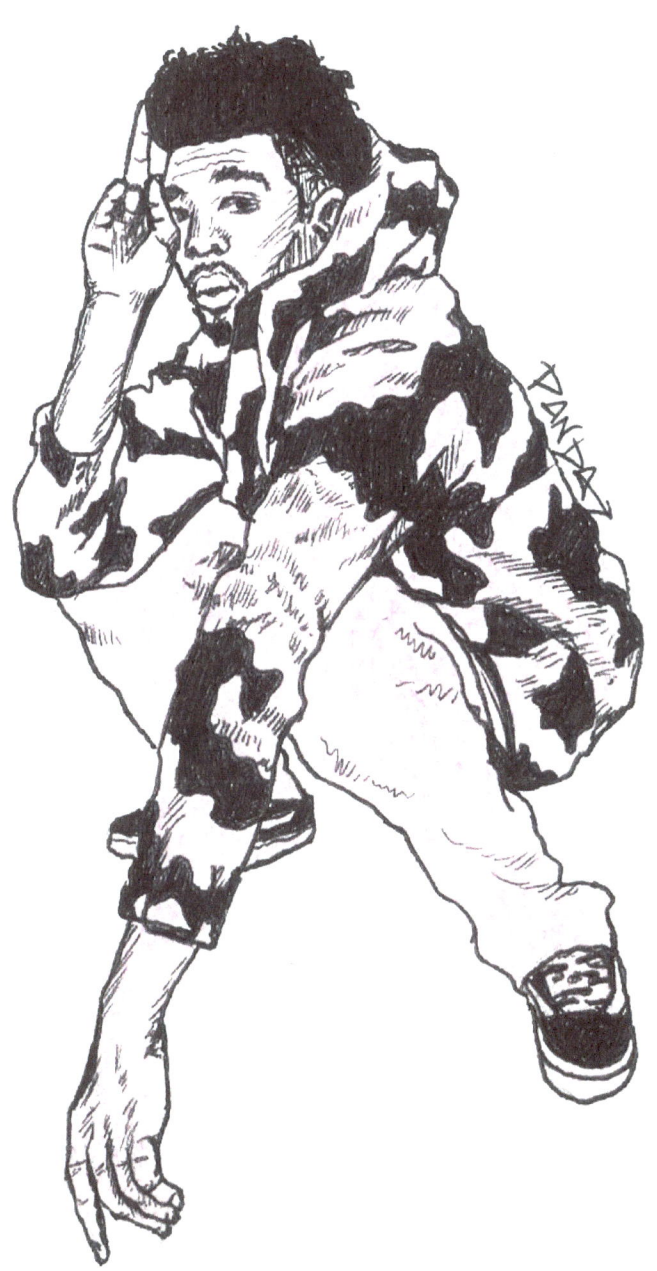

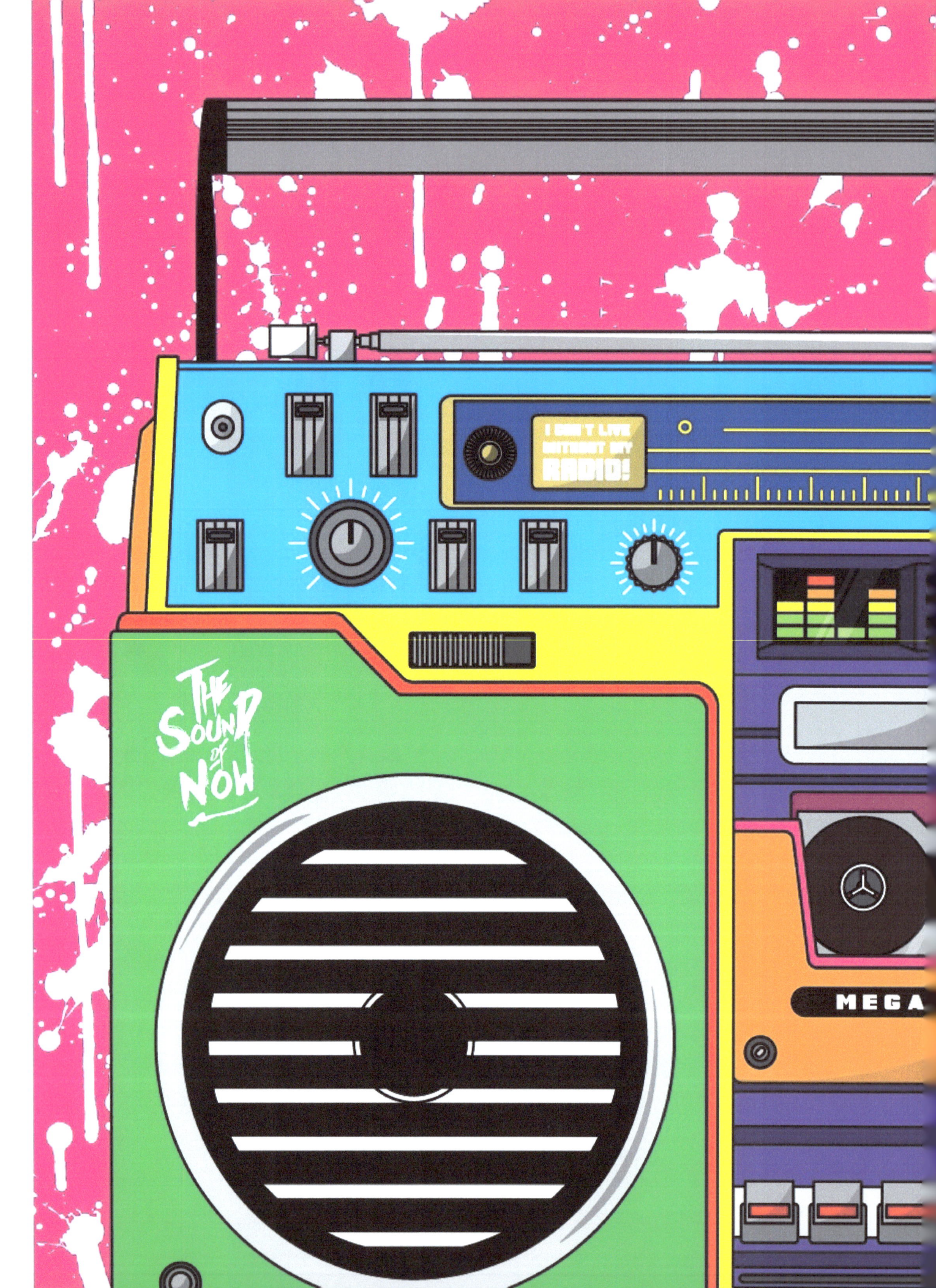

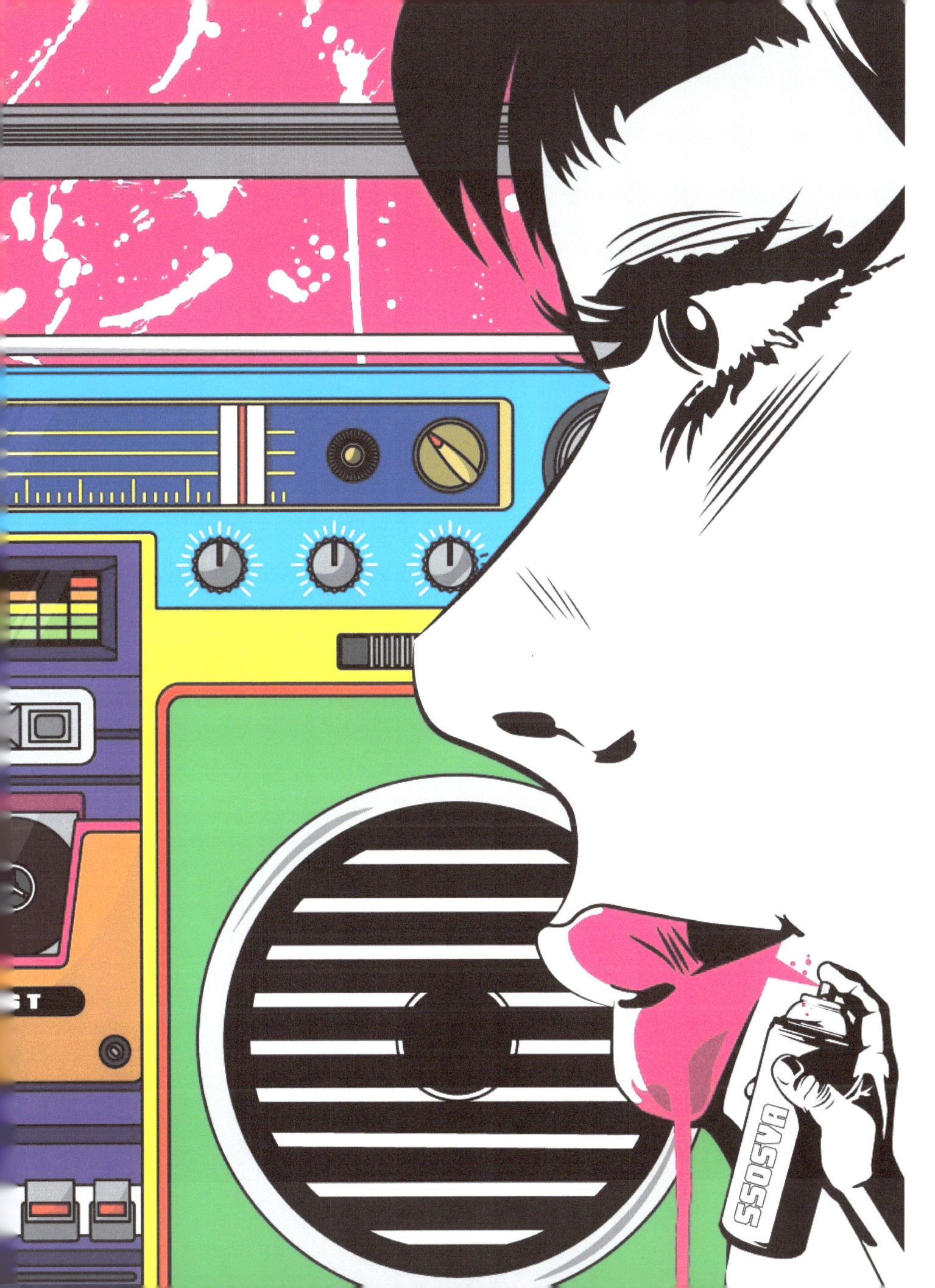

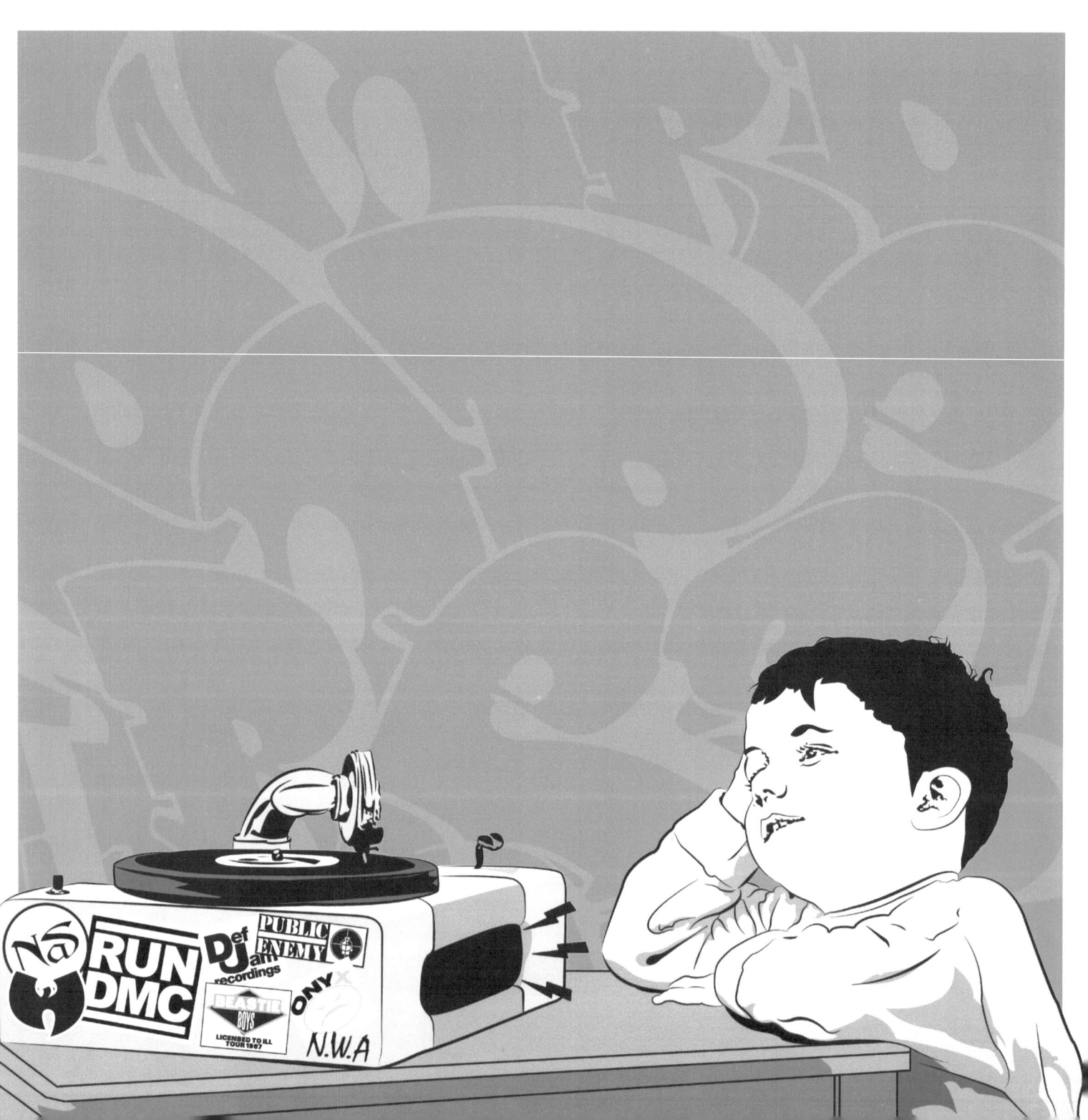

ARTISTS

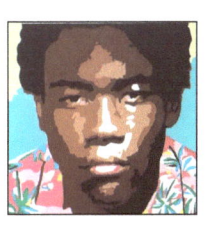 **@NDLOCAL** — Pg. 20, 28-29, 34, 36, 37, 41, 84, 107, 135, 149

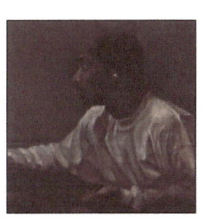 **ALEX MELAMID** — Pg. 9, 96, 125, 129, 142

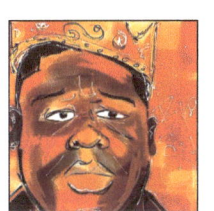 **@ARTGOON365** — Pg. 25, 48, 126, 127, 128, 146, 160

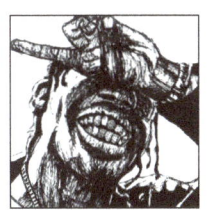 **@ART_OF_JIMMYCHAD** — Pg. 10, 23, 26-27, 54, 73, 150

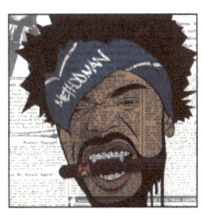 **@BAREFACEART** — Pg. 32-33, 58-59, 100, 104, 138-139, 143, 164, 168-169

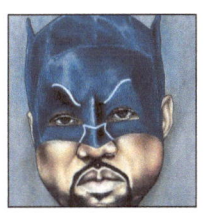 **@BRISCO_ART** — Pg. 16, 68, 78, 87, 148

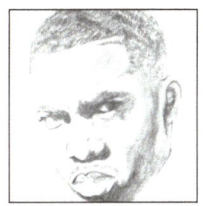 **@DAMOVDM** — Pg. 23, 35, 65, 93, 101, 102, 106, 113, 116, 121

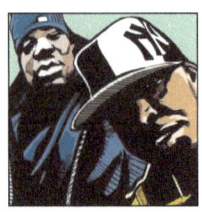 **@DOMDIRTEE** — Pg. 44, 109

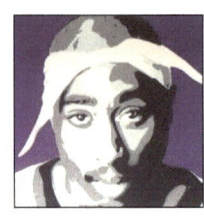 **@DURTYART** — Pg. 14, 15, 18-19, 21, 23, 45, 52, 53, 88-91, 118, 119, 145, 154-156

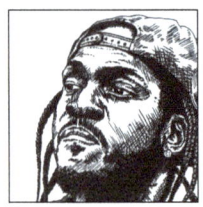 **@GROOVYPANDAB** — Pg. 56-57, 62, 63, 72, 74, 94-95, 98, 99, 103, 120, 136, 141, 144, 163, 167, 170-171, 172

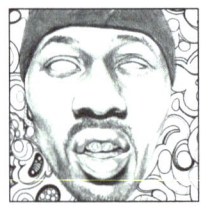 **@MIAAASCH** — Pg. 31, 50, 76, 86, 110, 111, 114, 123, 124, 130, 132, 133

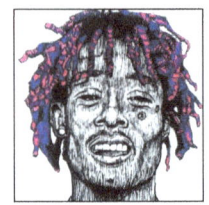 **@OLIVER_HASSELL** — Pg. 40, 47, 60, 79, 97, 106, 147, 150, 161, 165

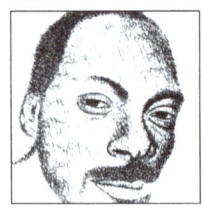 **@PAT_PRINT** — Pg. 77, 143

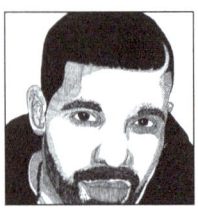 **@PHARAOHDRAWS** — Pg. 12, 13, 46, 49, 70, 71, 134, 161

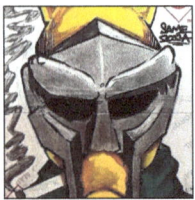 **@SAME_SOSA** — Pg. 21, 66, 78, 92, 122

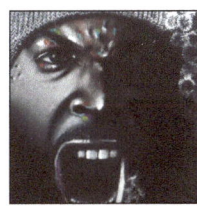 **@SHAPESWELLPLACED** Pg. 11, 55, 69, 83, 105, 131, 137, 151

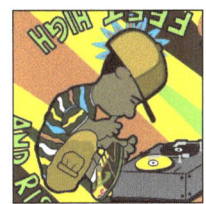 **@STICK_FIGURE_DRAWINGS** Pg. 16, 22, 38, 39, 67, 75, 82, 85

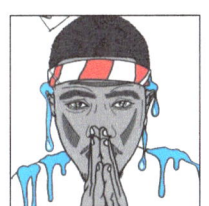 **@SYDTHEARTIST** Pg. 61

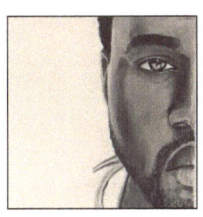 **@JUST_TYRA** Pg. 80, 81

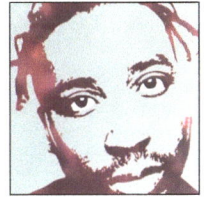 **@WICKEDWITCH333** Pg. 21, 24, 30, 42-43, 51, 115, 117

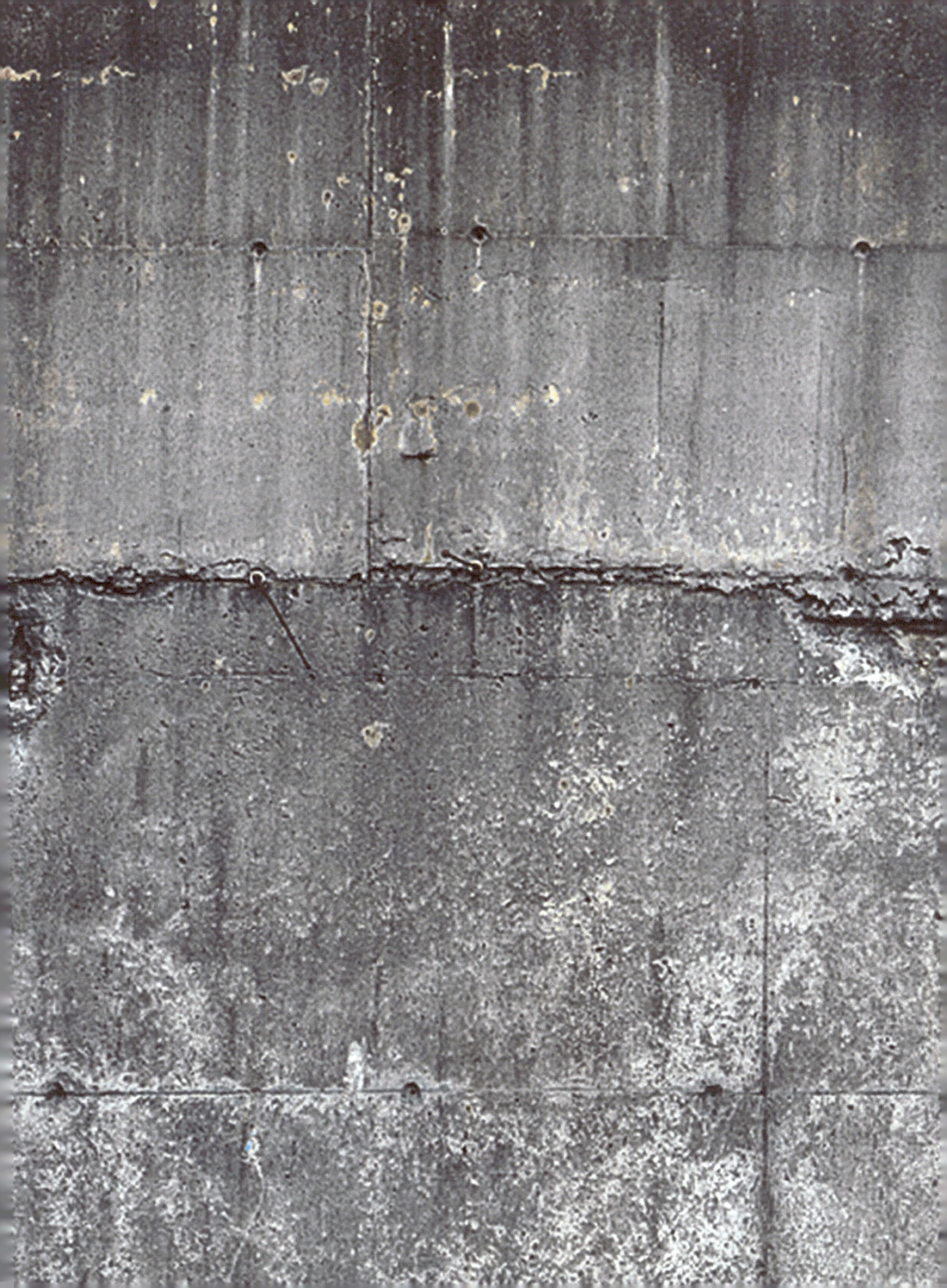